Praise for *Beyond*

"The story of how what seemed like Darryl Hunt's happy ending turned out to be a chapter, not an ending, and a testament to how profoundly post-traumatic stress disorder (PTSD) can affect prisoners for years after they are released. In a larger and more important sense, it is another reminder of how the United States' prison-industrial complex has ruined so many men in so many ways, especially Black men ... Zerwick's research is exemplary, and the story is a strong one." — *Atlanta Journal-Constitution*

"With the addition of *Beyond Innocence* by Phoebe Zerwick, my personal bookshelves hold no fewer than eighty-seven titles about wrongful convictions. Of the lot, none has made my blood boil more than Zerwick's chronicle of the life and death of Darryl Hunt ... Meticulously reported and eloquently written, a real page turner, journalism at its best ... Should be required reading for every legislator, prosecutor, and judge in the country."
—Rob Warden, *National Book Review*

"A moving account of a North Carolina man's wrongful conviction and incarceration, eventual exoneration, and lingering postprison trauma ... Richly detailed and lucidly written, this is a harrowing story of racial injustice and the lingering traumas of wrongful imprisonment." —*Publishers Weekly*

"Zerwick tracks Hunt's life as an exoneree and dedicated activist, whose advocacy helped lead to substantive reform for death row inmates until the burden of his trauma led tragically to his taking his own life. Zerwick's portrait of Hunt humanizes all who are incarcerated, opening out into a well-researched, frustrating, inspirational, and heartbreaking look at profound issues of equality and justice and how racism and injustice destroy lives." —*Booklist*

"The book's reconstruction of Hunt's last days is a powerful reminder of incarceration's effects on the large numbers of Black Americans who have spent time behind bars. Zerwick's portrait of Hunt is a reminder of the trauma caused by the American justice system and offers an essential narrative of the lasting impacts of incarceration."

—*Library Journal*

"Phoebe Zerwick's *Beyond Innocence: The Life Sentence of Darryl Hunt* exerts a grip on the reader equal to any true crime nonfiction, but it speaks far beyond that. I knew Darryl Hunt and many in these pages who championed his cause and his causes. I saw Darryl regularly for ten of the 32 years covered by this amazing book. I celebrated his freedom from 19 years of unjust incarceration, his nobility of soul, and his achievements for criminal justice reform. I wept in 2016 when I heard what I believed to be his full sorrow. But Zerwick's masterful detective work, relentless research, brilliant storytelling, and, more than that, her insights into the dark night and fragile light of the human heart illuminate not only the essential facts but the deepest truths of this profound tragedy. *Beyond Innocence* is anything but gooey polemic. But sometimes a single human story cracks open our once familiar worlds in ways that we cannot forget, and compels us either to admit that vicious, intentional injustice speaks for us, or to speak for ourselves in a call to higher ground. This story is an opportunity to rethink our lives that we cannot afford to ignore."

—Timothy B. Tyson, bestselling author of *The Blood of Emmett Till* and *Blood Done Sign My Name*

"In *Beyond Innocence*, Phoebe Zerwick provides a gripping account of the life and death of Darryl Hunt, and in the process explains how the trauma endured by those wrongfully convicted is fundamentally at odds with a happily-ever-after ending. Zerwick's unflinching, intimate portrait of Hunt, exonerated but never truly free, leaves the reader with a story that is far more complicated and thought-provoking. This book will stay with you."

—Lara Bazelon, author of *Rectify: The Power of Restorative Justice After Wrongful Conviction* and professor, University of San Francisco School of Law

"*Beyond Innocence* is a singularly important book about the extraordinary costs of a wrongful conviction, put in the larger context of a deeply flawed system that makes such convictions inevitable."

—James E. Coleman, Jr., Director, Duke Wrongful Convictions Clinic, Durham, NC

"[Zerwick's] moving and powerful book is truly special. There were times when I had to put it aside momentarily because I could feel the pain that Darryl and so many others experience in a system that is fundamentally racist. Thank you for shining a light on his story and the stories of so many others. There can be no change without truth."

—Judge Gregory Weeks, Retired Superior Court judge and former board member, The Sentencing Project

BEYOND INNOCENCE

BEYOND INNOCENCE

THE LIFE SENTENCE OF DARRYL HUNT

A true story of race, wrongful
conviction, and an American
reckoning still to come

PHOEBE ZERWICK

Grove Press
New York

Copyright © 2022 by Phoebe Zerwick

All rights reserved. No part of this book may be reproduced in any form or by any electronic or mechanical means, including information storage and retrieval systems, without permission in writing from the publisher, except by a reviewer, who may quote brief passages in a review. Scanning, uploading, and electronic distribution of this book or the facilitation of such without the permission of the publisher is prohibited. Please purchase only authorized electronic editions, and do not participate in or encourage electronic piracy of copyrighted materials. Your support of the author's rights is appreciated. Any member of educational institutions wishing to photocopy part or all of the work for classroom use, or anthology, should send inquiries to Grove Atlantic, 154 West 14th Street, New York, NY 10011 or permissions@groveatlantic.com.

Epigraph from "Essay on Reentry: *for Fats, Juvie & Star*" from *Felon: Poems* © 2019 by Reginald Dwayne Betts. Reproduced by permission of W. W. Norton.

Published simultaneously in Canada
Printed in Canada

First Grove Atlantic hardcover edition: March 2022
First Grove Atlantic paperback edition: March 2023

Library of Congress Cataloging-in-Publication data is available for this title.

ISBN 978-0-8021-5938-0
eISBN 978-0-8021-5939-7

Grove Press
an imprint of Grove Atlantic
154 West 14th Street
New York, NY 10011

Distributed by Publishers Group West

groveatlantic.com

23 24 25 26 27   10 9 8 7 6 5 4 3 2 1

Contents

Dedicated to Darryl E. Hunt

No words exist for the years we lost

...

to prison.

—Reginald Dwayne Betts, from "Essay on Reentry:
for Fats, Juvie & Star"

BEYOND INNOCENCE

Author's Note

Beyond Innocence is my attempt to finish a story I began long ago, in 2003, when I wrote about the wrongful conviction of Darryl Hunt for the *Winston-Salem Journal*. Hunt was in prison then for the 1984 murder of a newspaper editor who had been raped and stabbed to death, not far from the newsroom where I worked. But a claim of innocence is no defense, and only after 19 years of legal battles and the tireless effort of local activists was Hunt released. It was a triumphant moment for him, for his supporters, and for me.

It's not that case of innocence, however, that led me to this book, but rather what happened over the next 12 years, after Hunt was exonerated by DNA evidence, after he became a champion for justice, after the trauma he had endured finally caught up with him.

To the outside world, Hunt was the man who walked out of prison without rancor or regret. But the past haunted him, and the heroic narrative of a man who fought for justice masked a deep despair.

I first heard about his case when I arrived in North Carolina in July 1987, fresh out of journalism school, having headed south from New York City to a region that felt rich in stories. Most of the other reporters at the *Journal* were my age, in their mid- to late twenties, all of us looking to launch a career in a state known as a training ground for journalism. Two of my new coworkers proposed a tour one Saturday of local landmarks, ending with lunch of barbecue, pinto beans, and sweet tea.

The first stop was an overgrown park, two blocks away from the back door to the newsroom. I don't remember if we walked or drove, or if I noticed the odd fence made of wood pilings, or the trash that littered the hillside. They told me about Deborah Sykes, a copy editor at the former afternoon newspaper who, three years earlier, had been raped and stabbed to death there one summer morning. She was 25 when she died, young and ambitious like me. They told me, too, that a Black teenager named Darryl Hunt had been convicted in her death and that the case had become a flashpoint in the city's racial politics. Many Black people in town believed that he had been railroaded. It was a story I would need to understand if I was going to understand this place I now called home.

In the 1980s, Winston-Salem was an industrial city of the New South. The R. J. Reynolds Tobacco Company, headquartered in an art deco building that was the model for the Empire State Building, anchored one downtown corner, and Wachovia Bank, long considered one of the strongest banks in the nation, stood across the street. Piedmont Airlines, HanesBrands, and McLean Trucking were headquartered in town, too. Of these Fortune 500 companies, Reynolds defined the city, filling the air with the sweet smell of tobacco. The Camels my brother smoked were made here. So were Winstons, Salems, and Dorals. In the fall, farmers came to town to sell piles of flue-cured leaves at auction. And in the newsroom, in deference to our readers and to the city's largest employer, we didn't state as fact that cigarettes caused cancer but hedged with the attribution of "some medical experts say."

It was also a city divided by the murder of a white newspaper editor and the conviction of a Black teenager. I grew up in New York City and went to college on the South Side of Chicago, so I knew how crime can define a community, and I knew enough about American history to know, even to expect, that race would be the subtext of much of what I would write about.

I began working as a bureau reporter in Lexington, a furniture town a half hour south of Winston-Salem, with enough character to satisfy my romantic notions of the South. The sheriff, Paul R. "Jaybird" McCrary, ran the local Democratic Party machine. His detectives made fun of the New Yorker the paper had sent to town, but they were kind to me and let me read through their case files and follow them around crime scenes. And I learned about Southern justice from the district attorney, H. W. "Butch" Zimmerman, whose office was decorated with Confederate memorabilia. Defense attorneys would gather there on Friday afternoons while he read excerpts from his collection of slaveholder diaries, many about their sexual exploits with enslaved women, recited not as stories of rape but for the entertainment of the men in the room. Zimmerman tried the murder cases himself, and lawyers from as far away as Raleigh and Charlotte would come to watch him and to learn from his legendary courtroom theatrics. He rarely lost.

The subtext of racism was not as obvious in Winston-Salem as it was in small-town North Carolina, but it was far from hidden. The city council, then known as the board of aldermen, was divided by race, with four Black and four white members. Often the members agreed, but when they did not, the division typically fell along racial lines. Black aldermen supported naming the local coliseum after a Black Vietnam War hero; white aldermen did not. Black aldermen voted to establish a police review board. White aldermen opposed it. The mayor, a white woman and a Democrat, broke those ties, and when she sided with the Black Democrats on the board, business leaders saw her as weak.

Other reporters wrote about Hunt's case over those years in the neutral style we all accepted as objective journalism. The stories dutifully quoted his supporters—men like Larry Little, who in the 1970s had founded the local Black Panther Party, and Rev. Carlton Eversley, who had moved south from New York City in the hopes of becoming an activist—who claimed that Hunt was the innocent victim of a racist justice system. And the stories just as dutifully quoted police and prosecutors who insisted that the evidence against Hunt was rock solid. From that balanced perspective, it seemed impossible that after two trials, three layers of appellate review, and the tireless efforts of attorneys, that a truly innocent man could be imprisoned.

The series I wrote, "Murder, Race, Justice: The State vs. Darryl Hunt," was published in November 2003. Written as an eight-part narrative, the articles helped our readers—including the judge who had ordered DNA testing—see facts they thought they knew in a different way. A month later, threatened with a contempt order, the state completed its DNA testing of the evidence in the Sykes murder, ran the profile through its database of convicted felons, and found a match. Hunt was released from the Forsyth County Jail on Christmas Eve and exonerated two months later, in February 2004.

My work on Hunt's story was over.

Then, in March 2016, Hunt disappeared, setting off a frantic search. After nine days, he was found in the driver's seat of a pickup truck, parked beside a busy road, dead from what appeared to be a self-inflicted gunshot wound.

I grieved his death, not with the intensity of those who loved him, but with the knowledge that I, among others who had been a part of bringing about justice for him, ultimately had failed him, believing the stories we told about him, all the while missing a more complex and troubling tale.

I wasn't done with the story after all.

I started looking into his death soon after the funeral. Rather than tackle the big question of what it said about the failures of our justice system, I focused first on the facts, trying to track his movements in the days before his death. I talked with anyone I could find who had spent time with him in the weeks before he died and I pored over posts to his Facebook page, followed them to pages of his friends and relatives, studying photographs from birthday parties and beach trips, of people I had never met, searching for clues.

Part of me simply wanted to solve the mystery of his death. What compelled him to pick that particular parking lot by a diner, a gaming parlor, and a Family Dollar? Why, after 30 years of struggle, had it come to this? What had I missed?

Hunt left answers to many of these questions in his own words, in correspondence with his lawyers over the 19 years of his incarceration, in the public talks and interviews he gave after he was released, in journals he kept in prison, and in an unpublished oral history he had recorded. I found more answers in conversations with his friends and supporters, who shared their time and insights with generosity and trust. Like all stories, Hunt's was shaped by cultural forces and by history. For insight, I turned to other writers on the legacy of slavery and Jim Crow and on criminal justice and psychiatry, writers whose work has informed the way I tell Hunt's story.

Hunt's death taught me a great deal about the limits of journalism and forced me to question my motives. Does the public's right to know, that righteous principle we journalists invoke, justify exposing the secrets I hoped to find? Does shining a light in the dark places really help, as we claim it does? Who am I to tell a story Hunt himself had not told?

In life, he had been a heroic figure, wrongly convicted at 20, exonerated at 39, and at the time of his death a tireless advocate for reform. Like so many others who have been falsely imprisoned, Hunt was traumatized, first by the soul-shattering injustice of it all, then by the years in prison, often in solitary confinement, and finally by reentry into a culture that did not and would not understand him.

Some would have preferred that I left Hunt's secrets alone and his image undisturbed, but among his friends, at least those I have come to know, the myth matters less than the man. "I ain't no choir boy," his friend Ayyub Rasheed told me almost every time we met. "And Hunt was no angel," he said, as if to remind me that only the full story of Hunt's life could restore the humanity that was stolen from him.

Preface

When I met Darryl Hunt for the first time in June 2003, I wasn't concerned about his life in prison. In fact, I intentionally kept an emotional distance from him; my job was not to care about Hunt the man but to dissect the flawed case against him for an unsympathetic readership of the *Winston-Salem Journal*. I vaguely remember a prison guard watching at a distance, the distracting hum of the vending machine, and Hunt's uncanny memory for detail. If I wondered about his life in prison once the interview concluded and he shuffled away, his legs shackled at the ankle, or how those 19 years had harmed him, I didn't ask. But now those questions haunt me.

As of May 2021, 2,783 men and women in America have been exonerated of crimes they did not commit.[1] The National Registry of Exonerations, which tracks cases back to 1989, calculates the combined years they lost at 24,915. Some defendants were intentionally framed, but many more were wrongly convicted by a false confession, misidentification by witnesses, flawed forensics, jury bias, or incompetent legal representation. Some were convicted of crimes that had not even occurred, deaths of infants that should never have been ruled as homicides, or fatal fires ruled as arson that were, in fact, tragic accidents. No one knows with certainty how many more of the over two million people behind bars in the US are in prison for crimes they did not commit. One recent study of death penalty cases estimates that 4 percent[2] of people on death row may be innocent. It's clear to me now that the conditions of Hunt's imprisonment are part of a story of trauma and despair shared by thousands.

In 1985, when Hunt went to prison, there were 9,274 Black men and women incarcerated in North Carolina.[3] By 2003, the year I met him in prison, the number of Black men and women in North Carolina prisons had more than doubled to 20,463.[4] As far back as data exists, the Black prison population has outnumbered the white prison population, disproportionate to the number of Black men and women in the general population. Black men also outnumbered white men on death row, by nearly two to one,[5] and still do. And when Black people were convicted of killing white people, the chances of landing on death row were even higher. Today, in North Carolina, African-Americans represent just over 20 percent[6] of the general population yet make up more than half of the prison population in the state. In these patterns, North Carolina is no different than the rest of the country.

The fact that the United States imprisons a higher proportion of its population than any other country in the world is widely known, but the subtext of systemic racism is not as widely embraced. By 1993, the incarceration rate for Black US residents was seven times that of whites. In the last 15 years, that disparity has shrunk, but in spite of these improvements, Black people in this country are still imprisoned at five times the rate of white people.[7] The policies that led to these disparities destroy lives like Hunt's, and with them their families and entire communities.

Other writers and scholars have written with expertise about the history of mass incarceration, its roots in slavery and Jim Crow, and the ways in which it traps anyone with a criminal history in what some call "civil death." I write this in May 2021, at the end of the first year of a pandemic, numb to the half million deaths, which like our carceral state have claimed a disproportionate number of

Black lives. In Minneapolis, former police officer Derek Chauvin has been convicted for the murder of George Floyd, whose death, broadcasted around the world on social media, forced many white viewers to take a stand with the Black Lives Matter movement. In Hunt's hometown of Winston-Salem, the FBI has arrested a 33-year-old leader of the white supremacist organization the Proud Boys as part of the ongoing federal investigation into the January 6 storming of the Capitol Building. The conflict between the ideology of white supremacy and the struggle against racism, forces that so profoundly shaped Hunt's life, endures.

Beyond Innocence looks squarely at the toll of the carceral state on one man—a peaceful, tormented man no longer here to tell his own story—and calls for a reckoning with the failures of our justice system, with the scourge of prison, with the arrogant power of the state, and most of all with the intractable legacy of racism, all bearing down on one man who lay dead for days in a pickup truck in an obscure shopping center, alone and unnoticed.

Chapter One

The First Lie

The 911 call came in at 6:53 a.m. on August 10, 1984, shortly after sunrise. It lasted just 48 seconds, long enough to set off a series of events that would destroy one life and consume many more.

"My name is Sammy Mitchell," the caller said.

"Yes, sir."

"And I'm calling, I just want to report an incident I just saw."

"OK, where was it?"

"I just seen a lady which some guy was jumping on her, down here, you know where the fire station is downtown."

"There's several." A second dispatcher came on the line. "Are you talking about Engine 1 that's near the Hyatt House?"

"No, ma'am, down in there, Crystal Towers way," the caller said.

"On Claremont and 40, near 40?" she asked.

"Yeah, I guess that is 40. I seen some dude jumping on a lady, I thought I would call the police department."

"OK, is it in front of the station?"

"No, it's in that field, it's right there."

"Right there at Davis Garage?"

"Across the field right in front of the fire station is a big field there, and they was out there fighting pretty bad, so I think somebody ought to go see because she was hollering pretty hard."

"OK."

"OK, thank you."[1]

The caller got most of what he reported right. The firehouse. The Crystal Towers high-rise. The field. Some dude on top of a woman, and the woman hollering for help. All that happened, exactly where he said. But in those few seconds, so much was missed. First was the reference the dispatcher made to the Hyatt House, a hotel just two blocks away from the field where the woman was calling for help. "No, ma'am," the caller had said, not the Hyatt House. It's not clear why the caller didn't recognize the landmark, except that he spoke from one geography, the dispatcher from another. It's not clear either why the dispatcher ignored the landmark the caller used, Crystal Towers, the name of both a high-rise apartment building and a neighborhood, both of which anyone in emergency services would have known because of the large number of calls coming from each. Maybe the static on the line made it hard for the dispatcher to hear. Maybe the dispatcher wasn't paying attention. Or maybe it was the caller's speech, with its inflections and diction, that made the dispatcher think of another fire station, on the other side of the interstate that separated the Black part of town from the rest of the city, a world away from the field where some dude had jumped a woman. The dispatcher sent a police car to Claremont Avenue, on the east and other side of town. Finding nothing, the officer went on to other calls.

～

In the summer of 1984, Deborah Sykes had just started on the copy desk at the *Sentinel*, the afternoon paper in Winston-Salem, North Carolina. She was living with her husband's parents about an hour away, in Mooresville, near Charlotte, while she and her husband looked for a house in Winston-Salem. She was 25, with a degree from the journalism school at UNC Chapel Hill and some four years of experience at smaller newspapers in Tennessee and North

Carolina. Striking-looking at five feet ten, with brown hair and lively eyes, she had already impressed the other copy editors at the *Sentinel* by the care she took with her work.[2]

The small staff was a close-knit bunch, bound together by the odd hours required to publish an afternoon newspaper, often starting before sunrise to meet a late-morning deadline. The *Sentinel* shared downtown office space with the larger morning paper, the *Winston-Salem Journal*. The two newsrooms occupied the older part of the complex, and the press and business offices the newer portions. Staffers shared a back door, by the loading dock, which led up a metal flight of stairs to the newsroom. The shift at the *Sentinel* began at 6:30 a.m., and Sykes was never late. That Friday, when she wasn't at her desk by seven, her colleagues worried.[3] Within an hour, the area would be filled with people—the thousands who worked at the headquarters of the R. J. Reynolds Tobacco Company, or at Wachovia Bank, which boasted a reputation for conservative lending and Southern gentility, or at one of the dozens of smaller companies that supported these giants. But in the predawn hours, downtown Winston-Salem was deserted. The empty early-morning streets attracted vagrants, among them "Too Tall" Wall, a Black man well over six feet tall, who wore a floppy hat, muttered to himself, and had a habit of threatening women.

Sykes had parked about two blocks from the back door of the newsroom, on a stretch of West End Boulevard that winds between the grounds of the Crystal Towers apartment building on one side and an overgrown patch of park on the other. About halfway down the street, a fence made of stout, upright wooden posts separated the most overgrown part of the park from the sidewalk. News editor Jo Dawson and others who worked with Sykes on the desk started looking for the pickup she normally drove to work. When they couldn't find it, Dawson called Deborah's husband, Doug Sykes, waking him. He checked to see that her car was gone, and it was, but her colleagues were looking for the wrong vehicle. She had taken their blue Buick Opel that morning and left the pickup for him.[4]

The call worried Doug Sykes. He had known his wife since they were high school sweethearts at North Iredell High School, near Mooresville. He had been looking for a job in Winston-Salem that month, and on days he had interviews lined up, they drove together. That day, he was staying home to help his father in the yard. Something must have happened for her to be running so late. He called his sister, who worked for the police department in Statesville, a town on the way from the house to Winston-Salem, to find out whether the highway patrol had reported any accidents along the interstate. Then he set out to find her on his own, checking for the Opel at exits between the house and Winston-Salem.

Back in town, Dawson walked the two blocks to West End Boulevard and found the Opel. But there was no sign of Sykes. Dawson and the newspaper's managing editor, Fred Flagler, searched the newspaper building, thinking maybe she had been accosted in a stairwell or in the alley that ran next to the building.[5] There was plenty to be fearful of. Downtown was in the midst of a long and steady decline that often left its streets empty, especially so early in the morning. Winding West End Boulevard may have offered free parking, but it was a street where women knew to be wary of the panhandlers and men sitting around the picnic tables behind the high-rise, drinking and calling out lewd remarks.

Doug Sykes arrived in Winston-Salem around 11 a.m., driving directly to West End Boulevard. When he saw the Opel, parked where his wife always parked, he relaxed. He walked the two blocks to the newspaper office and made his way to the newsroom, thinking he would wait there for his wife's shift to end and they would spend the rest of the afternoon together. Her place at the desk was empty. By then, Flagler was frantic. At 58, he had a protective manner about him, especially toward younger staffers. Shortly after 11 a.m., he called the police to report a missing person. Over the five minutes he stayed on the line, he was transferred first to a supervisor, then to the records room, then back to the supervisor. Flagler overheard someone on the line refer to him as that "dumb ass" from the newspaper. Clearly they weren't taking him seriously. The advice from the police enraged him more. It's probably a family matter. Call her husband. Furious, Flagler called the police chief, whose direct line the newsroom had on file. He took Flagler's alarm seriously and was angry at his own staff for their lack of response, and by noon the search for the missing copy editor began in earnest.[6]

~

The Winston-Salem Police Department assigned detective Jim Daulton, an 18-year veteran, to the case. Daulton called the two hospitals in town before heading over to West End Boulevard, where he met up with Flagler and Doug Sykes. The Opel was there, neatly parked, Deborah's briefcase on the rear floorboard, behind the driver's seat. He asked Sykes if it was possible his wife had a boyfriend or maybe she'd gone off for a shopping day with a girlfriend. Next, Daulton spoke with a woman who lived around the corner in one of the clapboard houses that had been converted into apartments. She told him she'd been awakened shortly after six in the morning to a scream coming from the park. He dutifully wrote down her age and birth date, in case he needed it. By then, it was after one in the afternoon and no one had thought to look beyond the overgrown bushes on the other side of the fence.[7]

Daulton noticed two men near Sykes' car, one of them motioning to him. He was one of Sykes' coworkers from the *Sentinel* who'd been out looking for her. With him was Brian Watts, who was on his lunch break from a nearby textile factory. Watts had been planning to eat the two hot dogs and an ice cream he'd brought with him in the park when he saw a white handbag on the ground beside the fence, its contents spilled, as if it had been dropped. He picked up the 95 cents in change and put the coins in his pocket.

As he looked up, he saw a woman about 12 paces away, sprawled on the hill.

The crime scene photographs show Sykes lying face up, on a slope covered in clover, her legs bent slightly, her left arm outstretched. Blood stains her legs and knit top. Her underwear is torn, leaving her naked from the waist down. One picture closes in on her bare legs. Another on the jagged slit left by a knife in her knit top. Another on the wound on her neck. Altogether, the medical examiner counted four wounds to her chest, three to her neck, four to her back, one on her head, and a cut on her arm. The blood had already dried.

In life, Sykes was an ambitious journalist. She wanted children, but later, when she was further along in her career. She sailed and played tennis. As a child, she was voted "Little Miss Statesville." She gave spare change to homeless people. She doted on her grand-mother, even inviting her to live with her and her husband once they were settled. As a writer, she had an eye for detail. The day she was murdered, she wore sensible clothes, sandals and navy blue slacks. Police photographed them, too, near the fence where they were found. The slacks were stained with mud, the zipper torn.[8]

~

The police department tried to make up for lost time. Crystal Towers was what we would today call a transitional neighborhood, five blocks of winding streets, run-down cottages, and rambling Victorian houses that could be bought for a song, some divided into apartments and others owned by urban pioneers who didn't mind living beside a subsidized apartment building. To the north, the hilly neighborhood overlooked an industrial strip of textile mills, auto repair places, and warehouses. Officers canvassed the neighborhood, dutifully writing down the names, phone numbers, and dates of birth of people they spoke to. One woman heard screams. Another remembered seeing winos at the picnic tables. Someone else was afraid.[9]

A technician with the police department photographed the body and collected every bit of trash littering the field—an empty vodka bottle, a dirty pair of men's briefs, a piece of beige elastic, a green shirt, a leather coat, soggy tennis shoes, and a pair of black-and-white pants. Dark clouds filled the sky, and the technician worked quickly to beat the forecasted rain. Watts, the Black man who found Sykes, agreed to a formal interview, and police put the 95 cents he had picked up off the ground away as part of the investigation. Police also fingerprinted and photographed him. More officers canvassed the neighborhood and set up a checkpoint, stopping people driving down West End Boulevard, in the hopes of finding witnesses. Once word of the murdered copy editor hit the evening news, the calls came in to Crime Stoppers, dozens of them. All of these reports eventually went to Daulton, a 39-year-old who had spent many years as a motorcycle cop, writing traffic tickets and investigating car wrecks. Two years earlier, he had been promoted to detective, but for most of that time he worked the juvenile unit, looking into crimes committed by teenagers. He'd never once been in charge of a homicide investigation.[10]

~

The news coverage was unrelenting, with television cameras getting in the way at the crime scene and reporters at the *Sentinel*, where Sykes worked, and the *Journal*, the morning paper, demanding answers. "Woman's Murder Heightens Anxiety in Neighborhood,"[11] read one article, "Murder Case Has Boiled Down to Plain Old Footwork,"[12] another. The *Journal* published daily, with the first edition rolling off the presses around midnight, and the *Sentinel* five afternoons a week. The schedule meant that Sykes' colleagues had until the Monday afternoon edition to collect themselves enough to write about her death. The *Journal* tried for a more neutral tone. Not the afternoon paper. "Tragedy Hits Home, We Often Write of Death; This Time We Lived It,"[13] read the headline to the lead story by the *Sentinel*'s columnist. A picture was included of "Debbie Sykes," as she was known in the newsroom, in a striped blouse, looking serene with her lovely almond-shaped eyes.

The story described the search for Sykes by her coworkers, looking, as one reporter said, for "something I didn't want to find." A photographer knew he should be taking pictures, but couldn't. A writer lashed out at television reporters who were at the crime scene doing their jobs. Another remembered the scene in the newsroom of Deborah's mother, tall and striking like her daughter, arriving, and Doug Sykes breaking the awful news. "To have seen Doug, Debbie's husband . . . to have heard the screams of Debbie's mother when she heard the news—these are things not easily put aside." Even in the few weeks since Sykes arrived at the paper, the rest of the small staff had come to think of her as one of their own. Her death left them numb and afraid. "When I close my eyes, I feel the terror she must have felt when she realized what was happening to her," one unidentified female editor said. "I woke up early Saturday morning and couldn't get back to sleep. I was afraid to go out my back door and around the house to get the newspaper out of the front yard."

~

At the police station, the mood also was tense. A beautiful young white woman was dead, brutally raped and murdered on her way to work right downtown. There were 26 homicides[14] in the city and surrounding county that year, but the deaths, however brutal, mostly arose from long-simmering squabbles among people who knew each other or from domestic disputes turned deadly. In May, for example, a 59-year-old woman named Bertha Lee Caldwell was found stabbed to death in a motel room. Like most other homicide victims throughout the city's recent history, the victims were Black, a pattern that played out across the nation, the homicide rates among Blacks far exceeding the rate for whites.[15] The newspaper would report their deaths in brief, buried on the inside pages. When the cases were solved, the newspapers followed up with a brief notice; the same when the cases went to trial.[16] There was little public reaction to these crimes or to the lenient sentences often imposed. In Caldwell's case, her killer, a lover of three years, pleaded guilty to manslaughter and was sentenced to six years in prison.[17] But the rape and murder of a young white woman on her way to work would be different.

Even in the first hours of the investigation, police knew the public pressure would be intense. What's more, the crime scene was a mess, with officers trampling all over the muddy ground. The police chief was furious. They had the 911 call from a man who used the name Sammy Mitchell as a starting point, but they had so bungled the response that it brought added pressure to make up for the mistake. Then there was the humiliating fact that police searching for the missing copy editor hadn't even bothered to look over the squat fence where her bloody body lay for hours in the summer heat.

By evening, four eyewitnesses had come forward. Two painters who lived at the Rescue Mission, a shelter about three blocks from where Sykes was killed, came within 30 to 40 yards of the attack while walking across the field on their way to work. Bobby Upchurch and Ralph Nash took the shortcut through there daily. They both told police that they saw a Black person wrestle a white person to the ground on the hillside where Sykes was killed, but they often saw vagrants there and thought the two were drunks fighting. They didn't think to stop or get help, and they couldn't identify the victim or the attacker or provide a description of what they looked like. They couldn't even say for sure whether the victim was a woman or a man. Police also spoke with a man named William Hooper, who was driving north on West End Boulevard at about 6:20 that morning on his way to work at the Hanes Dye and Finishing Plant. Hooper didn't approve of mixed-race couples, so when he noticed a white woman with two Black men, he slowed his car. He saw one of the men, the shorter one, shake his fist at her. The other man kissed her on the mouth. But Hooper didn't think she was in trouble, just another white girl "gone bad," and drove on. Police showed Hooper a stack of mug shots, but none of the faces looked familiar. A block behind Hooper, Thomas Murphy was also taking his usual route to work at the Hanes plant. He, too, slowed when he saw a white woman he had seen before with a Black man. He told police they were leaning toward each other, as though they were drunk, with the man's arm around her neck. About 100 feet away from them, he saw another Black man. The woman wasn't struggling, so he, too, drove on. That evening, when he heard about the murdered copy editor on the news, he called the police department. "I knew I should have stopped," he told the police, repeating himself through tears. Murphy also looked through stacks of mug shots but, like Hooper, didn't see a familiar face.[18]

A police artist sketched composite drawings from the descriptions Hooper and Murphy gave. The first, based on Murphy's description, shows a man with high cheekbones, light brown skin, and a narrow nose. The next two drawings were based on the descriptions Hooper provided of the two Black men he saw with the white woman that morning. One man has a wide nose, broad forehead, narrow face, and dark skin; the other is lighter skinned, with a narrow nose and jaw. But it was Murphy, filled with regret, who was most eager to help. That night, Daulton took Murphy back to the crime scene and around downtown looking for the man Murphy had seen that morning with Sykes. The next morning, before he was due in at work, he and Daulton met on West End Boulevard, again, in the hopes that he would see one of the two men he'd seen the day before. Maybe the killer would return.[19]

Not until the evening of August 10 did Daulton learn of the 911 call reporting the attack. "Sammy Mitchell" was a name recognized by many in the police department. He was a young Black man who lived with his mother in a brick apartment building on Patterson Avenue and was always getting in trouble for fighting or worse. He was part of a rough crowd, men and women who hung around the illegal liquor houses operating in apartments and shotgun houses all over the east side of town. Another detective knew that Mitchell frequented a convenience store near his home, a place called the Service Distributor's Station on Liberty Street.[20] This was still part of downtown, but it was the Black downtown, near the tobacco factories that lined Patterson Avenue.

Since the turn of the century, the factories had employed so many Black workers that Winston-Salem became home to a solid Black middle class, one of the strongest in the South. In 1984, the sweet smell of tobacco still filled the air, especially on warm summer nights, but Mitchell's family had never made it to that solid middle class. Mitchell worked a few odd jobs that summer, but mostly he could be found on the streets or behind his mother's apartment building, playing cards in the shade of a tree.

The detective who worked with Daulton left his card at the Service Distributor's Station. When Mitchell showed up later that night, the clerk called the detective back. By the time the detective arrived, having driven the half mile over from city hall, Mitchell was gone, but another man, thinner and younger than Mitchell, met him in the parking lot. The detective told Daulton he thought the man in the parking lot said his name was Darryl Hunt and that he was Mitchell's "brother."[21]

Newspapers strive for neutrality, but with one of its own murdered, the *Sentinel* offered $2,500 for a reward for information leading to an arrest. The *Chattanooga Free Press*, where Sykes worked before joining the *Sentinel,* matched that reward with another $2,500. Across the street, executives at the Integon Corp. insurance company pledged $1,000. An anonymous donor added $2,000 to the reward fund. The local chapter of the Communications Workers of America contributed $500, and other contributions came from individual donors, $10 and $20 at a time. The reward fund grew to more than $12,000 and, matched with widespread publicity about the case, produced dozens of tips to Crime Stoppers. Women called about their ex-boyfriends. People called about their neighbors. Some suspects had alibis. Others did not resemble the composite drawings. The number of tips was overwhelming, and they landed on Daulton's desk.

The detective looked into several tips that the man known around Crystal Towers as "Too Tall" Wall had been seen lurking around the park where Sykes had been stabbed. Sykes' coworkers at the newspaper knew Too Tall too, the menacing man in the floppy hat who made threatening comments to women. Daulton showed Murphy a picture of Too Tall, whose real name was Charles Wall, and Murphy identified him as the second man he'd seen 100 feet down the block from the Black man embracing a white woman. Someone else saw Too Tall running from the park hours before the crime. Daulton and another detective, a woman named Teresa Hicks, brought Too Tall into the police department for questioning. He kept jumping up, saying that a ghost had killed the woman in the park. Then he left. None of the witnesses had described an attacker of six and a half feet, and if Too Tall was a witness, he wasn't much use. Daulton needed something more to go on than a ghost.[22]

On August 14, a Tuesday, a police officer left a card again for Sammy Mitchell with the clerk at the service station. That afternoon, Mitchell and Darryl Hunt, together as usual, picked up the card on their way downtown. This time, Mitchell flagged down a patrol car. The officer got in touch with Daulton, who arranged to meet Mitchell and Hunt outside a downtown pool hall. Mitchell wore a heavy beard that summer and was the stockier of the two men. Daulton noticed that they wore black hats and that Mitchell's breath smelled of alcohol. Daulton had the tape of the 911 call in his police car and asked them both to listen. Hunt didn't recognize the voice of the caller. Neither did Mitchell. And once he heard Mitchell's voice, Daulton could also tell that it wasn't the voice on the tape. "Both of these guys were laughing and they didn't take it very seriously," he noted.[23]

A new break in the case came the following week, on August 22, when a man motioned to a downtown patrol officer, pointing to another man getting on a city bus. "That man, the one in the orange shirt, that's the one who had killed the Sykes girl," he was saying. Police stopped the bus and brought the man in the orange shirt into the police station for questioning. One of the officers recognized the accuser right away as one of the regulars from the Trade Street pool hall, a guy named Johnny Gray, with a police record that should have given officers pause. Soon it was clear to police that he was the eyewitness they'd been looking for over the past two weeks, the man who gave his name as Sammy Mitchell on the 911 call because, as he was saying now, he feared getting involved. Gray told police that after he saw the attack, he headed north down the hill near the Hanes plant to the nearest pay phone he could think of, about half a mile away. "I told them, I said it was behind Crystal Towers by the fire station in the field," Gray told the detectives. "And they said they would check on it, so I just hung up the phone. I did do that, and I did recognize the man, and now if we have to come to a court of law to say that, I will do it, because I know this is the man I saw."[24]

Gray went on to describe what he saw the morning of the murder, all recorded and then transcribed. He was walking north on West End Boulevard, on his way to visit a friend, when he heard a woman hollering. The sound was coming from behind a wood fence. Gray peered over the pilings and saw a Black man straddling a white woman. She was naked from the waist down, and the man was hitting her. The man turned and looked toward Gray, then took off running through the field. He crossed Marshall Street, a mini thoroughfare, and disappeared in the alley beside the fire station. Gray said he got a good look at his face. He would never forget it. And he said that the man in the orange shirt the police had in custody in the other room was the same man. "I didn't see nothing in his hands, nothing like that, just seen what he done, and I seen him get up, took off running. I recognized the man and I'll put my life on the line that this man is here today." The detectives didn't hide their excitement. Would he testify in court? Yes, Gray told them; he just wanted to help. "Well, you know you'll be our witness 'cause we don't have an eyewitness to the actual crime itself," Daulton told him. "You got one now," Gray replied.[25]

News spread around the police station that a suspect in the Sykes murder was in custody. His name was Terry Thomas. After the interview with Gray ended, the officers turned off the tape recorder and walked with Gray down the hall to the room where Thomas sat. The door was open so that Gray could get a good look. "Terry Thomas was sitting in a chair facing directly toward Johnny Gray," a detective later wrote. "Gray and Thomas were approximately 15 feet away from each other. I don't remember how he said it or acknowledged it, but in my opinion, Johnny Gray insinuated that the Black man in the interview room [Terry Thomas] was the same Black man he had seen assaulting the white female near the bushes on West End Blvd. on 8-10-84." Police called the district attorney's office and began drawing up a murder warrant.

It didn't take long for their exuberance to come crashing down. Thomas had an ironclad alibi. The morning of the murder, he was in jail on a trespassing charge.[26]

Chapter Two

The Blues Brothers

The Service Distributor's convenience store, a low cinder block building at the corner of Chestnut and Liberty, served as an informal meeting spot for Darryl Hunt and Sammy Mitchell. They could sit on the low wall at the edge of the parking lot, drink their first beer of the night, and check on Ann and "Little Bit," two prostitutes who worked Liberty Street just north of the store, on a stretch they called "the Block."[1]

When Hunt and Mitchell reached the corner on the evening of August 10, the store clerk called their names out over the loudspeaker. The police were looking for Mitchell again, no surprise. At 29, Mitchell had never been able to stay out of trouble, getting into fights and, even when he wasn't involved, getting blamed anyway. Most of the officers who patrolled the east side of town knew him by reputation as a tough guy, with scars all over his chest and face to prove it. There were other reasons Hunt could think of that the police might be looking for them that night. Maybe Ann or Little Bit had gotten busted again. Or maybe it was Sammy's girlfriend, after him for not paying child support for Sammy Jr. Hunt went in and told the clerk to go ahead and let the police know he and Mitchell were there. Whatever it was, Hunt wasn't worried. Had he known about the rape and murder of the young newspaper editor that morning, or that there was a manhunt on to find the Black man who killed her, he might have been more concerned. But he hadn't heard the news.[2]

The evening was unfolding much like every other that summer. Hunt and Mitchell had met up at the apartment on Patterson Avenue where Mitchell's mother lived, then headed out for the night. They'd known each other for about five years, but had grown tight in the past year, ever since Hunt came home from California at 18 to collect an inheritance from his grandfather, who had managed to leave his grandson $8,000 from working at the city streets department.[3] Despite their age difference, Hunt and Mitchell spent so much time together that year that people they knew around the neighborhood began calling them "the Blues Brothers" or "the Gold Dust Twins." In a Polaroid shot taken the night before Sykes' murder, Hunt wears a white shirt, unbuttoned almost to his navel, and a ball cap, his head cocked to the side, the tail end of braided cornrows visible behind his left ear. Mitchell, heavier and bearded, wears a golf cap, tilted jauntily, his arm thrown casually over Hunt's shoulder in a brotherly gesture.[4]

Neither man had a job that summer, or his own apartment, so they depended on any number of women they knew from the neighborhood for a place to sleep. Hunt had learned in his early teens to survive by picking up women.[5] Mitchell was equally charming. They had their choice of women that summer. For starters, Little Bit often gave Hunt money from the tricks she turned, though Hunt never thought of himself as her pimp. People in the neighborhood gossiped about Hunt and Little Bit because she was white. Sometimes, white people driving by would call out at her: "Why are you with that nigger?" Hunt didn't care. He had grown fond of Little Bit and was trying to help her get off drugs. Little Bit was fond of him, too. After checking in with the two prostitutes, Hunt and Mitchell usually ended up at one of the dozens of illegal liquor houses that operated out of apartments and shotgun-style rental houses all over the east side of town, where most of the city's Black population lived.[6]

Like many places in the heavily Baptist South, North Carolina discouraged drinking through laws that required food sales for a liquor license. More prosperous neighborhoods on the west side of town had their country clubs and high-end restaurants that sold fine wine and booze. Poor people had their liquor houses. Sometimes, "Guitar Gabriel" and other local blues players would show up. But most liquor houses were more basic: a couple of tables and some chairs for serious drinking. The night before Sykes' killing, Hunt had paid a bartender at one of the liquor houses they frequented a dollar to take the Polaroid picture of him and Mitchell. Later, he and Mitchell spent the night with the McKey sisters, Cynthia and Mary, over on Dunleith Avenue.[7] As he waited for the police, Hunt would not have known yet where the night would end. Maybe Little Bit would rent a room for the night, or they might end up with the McKeys again. They never had a clear plan, but whatever they did, Hunt would remember. He had an uncanny memory for events.

By evening, the morning fog had lifted and a light drizzle fell,[8] a relief from the heavy heat of August. Hunt waited outside the convenience store for the police, while Mitchell went down the street to pay off a tab at Pookie's Lounge. Hunt hadn't been waiting long before the police pulled up. He waited when officers went into the store, where the clerk told them to look outside. He had nothing to hide and as far as he knew, neither did Mitchell. And he was still outside, waiting, when the two officers came out looking for Mitchell. They asked his name and where he'd been the night before. "We stayed over at Cynt's house," Hunt told them. "Did Sammy make a phone call?" "No." As the police car pulled out of the parking lot, it passed Mitchell heading back to the store. The officers waved at Mitchell and drove on.[9]

At the time, the questions meant little to Hunt, though later he would remember the details of the exchange as the beginning of a series of events that would change his life forever. He didn't know that the name Sammy Mitchell was the only solid lead police had in the murder that morning. If anything, the questions made Hunt see how little police really knew about his friend or about the life they lived on the east side of town. If they really knew Mitchell, like he did, they would have known that he only called two people, ever—the bail bondsman and his mother.[10]

~

As a child, Hunt had looked forward to regular weekend excursions to Patterson Avenue with a relative he knew only as Jean. She was part of the large extended family always welcome at the house on Maryland Avenue in the City View neighborhood, where Hunt had lived with the couple he knew as his parents, Willie and Hattie Stroud, and his older brother, also named Willie. Until he was nine, it wasn't exactly clear to him how he and his brother were related to Jean. He thought of her as an older sister or an aunt. But there was something about Jean that drew him in. Maybe it was the way she held the boys close when she hugged them. Or her smile. Or that she was so much younger and more light-hearted than his parents, both in their fifties. Most weekends, Jean would take the boys downtown for the day, to her apartment on Patterson Avenue, and show them off. City View was a quiet residential neighborhood, but Patterson, on the eastern edge of the city's downtown, was always full of people: women pushing baby strollers, children playing, men and women getting off work at the tobacco factories down the street. Sometimes, Jean would take the boys out to eat or to shop for clothes. And she seemed to know everyone: the waitresses at the cafés, the sales clerk at the shoe store, the men playing cards in the parking lot.[11] A picture from that time shows Jean with a short, stylish haircut, in a sleeveless blouse.[12] Her friends on Patterson Avenue would comment on the resemblance between her and the boys. Darryl loved the commotion and the people who would call out their names when they passed.

He felt at home there and hated it when the visits ended and they returned to their mom and dad on Maryland Avenue.[13]

Hunt was born in 1965, the year after the Civil Rights Act passed, a law that tore down the legal framework for the segregated South but did little to change life on Maryland Avenue. The freeway, which had expanded US 52 from a two-lane road into a four-lane highway, opened the year he turned four, cutting off the east side of town from the rest of the city, a physical reminder of the city's entrenched pattern of segregation. Maryland was just two blocks long, in a neighborhood tucked behind a park. The Kate B. Reynolds Hospital, established for Black residents by the wife of the tobacco magnate who founded the R. J. Reynolds Tobacco Company, was within walking distance. So were other institutions that gave stability, if not equality, to the east side of town. The campus of Winston-Salem State University, founded in 1892 as an African-American teachers college, was on the other side of Interstate 40, the east-west thoroughfare through town. Within half a mile were dozens of churches, including Goler Metropolitan AME Zion Church, a brick building with an imposing Greek Revival façade that had twice hosted Rev. Martin Luther King Jr., and First Calvary Baptist, also in the Greek Revival style, which Hunt's family attended.

A school picture of Hunt from the time shows a skinny kid with thick glasses.[14] He and his brother rode their bikes around the neighborhood, played baseball with the other kids, and made sure to do their chores. If they missed curfew or skipped their chores, they'd get a beating. The Strouds were loving but believed in discipline at home. Better to get a beating from those who loved you than to fall into the dangerous hands of outside authorities. Hattie Stroud worked for a dry cleaner for 20 years, until she became disabled with diabetes.[15] Her husband, stocky, with a powerful build and a mustache, worked for the city streets division and paid his bills in cash on time and in person, often taking Darryl with him, to teach him about handling money. The night before, they would sit at the kitchen table and count out the bills from the several thousand dollars in cash Stroud kept hidden at home. Stroud didn't trust banks and kept most of his money in jars in the attic or buried in the backyard.[16] He was a proud man, too. When his wife became disabled, having lost both legs to diabetes, Stroud applied for medical assistance and food stamps. In their reports, social workers noted with admiration his reluctance to apply for these benefits; they called him "exceptional."[17]

When Hunt was eight, Hattie died[18] and the mysterious woman whose visits he always anticipated started spending more time with him and his brother. One afternoon, their father called Darryl and Willie into the living room. There were some things they needed to know about Jean, some things that would be hard for a nine-year-old boy to understand, but it was time they knew the truth. Jean was their mother, but when they were born, she was too young to take care of them, so he and Hattie raised them. And now that Hattie was gone, and Jean was a little older, she was going to be more of a mother to them. Her neighborhood, the one Darryl liked so much, wasn't a good place for children. It was too crowded and dangerous, so the plan was that Jean would move back home with them. A week later, their grandfather sat them down again. The woman they'd only just discovered was their mother was dead, murdered on the street outside her apartment building. She was 24.[19]

Years passed before Hunt learned the full story of the shooting. In the 1970s and into the 1980s, Patterson was a close-knit but violent neighborhood. The street was still the center of a prosperous Black business district, lined with lunch counters, grocery stores, and other small businesses. Black doctors, lawyers, and funeral directors had their offices there, too. There was a YMCA, separate from the Central YMCA on the west side of town, and two churches, another AME Zion Church, called Goler Memorial, and the wood-frame Lloyd Presbyterian Church with an apricot tree in its yard. But middle-class Black people, those who made good money working in the tobacco factories on the southern end of the street, had long since moved out to suburban-style neighborhoods, still on the east side of town, where they could buy a brick split-level with a yard, leaving the neighborhood's cheap rentals, the shotgun-style frame houses and run-down apartment buildings, to others less fortunate.

During the day, the sidewalks were crowded with people heading off to work and school or out shopping. At night, neighbors headed out to drink at one of the liquor houses operating out of one of the frame houses or one of the apartment buildings in the neighborhood, places with nicknames like "the Pink Palace," for its pink stucco exterior, and "the Island," for the tall trees growing beside it that swayed in the breeze like palm trees. Known around the neighborhood for fighting with the ferocity of a man, Jean Hunt was part of this hard-drinking crowd. The boyfriend she'd been with since her early teens, a man named Frankie Crosby, was always in and out of jail. She also had a younger boyfriend, a teenager still in high school, who went by the nickname "Man." Something happened between Jean and Man that enraged the teenager's sister. Some said Jean had beaten Man up. Others said the sister, Jimmie Lee, was angry that a grown woman was dating her little brother. Whatever the reason was, she confronted Jean, making sure to bring a gun, and in the squabble, shot her dead.[20]

It was a lot for a boy to make sense of, and in a way Darryl Hunt never did. He'd already lost Hattie, the woman he thought of as his mother. Then he lost his real mother before he ever had a chance to get used to calling her "mama" or to know all the normal things he imagined boys know about their mothers—her favorite color or what she liked best to eat or the kinds of flowers she would want on her birthday. And it was never even clear how his murdered mother and his grandparents were related, except that they had raised her the way they'd raised him. In one version of the story, William Stroud came home from work one cold day to the sound of a baby's cries coming from the vacant house next door. He followed the cries to find an abandoned baby girl with a note from a woman he was seeing on the side pinned to the baby's blanket, telling him that she was leaving his baby in his care and heading out of town. In another version of the story, the baby's paternity was unclear, but she was a helpless infant in need of a home, and William and Hattie gave her one. William and Hattie were strict with Hunt and his brother, so they must have been strict with Jean, too. Still, she grew up wild and by the time she was 13, she was sent to a juvenile detention center, where she gave birth to Willie. Darryl was born next, when his mother was 15. At 17, she gave birth to a daughter, Doris. The Strouds took all three babies in, and raised them as their own, though Doris soon went to live with Jean's mother. When Jean died, Stroud looked after the two boys as he always had.[21]

～

Darryl was never much of a student. For one thing, he had trouble reading. And he didn't care much for most of his teachers. But there was something about his sixth-grade teacher at Mebane Elementary School that made him feel at ease. Jo Anne North had grown up poor in the mountains, about an hour north of Winston-Salem, and was the first in her family to finish school. She understood in her bones the lives led by her students, white and Black, and she made her classroom a sanctuary. She covered the walls with colorful posters and the children's art. She placed plants on the windowsill to hide the view.

It wasn't easy managing a class of 30 students. One day, she put the boys in one line and the girls in another. It was time for them to get their eyes checked in the nurse's office. She worked her way through the line of girls, handing out health cards, and was halfway down the line of boys, when one of them, a boy named Nathan, threw his card on the floor. "I'm not taking it," Nathan said. "You gave them to the girls first."

Darryl could see North hesitate, trying to decide what to do, a sign of weakness he knew would only make things worse for her. "Pick up your card," he told the other boy. Nathan stared at him; Hunt stared back. "Pick up your card. The girls go first. That's the rule." His quiet authority worked, and his teacher was forever grateful.[22]

Before the schools in Winston-Salem were desegregated in 1969, Mebane Elementary School had been a school for Black children, and by 1977, the year Hunt was in the sixth grade there, it had yet to be renovated. The brick outside was chipped. The worn wooden floors were hard to keep clean. And one of the houses across the street was reputed to be a whorehouse. When Jo Anne North started working there three years earlier, her friends warned her away, telling her it was too dangerous.[23]

With its entrenched, segregated housing patterns, Winston-Salem relied on a busing plan to desegregate its schools, sending Black children to white suburban schools during the first three years of elementary school and white children to inner-city Black schools for the last three years. Darryl was one of eight Black children in a class of 30 sixth graders. And once he stood down the class bully over the health form, North came to count on him. She'd been warned, for example, that there was a good chance her car battery would be stolen during evening PTA meetings. She stopped worrying when she found Hunt standing by her car in the darkness, on guard.

North liked to reward her students on Fridays with bingo games and candy for prizes. But the school was infested with mice, which would get into the candy she had stored in the closet. When she complained to her students about having to set traps and, even worse, clean them out in the morning, Hunt volunteered to come in early, after his paper route, and set the traps. The routine left them plenty of time to talk before the other children came to school. North knew he didn't have a mother and tried to give him extra attention.

Sometimes Hunt complained about his brother and his grandfather, like the time he took a beating because his brother blamed him for not mowing his part of the yard, when really it was Willie who hadn't mown the grass. "Life isn't always fair," North told him, hoping that would be a comfort. She admired Hunt's grandfather, who came to every parent-teacher conference. Stroud told her how he had gotten his GED so that he could be promoted to foreman with the city streets division. He wanted Darryl to be educated, too. "Darryl's a good boy," he would tell her. "Now, Willie. He's a different story. But Darryl, that boy never gives me any trouble."[24]

~

Darryl Hunt would remember the first time he met Sammy Mitchell for the rest of his life. At the time, he was 14, a skinny teenager who had started hanging around his mother's neighborhood in search of her old crowd. Hunt had already tracked down the man Jean was dating when she died, not the high school kid she was seeing on the sly, but Crosby, the grown man who was her longtime sweetie, the one who claimed to be Hunt's father. Crosby seemed to know everyone in the neighborhood, just like his mother had. Crosby taught Hunt survival tips, how to pick up women and crash with them when he needed a place to sleep. And Crosby introduced him to Sammy Mitchell. They were hanging out across the street from his mother's old apartment building, where Hunt remembered the excitement of visits with his mother and all the people on the street who knew them by name. The memories made Patterson Avenue feel more like home than anywhere else. But it was also the place where his mother had been shot to death. At 14, he must have imagined that moment, the sound of gunshot and the woman he longed to know falling to the sidewalk. Mitchell, who carried himself with the swagger of a 24-year-old man with a tough-guy reputation to uphold, recognized Hunt right away. "Man, you've grown since I last saw you," he said. "What's been up?" They talked some about Jean, and how Mitchell had always admired her for the way she carried herself. More than anyone, Mitchell gave Hunt a way of seeing his mother in a new light, as a respected figure. That was more than enough to seal his loyalty.[25]

By the summer of 1984, Darryl Hunt was 19 and trying to get his life back on track. After his grandfather, William Stroud, died in 1977,[26] he was sent to live with his grandfather's sister in Winston-Salem, while his brother was sent off to other relatives. The separation hurt. "The passing of granddaddy changed the course of our lives," Hunt wrote years later in journals he kept in prison. "When there was security, after granddaddy passed everything was unsure."[27]

As a teenager, he took a bus to Charlotte, hoping to track down his grandmother on his mother's side and find his baby sister, Doris. The police found him in a liquor house and sent him home. By high school, Hunt had dropped out. He moved to Monterey, California, to live with a cousin, a woman he thought of as a half-sister. He worked there, first in a restaurant, then for a landscape company, often babysitting his sister's children. Before he left for California, he had learned that his grandfather had left him money that would be his when he turned 18. As that birthday drew near, Hunt moved back to Winston-Salem and settled in with his mother's old crowd. The inheritance came to $8,000, a vast sum to an 18-year-old in a neighborhood where most everyone lived paycheck to paycheck, if that. His first act as a man of means was to rent an apartment, paying six months up front, for Crosby, the man who claimed to be his father. Hunt lived there, with Crosby and Crosby's girlfriend.

Soon Hunt started dating a woman named Renee Boston, and her father gave Hunt a job in his construction company. Renee was pregnant by another man, but that didn't bother Hunt, and the couple started making plans for a life together. At first, they lived with Renee's parents, but with money left from his inheritance, Hunt rented an apartment for himself and Renee, and spent most of what was left buying furniture for them and the new baby. When Tahara was born, Hunt looked after her, much the way his grandparents had looked after him, loving her as his own. He played with her, changed her diapers, and babysat when her mother went off to party. Later, when he dreamed of starting a family of his own, he would imagine Tahara as the eldest of five, teaching the younger ones how to do right in the world. But the romance didn't last. When he and Renee split up, Hunt was broke, homeless, and heartbroken.[28]

In 1983, he got into a fight and was charged with the misdemeanor of damaging property, which carried a fine of $975.[29] Out of work, he decided it would be simplest to serve a six-month jail term in lieu of paying the fine. Mitchell also had a sentence to serve. In December, they turned themselves in to the Forsyth County Jail, hoping they would be assigned to the same cell block. Mitchell knew his way around the jail. At least they would be together. When Hunt's six-month sentence was up in June, he settled into a routine that revolved around Patterson Avenue. With no permanent address, he kept his clothes at the apartment of Mitchell's mother, Mattie, in the brick building across the street from his mother's old place, and would stop by there at least once a day to get cleaned up. During the day, he would look for a job, stopping at construction sites or the city's streets department, where his grandfather had worked. Then he and Mitchell would meet up, drink a beer, and decide on a plan for the night. He knew about Mitchell's bad reputation, but he saw a softer side. Mitchell ran errands for elderly neighbors, defended women whose boyfriends hit them, and loved his children and his mother. Most importantly, he could tell Hunt stories about his mother and introduce him to her crowd. And that was enough. If anyone ever questioned Hunt's choice of Mitchell as a friend, he would say: "He's all I got."[30]

~

Detective Daulton had been working around the clock all through August and into September, and still there was no arrest in the Sykes case. But he could a feel a break in the case coming. He had the teenage prostitute, the one known on the street as Little Bit, in his office at the police department on a runaway charge, and she was talking. She had been nervous when he first met her in the courthouse, more than a week earlier, where he found her waiting for a hearing on a prostitution charge. That was when she had blown Hunt's alibi by telling Daulton that Hunt had been with her the night before the murder, way up on the north side of town at the Motel 6, not over on the east side of town the way Hunt had been saying. Daulton could tell she liked Hunt and would have done anything for him, though he couldn't understand why. She had looked at Daulton with those sunken eyes and told him as much. If he gave her a date, she would provide Hunt with an alibi.[31]

Hunt had accidentally given Daulton Little Bit's name at the end of August. Daulton had been working closely with his eyewitness Thomas Murphy all that month, a practice that violated just about every principle of criminal investigation, but having spent most of his career as a traffic cop, he didn't know better. What's more, the pressure on the department to solve the case was relentless, and it all flowed downhill, which would have made any investigator feel overwhelmed and alone. At least Murphy wanted to help. They'd been meeting outside the factory where Murphy worked at 5:30 in the morning, before the day shift began, and driving over to the crime scene together, looking, as Daulton would say, at foot traffic, in case the killer returned. On mornings when Daulton wasn't available, Murphy would do the surveillance work on his own. He still couldn't shake the feeling that if only he had stopped, he might have been able to save Sykes. Maybe now he could at least help find her killer. One morning late in August, more than two weeks after the murder, Murphy saw a man he recognized as the one he'd seen leaning into Sykes, with his arm around her neck. He was sure he'd be able to recognize the man if he saw his picture in a photo lineup.[32]

Daulton left word for Hunt and his sidekick, Sammy Mitchell, at the convenience store that he wanted to see them again, and this time they went downtown to the police department to see what he wanted. Daulton felt something was fishy about those two, the way they'd stop him on the street and ask him whether he'd figured out yet who made that 911 call. He felt like they were mocking him. More recently, he was hearing from officers who worked the streets that their sources were telling them that Mitchell and Hunt were bragging about killing the newswoman. It had been more than two weeks since the murder, and Hunt's and Mitchell's names kept coming up. Now that his eyewitness had seen the suspect again, Daulton wanted to know where Hunt and Mitchell had been that morning, the 28th of August. Maybe he could link them to the man Murphy had just seen. Hunt told him he'd been at the Motel 6 with Little Bit. Hunt gave Daulton Little Bit's real name too: Brenda Rene Morino. Daulton wrote her name down, for later. And he also asked whether the two men would take a polygraph. They would, they said, though Mitchell, the cocky one, said he knew a way to beat it. That pissed Daulton off. This was serious business, and here they were mocking him again.[33]

He took Little Bit into custody on a runaway warrant from her hometown of Eden, about an hour east of town. She was only 15, and it turned out her real name was Margaret Crawford, not Brenda Morino, the name she was using, so she, too, had been lying. He could tell she was scared and that most of all, she didn't want to go back to her hometown. All this—her youth, her drug habit, her fear—should have given him pause. But the threat of arrest on the runaway warrant was working. Once again, she told Daulton that she and Hunt had spent the night of August 9 together at the Motel 6, which contradicted what Hunt had been saying, that he'd been with the McKeys on Dunleith Avenue the morning of the murder. There was no good reason for Daulton to believe her without corroboration, nothing that made her any more or less reliable than Hunt. But as the more experienced detectives in the department liked to say, you can't choose your witnesses. And now she was talking in a way that made all the pieces come together. She told Daulton that Hunt left the motel in a taxi at six in the morning of August 10. That put Hunt on the scene at the time witnesses saw a Black man with a white woman.

And there was more to her story. Crawford said that Hunt returned to the motel room three hours later, about 9:30 a.m. He was nervous and she noticed grass stains on his pants. The story she provided continued. About two weeks after the murder, she and Hunt had been watching TV together when a report came on about the reward in the Sykes case. "I wish I knew who killed that lady, because I could use the money," she remembered telling Hunt. Then she gave Daulton exactly what he needed, repeating what she said were Hunt's words: "Sammy did it, and he fucked her, too."[34] The damage was done. Try as she might, she would never be able to retract her words.

Daulton was determined not to screw this up. Crawford's statement wasn't enough to get a murder warrant drawn for the two men, but it was enough to get a warrant drawn up for Hunt's arrest on a charge of taking indecent liberties with a minor. That would get Hunt into custody and give Daulton time to figure out what had really happened out in that field the morning Sykes was killed.

～

Summer in North Carolina lasts well into September, with warm days and balmy evenings. Hunt and Mitchell planned on spending Tuesday evening, September 11, together as usual. They had just met up in the parking lot outside Mattie Mitchell's building when Daulton pulled up in his squad car wanting to talk with them yet again. They told him they were getting fed up with all these questions about a crime they knew nothing about but climbed into the back of his car anyway, for the quick ride downtown, hardly the behavior of two men trying to dodge a murder charge in the most high-profile case of the decade.[35]

The police department had its offices on the third floor of Winston-Salem's elegant city hall. Daulton brought Hunt upstairs to an interview room and asked Mitchell to wait outside. Hunt didn't know the other officers in the room, but it was clear they meant business. They asked him again about the night of August 9 and the morning of August 10. Then they started yelling at him, accusing him of the killing. After what seemed like an hour, Mitchell knocked on the door to tell them he was leaving because he needed to go across the street to pay down a bond for the last time Ann, the prostitute, had been arrested. None of the officers stopped him. In fact, Daulton was glad to see him go because he wanted Hunt in the room alone. "You're a lying nigger," an officer said. "We got witnesses who can put you at the scene." Hunt thought it was all some kind of sick joke. "You can't charge me with something I haven't done," he told them. One of the officers left the room, and Daulton told Hunt they had Little Bit locked up. He wanted Hunt to talk with her and dialed the phone number. She was crying, saying something about how she was going to be charged with murder and begged him to tell them what he knew. "I don't know nothing about this shit," he told her. Daulton took the phone away and hung it up. Another officer appeared and threw a warrant on the table. "Are you going to tell us the truth?" one of them asked. "I been telling you the truth," Hunt replied. "I don't know nothing about a murder."[36]

Next, the detectives brought in a uniformed officer, who handcuffed Hunt and went through his pockets. Daulton read the arrest warrant, charging him with taking indecent liberties with a minor. Hunt didn't know what the words meant, until Daulton explained that Little Bit was a juvenile and he was being charged with having sex with a minor. The charge made no sense. Little Bit had been on the streets turning tricks long before he met her. It never occurred to him to check her age. One day she'd say she was 22, the next day

19. What did it matter anyway? He could manage a night in jail. His first appearance in court was the next day. Surely a judge would see that this was all a terrible mistake.

~

The county jail occupied a three-story brick building on Church Street, across from the back door to city hall. There wasn't a lot of room in the jail then, so the system the police had developed for witnesses to identify a suspect was to line up a group of men, all imprisoned in the jail, in front of the elevator door on the third floor. They'd bring a witness up in the elevator and let them look through the elevator window at the line of men. With Hunt in jail, Daulton could put him in one of these live lineups.

He'd already shown Hunt's picture, which the department would have had on file from Hunt's earlier arrest, to his witnesses. That was a couple of weeks earlier, after he'd been hearing that Hunt and Mitchell were bragging about killing the newswoman. Daulton thought about showing Mitchell's picture to witnesses. After all, he was the one with the criminal record and the reputation for violence, but the trouble was none of the witnesses had described seeing a man with a beard, so there was no sense in showing them Mitchell's bearded face. Instead, he settled on the photograph of Hunt.[37]

Everything about the way Daulton assembled the photo lineup violated procedures police departments now use to guard against misidentification. First of all, Daulton should never have been the one to show witnesses photos of suspects. He and Murphy had developed a relationship, which meant there was a chance Murphy would pick up on body language and other signals to select the photo Daulton wanted. A better practice would have been for an officer with no knowledge of the case to show Murphy the photos. The photos themselves also made it more likely that Murphy would pick out Hunt. The mug shot of Hunt is shot against a light brown background. The other photos of Black men Daulton used to fill out the lineup were shot against a light gray background. The difference in background color would have made Hunt's picture stand out from the others, making it more likely that a witness would select him. Daulton had noticed how Murphy took his time looking at the pictures before settling on Hunt. Daulton had noticed, too, that Murphy picked the picture up, closed his eyes, and looked again, before saying, "Maybe I'd like to see this one in person."[38]

Daulton had also tracked down his other lead witness, the 911 caller named Johnny Gray. He had his misgivings about Gray. After all, Gray had lied when he called 911 and he had picked out the wrong man once before. Daulton had even shown Gray's photo to Murphy in case he should be thinking of him as a suspect. All that aside, Gray was the only witness who had actually seen the attack. Daulton found Gray at the pool hall on Trade Street. Gray came outside, got in the car, and looked through the six photos Daulton had shown to Murphy, settling on the picture of Hunt. "I'm telling you this guy looks good, you need to pick him up," Gray said.[39]

The day after he'd picked Hunt up on the sex charge, Daulton asked the jail to recruit volunteers to stand in a lineup with Hunt. He lined the five men, all Black, up in front of the elevator, their backs against the wall, and gave them each a sheet of paper with a number scrawled across the front. Hunt, dressed in jeans and a white-collared knit shirt, was number four. Murphy and Daulton rode the elevator up to the third floor, with the light inside the elevator shut off, so that Murphy could see out through the window but the men in the lineup couldn't see him. The five men turned so that he could see them in profile. Daulton gave him a couple of minutes to look, then asked if he was through. Murphy nodded his head yes. Back downstairs, in the warden's office, Murphy sat down and held his hand over his heart. "Dammit, I didn't never think I'd see that face again," he said. Daulton asked him which man he had recognized. "Number four," Murphy replied. "Damn, Daulton, you've got him."[40]

~

Now in his third term as district attorney, Don Tisdale had little patience for obstruction or denial. He had studied Latin and history in college, which gave him an appreciation for language and clarity. At home in the courtroom from the get-go, he'd been elected DA just six years out of law school, and he well understood the politics of his office. The investigation into the murder of the newspaper editor had already gone on way too long, and the public wanted justice. Now 40, with thinning hair and a complexion that grew red with anger, he was ready for a fight. He leaned back in his chair and took a hard look across his desk at Hunt. "We know you didn't kill Mrs. Sykes," Tisdale said, leaning forward. Then he pulled out a heavy stick with an evidence tag on it. At first, Hunt thought the district attorney was going to strike him. Instead, he told Hunt that Mitchell had used the stick to rob a man back in 1975, and that he kept it in his office as a reminder of his first jury case, the one he lost. "We want Sammy," Tisdale said, slamming the stick down on his desk. "He got away the first time, but I'm going to get his ass this time."[41]

Tisdale offered Hunt a $12,000 reward if he would testify against his friend. Hunt wouldn't do it. "I'm not going to lie on anyone," Hunt told him. Then Tisdale told him they would charge him with the murder instead. Back and forth they went, the DA growing angrier and Hunt more determined. "We're going to put your Black ass in another lineup," Tisdale said. This time, Daulton allowed Hunt to pick the four other men he wanted in the lineup with him. He was number four again, and another man in jail with him was number one. They lined up on the third floor in front of the elevator and waited. Daulton went downstairs. Minutes later, the elevator stopped. Hunt could see a Black man in a red hat looking out at him and the others in line with him.[42]

A day passed before Hunt saw Tisdale again. Friday morning, September 14, Daulton handcuffed him, signed him out of jail, and took him back to the county courthouse, a 1970s-era building made of concrete and brick, a style of architecture that projected brute force more than justice. This time, Tisdale's office was filled with police officers. "All you have to do is say that Sammy did it," Tisdale said, repeating the earlier offer. "And you'll walk with $12,000." Hunt refused. The shouting began, with threats of a murder charge and the gas chamber. After what seemed to Hunt like half an hour had passed, Tisdale leaned back in his chair, held up a piece of paper, and handed it to him. "Read it," he said. It was a letter from Little Bit, begging him to tell them what he knew. She loved him, she wrote. And she was pregnant, with his child. Moments later, Daulton brought Little Bit into the room and led her to a chair beside Hunt. Tisdale turned on Little Bit next. He'd send her to "the gas chamber" with Hunt if Hunt didn't give Mitchell up. Little Bit wept and begged Hunt to tell them what he knew. Hunt fell silent. There was no sense in saying anything more.[43]

Hunt watched Tisdale pick up the phone and heard him ask the magistrate to draw up a murder warrant. An officer led Little Bit away. Daulton and another officer took him by either arm, led him to the elevator and downstairs to the magistrate's office, where the magistrate read him the charges. He'd been in trouble before, for petty stuff. But this was some kind of terrible mistake. If only someone would listen, Hunt could explain that he was no killer. Outside the magistrate's office, Hunt moved as if in a dream. A newspaper photographer snapped his picture. The officers led him back outside and down the street to city hall, where they took his mug shot and fingerprints, then outside again for the short walk back to jail. "Niggers like you should be hung," an officer said. "When we walk back to the jail, nigger, if you slip, trip or raise your head, I'm going to shoot you in the middle of the street," another officer

said. "We'll just say you tried to run." Hunt prayed there would be
people outside to watch and keep him safe.[44]

Back in jail, Hunt felt safe on the third floor, in a group cell
with men he knew from the neighborhood. But the thought of the
first floor filled him with terror. It was well known around the jail
that guards routinely beat up men hidden away in the single cells
downstairs. News had spread quickly around the jail that Hunt had
been charged with the murder of the white woman, the one who'd
been raped and stabbed to death. It would have been clear to the
other Black men locked up with Hunt from their own experience
and the weight of history that his race put him in danger. That evening, when jailers came to move Hunt to the first floor, the others
in the cellblock protested. "He's alright here," one said. "Let him
stay," the others shouted. Fearing violence, jailers began to call for
backup. Hunt wanted to stay with the other men, more than he
could say, but at the same time he didn't want to cause a riot, not
on his account. The sergeant on duty was a Black man, a man Hunt
had seen at some of the illegal liquor houses, so he felt a little less
afraid as they made their way downstairs to the first-floor cellblock.
It was hotter than hell down there and dark, especially at the end
of the corridor, where Hunt was locked up in a single cell, with a
bunk and a toilet.

Soon, the shift would end and the sergeant he knew would be
gone. At the start of the third shift, two jailers Hunt recognized came
to make their rounds. They were well known among the Black men
Hunt knew in jail, with a reputation for membership in the Ku Klux
Klan. There'd be no one to hear him down there if he screamed. He
stood up, ready for a fight, just in case. The jailers kept the cell door
locked, which might have given Hunt a moment of ease, until he
heard what they had to say: "The last nigger in this cell was found
hanging from these bars right here."[45]

Chapter Three

Darker Than Blue

Hunt's mug shot appeared in the *Winston-Salem Journal* the morning after his arrest. He was dressed in a white T-shirt, trimmed at the neckline in red, his head cocked slightly to the right, the cornrows he wore that summer sticking out around his ears. It's hard to read his expression. Police would later talk about his smirk. But people who knew him from the neighborhood saw the familiar hint of a smile and a faraway look. Larry Little, then the alderman from the North Ward, recognized Hunt right away from pickup basketball games they had played at the Patterson Avenue YMCA.

Other Black aldermen had followed a traditional path to politics, from teaching, the ministry, and business. Little was an activist. He had grown up in the projects and, in 1969, inspired by organizers from Greensboro who had come to town dressed in black with shotguns and revolutionary talk, he had dropped out of Winston-Salem State University to help start the local chapter of the Black Panther Party. Little was 19 that year and went out to California for training, returning to town with a mission.[1] The local chapter he led, the first in the South, ran a free ambulance service, a food pantry, and children's programs, but right away it fell under suspicion by the FBI. In 1970, the newspaper ran a picture of Little in a black leather jacket and armed with a shotgun, standing guard at the house of an older woman to stop her eviction.[2] The image established his reputation among many white people as a defiant and fearsome figure. When Little was elected to the board of aldermen at 27, he decided to stay in the neighborhood, living in a rat-infested apartment on Patterson Avenue, beside a barbershop and a funeral home.

"This is crazy," his mother told him. "We came out of the projects. It don't make no sense for you to live there."

"Maybe I can draw attention to these conditions," he replied.[3]

Now he was 34, in his second term in office, still on a mission. He stared hard at the mug shot reprinted in the newspaper, at Hunt's impish smile, and thought about the teenager he knew from the basketball court. He knew Hunt ran with a rough crowd, but his gut told him that the kid with the faraway look wasn't capable of the brutal rape and murder of the young newspaper editor.[4]

The more Little learned, the more he came to believe his hunch. With his Panther background, Little didn't have much patience with the police, or much faith in lawyers, especially the ones the court appointed to represent a poor Black kid charged with murder. He went to see Gordon Jenkins and Mark Rabil, the two lawyers appointed to represent Hunt. Neither of them had ever handled a murder case before. Little was not impressed. "I just want you to know there are some people concerned about him,"[5] Little told the two. They asked if he could help raise money for Hunt's defense, but before he made a move, he asked around the police department, seeking out Black officers who often confided in him about their own problems with the top brass. "Have they got the goods on this boy?" Little asked them about Hunt. They would whisper back that the case was weak. He also sought out a Black lawyer in town, who was close to the DA. He didn't want to stake his reputation on a hunch. "Larry, they ain't got no case on this boy," the lawyer told him.[6] The more Little learned, the less he liked what he was finding out. The composite drawings, the ones that showed a man with medium-brown skin, looked nothing like Hunt. Witnesses

described the attacker as taller than Sykes; at five feet nine, Hunt
was an inch shorter than she was. And no one, not a single witness,
had described the cornrows Hunt wore that summer.

This wouldn't be the first time a Black man had been framed
for the rape of a white woman in town. Black people knew all too
well about police brutality, harassment, and the history of lynching
in the South, which in 1984 was not that long ago. Little organized
the first meeting of what became Hunt's defense committee by
handing out flyers in the street. The first volunteers, mostly from
the Patterson Avenue neighborhood, met upstairs at the YMCA.
Estella McFadden, a friend of Sammy Mitchell's mother, was there
with her daughter. They knew Hunt and could not believe that the
quiet teenager, who was always so polite, could be a murderer. As
support grew, Little moved the meetings to the white-frame Lloyd
Presbyterian Church across Chestnut Street from Mitchell's building, where McFadden was custodian and had the key.[7] "We all know
that Darryl Hunt is darker than blue," Little would tell people, his
voice rising in indignation, pointing out the lighter-skinned faces in
the composite drawings. His words rang true. As McFadden, who
would later send Hunt ten dollars a month in prison for spending
money, said years later: "You see, we're Black people, and usually
when bad things happen—they'll snatch just about anyone."[8]

∼

Black men had been snatched throughout the South ever since the
first enslaved men, kidnapped from what is now Angola, were sold
near Hampton, Virginia, in 1619.[9] Scholars now make the case that
our entire system of mass incarceration and the failure of Reconstruction and the Civil Rights Movement to protect young Black
men like Hunt from false arrest and conviction are all legacies of
slavery. All but 16 of the 65 known cases of wrongful conviction
in North Carolina are Black defendants, with more than half the
cases dating back to the era of Hunt's arrest.[10] In 1976, for example,

Charles Finch was arrested in the death of a store clerk and sent to death row, with a single eyewitness the only evidence against him. In 1984, Henry McCollum, 19, and his half-brother, Leon Brown, 15, were arrested in the rape and murder of an 11-year-old girl. There was no physical evidence to tie them to the crime, but they both confessed and both were sent to death row. A month before Hunt's arrest, Ronald Cotton was mistakenly charged with the rape of another white woman, 22-year-old Jennifer Thompson, and sent away for life.[11] These men wouldn't be exonerated until years later, but the patterns of police misconduct, coerced confession, and hysteria over the idea of a white woman raped by a Black man were well known to people who rallied to Hunt's cause. If it could happen to Hunt, it could just as easily happen to them.

Little was the youngest of four, the only boy, raised by his single mother, who supported the family by working at a tobacco factory. He played basketball at Reynolds High School, one of the few Black students in the school. But with a failing grade in geography, he didn't graduate. He went on to complete high school through a correspondence course, but the humiliation made him feel used.[12] During a trip to New York to visit a sister, he was introduced to *The Autobiography of Malcolm X* and the politics of Black liberation. The Panther chapter he helped found in Winston-Salem with another young idealist named Nelson Malloy focused on the free-breakfast program and ambulance service. The chapter soon became caught up in the divisions that eventually destroyed the Panthers, and Little left the movement, disillusioned with its national leadership.[13] As a city alderman, Little surprised people by his willingness to work with conservative white aldermen. But he remained a champion for Black causes. The year before Hunt's arrest, for example, he led the opposition to a proposed bond referendum because Black contractors were getting shut out of city construction jobs.[14] And in the spring of 1984, he organized for Jesse Jackson, the first Black man to run for president, registering voters and organizing turnout that carried Jackson to a primary victory in the county. Hunt's case was right in Little's wheelhouse.

The Darryl Hunt Defense Committee soon attracted a new generation of African-American clergy in town who saw social activism as a religious calling. The first minister recruited by Little was a 27-year-old Presbyterian from Brooklyn named Carlton Eversley. Eversley had come to town with his wife, Luellen Curry, a young lawyer from nearby Lexington who had found a job as a legal aid attorney. They had met at Oberlin, a small liberal arts college in Ohio, then moved to Chicago, where Curry went to law school and Eversley studied at Garrett Evangelical Theological Seminary and immersed himself in Black liberation theology. Dellabrook Presbyterian, with a small congregation of teachers, lawyers, and other professionals, appreciated his learned style. He and Little met on the basketball court, and Little was impressed enough with the new minister in town that he soon joined Eversley's church. "I'm not joining a Presbyterian church," he would tell people. "I'm joining Carlton."[15] Eversley's older brother was a cop in Boston, but it wasn't hard to draw him to Hunt's cause. There were some among Eversley's congregation who thought he had taken his politics too far by supporting a kid charged with murder, but if they couldn't support Hunt, they did give their young minister the leeway to speak out. And he did.[16]

John Mendez, 34 and also from New York, moved to town the year before Hunt's arrest to lead Emmanuel Baptist Church, with a congregation of about 600 in an African-American suburban community on the southeast side of town. Like Eversley, Mendez was also well schooled in liberation theology and in the Black freedom movement that spanned the US and Africa. He had moved south for college at Shaw University, a historically Black school in Raleigh, where he first met Little, who had come to campus to recruit for the Panthers. After working and organizing custodians at Duke University Hospital, Mendez finished seminary at Southeastern

Baptist Theological.[17] Even after a decade in the South, Mendez was surprised by the conservative church culture he found in Winston-Salem, where many ministers still drew their sermons from manuals provided by the R. J. Reynolds Tobacco Company. He wanted to be a different kind of church leader, one who turned the pulpit into a platform for social justice. Hunt's case fit that vision.[18]

Khalid Griggs, then 35, led a small Muslim congregation at the Community Mosque, on the third floor of the Bruce Building on Patterson Avenue, and he worked with the Winston-Salem Improvement Association, a community development organization. Griggs wasn't making much money leading Friday prayers and running a nonprofit, but it was a life he wanted. Raised in Winston-Salem, where he graduated from Reynolds High School a year behind Little, he'd gone to Howard University, a historically Black college in Washington, DC, to study political science. In their quest for Black identity, Griggs and his friends were drawn to early-twentieth-century Black intellectuals such as W. E. B. Du Bois and Carter G. Woodson. The Nation of Islam recruited on campus, but its brand of Islam, with its devotion to Elijah Muhammad, didn't sit well with Griggs, whose childhood was steeped in the Black church. Traditional Islam, with its theology of peace and justice, spoke to him. And so did Hunt's cause.

A decade earlier, when Little was still running the local Black Panther Party, he had learned how to use protest and publicity to rally support around a defendant in another racially charged murder, in this case a Black woman in eastern North Carolina charged with capital murder for killing a white man. In 1974, Joan Little (no relation to Larry Little), then 20 and serving time in the Beaufort County Jail on charges of larceny, killed a guard who was forcing her to perform oral sex. During the attack, she wrestled the ice pick he had brought as a weapon away from him and stabbed him to death. By any standard of justice, it should have been a clear case of self-defense, but it wasn't, not when the guard was a 62-year-old white man and the defendant poor and Black. In cases of sexual assault by white men, Black women had been denied the right to self-defense since slavery. Terrified that no one would believe her, Joan Little fled and only turned herself in when she realized she could be shot dead as a fugitive.[19]

When the Panther chapter from the other side of the state heard about the Black sister from down east who had killed her attacker with the very ice pick he had used against her, its members rallied to her cause, and Larry Little became one of Joan Little's closest advisers.[20] With help from national activists such as Angela Davis,[21] the Joan Little Defense Committee staged protests around the country, raising $350,000 to mount a vigorous defense. The following year she was acquitted of murder, an unimaginable victory in a region where it was still legal for a man to rape his wife[22] and where for generations a white man could get away with raping a Black woman with impunity. If the strategy of public pressure could undo this legacy of slavery, there was a chance it could work for Hunt, his supporters believed.

With clergy on his side, Little was able to bring Hunt's cause to a larger audience than the Patterson Avenue crowd. To be sure, not every Black person in town supported the cause. Hunt's connection to Mitchell made him suspect, especially among Black professionals. Mendez, for example, lost some members of his congregation, who felt that it was best to let the system handle Hunt's case.[23] Even if at first he wasn't absolutely persuaded of Hunt's innocence, Eversley was certain of the tremendous power of the state to railroad him. "If we don't help him, his life will be flushed away,"[24] the erudite young preacher would tell people. The state would provide court-appointed attorneys, but there was no money to pay for a private investigator or the experts Hunt would need to defend himself. As support grew, the money Little raised paid those costs.

Little was confident in Hunt's innocence, but not as much in Mitchell's. During his visits with Hunt in jail, he would test Hunt's story with a lie, telling him that his friend Sammy Mitchell had ratted on him. Give him up, Little would say, and save yourself. But Hunt would never budge.[25] Little also continued to do his own detective work. He found Johnny Gray in a café on the north side of town. Gray didn't say much, but Little had learned his real name, Johnny McConnell, a fact police had failed to uncover. A search with Gray's real name produced a long criminal record, more information the police had overlooked.[26] Little also helped track down alibi witnesses and, more importantly, persuaded them to meet with Hunt's white lawyers.[27] And he made sure, after the private detective confirmed an anonymous tip that Thomas Murphy had been a member of the Ku Klux Klan, that word got out to the Black community that the state was relying on a Klansman to railroad one of their own.

The gravity of their work was clear to defense committee members from the start. An older member provided Little with a haunting reminder, pulling him aside to show him a drawing from a 1950 pamphlet civil rights activists had printed of a young, clean-cut man with a hint of a mustache. Little had grown up hearing stories about Clyde Brown, how at 19 he'd been charged with the rape of a white teenager and executed. There was no clear evidence of rape, but Brown had confessed to beating the 17-year-old girl in her father's radio shop during a botched robbery of $3.50 from the cash register. The father found his badly beaten daughter unconscious in the back of the store, covered by a mattress. She remained in a coma for almost a month, with no memory of the attack. Evidence of a sexual assault was slim, but a doctor at the hospital eventually testified that she had been raped.

In the 1950s, rape was a capital offense in North Carolina. In practice, however, the death penalty was almost exclusively reserved for Black men found guilty of attacking white women. Between 1910 and 1961 (when legal challenges to the death penalty led to a temporary moratorium),[28] 67 of the 78 men executed for rape were Black. Tracking down the race of the victims has been challenging for scholars, but they have been able to confirm that at least 58 of the victims were white women. In some of these cases, there is also evidence of innocence. White men, meanwhile, were executed only in the most horrific cases that involved white teenagers or even younger girls. No white man was ever executed for the rape of a Black woman.[29]

Because of the scant evidence, Brown's case inspired a movement, similar in spirit to the movement Little was now building in support of Hunt. Many of Brown's supporters were veterans of the union-organizing efforts of local tobacco workers in the 1930s and 1940s. Calling themselves the People's Defense Committee, they raised money at churches and fish fries, in nickels and dimes, to pay for legal fees for Brown's defense.[30] When Brown was convicted by an all-white jury and sentenced to death, his supporters raised more money to take his case to the US Supreme Court. When that failed, they petitioned for clemency from the governor, with letters of support coming in from around the country from union leaders and academics.[31]

Brown was executed May 29, 1953. An article in the next day's *Winston-Salem Journal* made no mention of questions of his innocence or of the defense committee fighting for him back home. Rather, his death was portrayed in the lurid language that had been used for generations to fuel the myth of Black men as sexual predators.

Clyde Brown lived a fast life and became a corpse at the peak of his manhood. Yesterday, less than a month before his 23rd birthday he walked into Central Prison's execution chamber and was put to death for the rape of a 17-year-old Winston-Salem high school girl who was brutally beaten June 16, 1950.

The muscular negro held his head aloft as he entered the gas chamber from Death Row which had been his home for nearly three years. He was silent, but months before he had told prison authorities that he had made a "clean confession" of his guilt.

Clothed only in a pair of white undershorts, he stretched to his full five feet nine inches and flexed the powerful muscles of his shoulders and chest. The taut muscles took the slack from two strips of white tape that held to his chest a medical instrument that was to record his heartbeat.[32]

There was a second man scheduled to die with Brown that day, a 45-year-old Black man named Raleigh Speller, convicted of raping a deaf white woman.[33] He had been tried in Bertie County, in rural eastern North Carolina, where 60 percent of the population was Black, though as far as court officials could remember, not a single Black person had ever sat on a jury. The process for selecting jurors in Bertie County guaranteed Black disenfranchisement. A child would arbitrarily pull the names of potential jurors from a hat, with those of Black residents in red ink. When the prosecutor selected a name written in red, the juror would be dismissed "for want of good moral character or sufficient intelligence."[34]

Brown and Speller were strapped in wooden chairs, side by side, each of their faces covered with a mask. A chaplain gave a prayer and left. The room, then, was sealed shut, and at ten in the morning the warden gave the signal to release cyanide gas into the death chamber. The article describes the deaths with clinical precision. At 10:02, Brown clenched his fist. His head jerked. His breathing slowed. Speller was declared dead at 10:07. It took ten full minutes for Brown to die.[35] Those among Hunt's supporters who remembered the effort to save Brown made sure Little knew what was at stake.

"Larry," they would tell him. "You can't let happen to Darryl what happened to Clyde Brown."[36]

Chapter Four

She Trusted the Police

The Integon Corp. insurance company had its offices in a 21-story glass-faced building across from the Spruce Street loading dock to the newspaper. Visitors used the main entrance, which led to the lobby, at the corner of Fifth and Spruce, but the people who worked there tended to use the back door on Poplar Street, just across from the company parking lot. A pillar of the city's corporate culture, Integon specialized in high-risk automobile insurance and other niche policies. Eighteen-year-old Regina Kellar was thrilled to have a job there, making enough money to share an apartment with a roommate. In her first year at Integon, she had already been promoted three times. Most days she came in at 6 a.m., before dawn, and with her latest promotion to the commercial department, she often needed to work a few hours each Saturday to stay caught up. The first Saturday in February 1985, she got up early, put on a short, quilted coat against the chill of the damp morning, drove downtown, and parked her yellow VW bug in the lot by her office.[1]

Crossing the street, Kellar noticed a man in a gray hooded sweatshirt headed her way. They reached the back door to her office building at the same moment.

"Don't scream," he said, as he stuck a gun in her side. "Let's go back to your car."

Continuing to press the gun against her and pulling her so close that she bent over to keep her balance, he led Kellar across the street to her car. Once inside, he had her drive east through downtown to a part of town she didn't recognize.[2]

"Don't look at me bitch," he told her, his voice deep and raspy.

She thought of crashing the car into a brick wall but was afraid he would shoot her, so she kept driving, keeping her eyes on the road. Drawing on her deep faith, she prayed. "Lord, I may not always have lived the way you wanted me to, and I have made mistakes. I trust you and love you. Give me the strength I need to escape."[3]

The man spoke again. "Do you have any kids?"[4]

The question chilled her.

Soon they were on a street with houses, then a wider road, which led to the Flamingo Drive-In Theater. She'd driven barely two miles, but time had slowed and distance lengthened. Her abductor had her turn at a dirt road, muddy from the night's rain. She worried the car would get stuck, but she drove until he made her stop in a wooded area littered with trash. Still holding the gun, the man took the $300 she carried in her purse. She prayed again, silently, with the words of a familiar psalm: "I sought the Lord, and he heard me, and delivered me from all fears." The words gave her courage.

"You know what I want, bitch,"[5] the man said.

He ordered her to undress in the back seat and raped her. Then, without explanation, he ordered her to get out of the car and put her hands on the roof. He tried to rape her again, from behind, but this time, she summoned all her strength, from her years playing softball in school and church, and began to fight back. In the struggle, he laid the gun on the roof of her car. Kellar seized the moment, grabbed it, and pointed.

"I will blow your Black ass off the face of the earth," she said, pulling the trigger.[6] Nothing happened.

"Stupid bitch," the man said, laughing. "It's not loaded, but I have a knife that is going to kill you dead."[7]

She felt the butt of the gun strike her head, then caught a glimpse of a blade coming for her neck. She tilted her chin and felt the knife cut her face. It was at her throat now. She grabbed it, with one hand on the handle and one hand on the blade. He grabbed the knife too, his hand protected by a glove, which she now noticed. With his gloved hand between hers, they wrestled for the knife and stumbled to the ground. With his free hand, he searched through the pile of trash they had fallen in. She felt him cut her face with a shard of glass. She held on, and with a burst of strength, she pushed against the ground until they both were standing, face to face. She studied his face, his dark brown eyes, his wide nose, and the gap between his front teeth.

"Let go of the knife," he shouted.[8]

"No."

"Let's count to three," he said. "And throw it into the woods."

As he swung his arms, she pulled in the opposite direction, so hard that her attacker lost his balance and, with that, his grip. Still holding the knife, Kellar ran to an opening in the woods, then on to an apartment complex, and pounded on the first door she came to.

"Please help me. Someone is trying to kill me."[9]

A curtain parted. A man looked through the window, then opened the door. He wrapped her in a bedspread, and she fell to the floor, exhausted.

~

The police sent a detective to interview Kellar in the emergency room at Forsyth Memorial Hospital. Her parents and her fiancé, an electrician named Scott Lane, met her there. Her father had moved the family from Michigan to North Carolina when Kellar was in elementary school to work at the glass plant just south of Winston-Salem, in rural Davidson County. Her mother stayed home to look after Regina, her two older brothers, and two younger sisters. A doctor in the emergency room took vaginal swabs for a rape kit, though he noted that he was unable to find semen,[10] and cleaned up her wounds. There were at least a dozen, none life-threatening. A detective took pictures of her face and neck with a Polaroid camera, close-ups of the slashes across her neck and puncture wound near her ear, before and after they were sutured.

The questions detectives asked about the rape were humiliating, but Kellar did her best to answer them. That's how she'd been raised, to treat people with respect and obey authority. She was released from the hospital shortly after 11 that morning and went straight to the police station to meet with Detective Bill Miller for another round of questions. She described the rape and the struggle she put up in graphic detail. She later noticed that Miller left details out of the written report, details she felt were important, such as the fact that the way the man pulled her close as they walked to her car made it impossible for her to stand up straight, or the fact that he had only succeeded in raping her once, inside the car, and that she was able to resist his efforts to sodomize her once they were standing outside the car. The explanation he gave for the missing details, that there was no need to put all the details in the report, bothered her. Miller said the details would come up in court once an arrest was made, but Kellar had the sense that Miller didn't believe her and that he thought the whole ordeal had been her fault. Why else would he tell her that, even with a gun against her, she never should have obeyed the order to walk to her car?[11]

Police spent two days at the crime scene. They found the footprints in the woods Kellar left when she fled and a set of prints that followed hers through the clearing and then turned left toward the road. They also found her attacker's glove and a bus transfer near the drive-in and interviewed the bus driver on duty the morning of the crime, hoping he would remember a man in a gray hooded sweatshirt. They recovered the knife where Kellar had dropped it in

the apartment to which she had fled and searched her car for fingerprints and any other evidence that could help identify the rapist.[12]

Kellar stayed with her parents for the week. That Sunday, a
reporter for the *Winston-Salem Journal,* Tracie Cone, came to see
her. Kellar declined the interview after learning that her name would
be printed.[13] Three days after she was attacked, Miller asked her
and her fiancé to retrace the route to where the man had raped her.
From Poplar Street, they headed east on Fourth Street toward Old
Greensboro Road, to the dirt road that led through the woods. Her
fiancé asked if they could bring dogs out, to trace the scent from the
glove and the footprints, but police said that wouldn't work because
the grass had been wet. Miller had Kellar repeat her description of
the entire ordeal again.[14] She asked why.

"You would be amazed at how many people accuse others of
rape and then we find out it's consensual," he told her.[15]

Kellar and her family had talked about the attack all weekend. Her future mother-in-law was outraged about the way the
police were treating her. Mary Lane was the opposite of her son's
fiancé, outspoken, opinionated, and suspicious. She didn't trust the
police, especially after hearing all about the mistakes they'd made
with the murder of the young newspaper editor that was all over
the news.[16] She couldn't believe the police weren't connecting her
future daughter-in-law's case with the Sykes case. Sure, they had
arrested a man in the Sykes case, but the similarities were so clear.
Both women were attacked early in the morning, on their way to
work, within three blocks of each other. They were both raped and
stabbed multiple times. With their brown hair and athletic builds,
they even resembled each other. Her fiancé's mother had a point.
Kellar promised her she would ask.[17]

Later that week, she met with a police artist to pull together a
composite sketch of the man who attacked her. The drawing would
be released to the morning and afternoon newspapers. Maybe someone would recognize him and call in a tip. Kellar wanted to know

if there had been any other rapes downtown that year. Miller told her he didn't know but would find out. And what about the Sykes case? Could the same man have raped them both? They were both assaulted downtown, early in the morning. They were both stabbed. And in both cases, the attacker was a Black man. The only real difference she could see was that she survived and Sykes did not.

Miller left the room, as if to consult with someone else. When he returned he told Kellar to forget about the similarities between her case and Sykes'. That case was closed, and her questions would only harm the state's case against the man they had in jail.[18]

The answer stunned her, but she figured he knew best. In the coming weeks, even after she went back to work, she checked in with the police at least once a week. Sometimes she'd ask again about the Sykes case. It seemed the investigation into her case went awfully slowly. But she trusted the police would do their job.

Chapter Five

A Decent Life

The months following Hunt's arrest were all-consuming for his legal defense team. Gordon Jenkins, appointed by the court in September, and Mark Rabil, appointed the following month to assist him, quickly came to believe that the only way to save their client was to find the man who had committed the brutal crime Hunt was wrongly accused of. If Hunt were white, maybe they could rely on the law. But the law couldn't be counted on to protect a Black man accused of raping a white woman. History told them as much and so did literature. Rabil didn't need to look much further than *To Kill a Mockingbird*, a favorite book from college, to understand the task ahead. Just four years out of law school, Rabil had tried several felony cases, and even won one defending a white man charged with rape,[1] but this was his first murder case. Jenkins was ten years older and more experienced with felony work but, like Rabil, had never defended a murder case, much less a death penalty case. The burden of defending a Black man accused of raping and killing a white woman weighed heavily on both men. If they failed, Hunt could lose his life.

When they weren't studying case law or consulting with lawyers who had more experience with capital murder cases, they tried to figure out who had killed Deborah Sykes. Their private investigator,

Charles "Slick" Poteat, ran down leads for weeks without any real breaks. Johnny Gray, the man who made the 911 call, topped their list of suspects. They were certain, too, that Charles "Too Tall" Wall, who'd been seen near the crime scene by a number of witnesses, was involved. The Integon rape was another lead.

Hunt turned 20 in February 1985, still cooped up in jail, where the blistering heat had turned to a damp chill. He still couldn't understand why he was there for a crime he had nothing to do with. In jail, other prisoners were talking about this new rape case and the obvious similarities with the crime Hunt was locked up for. A sympathetic jailer even brought him a copy of an article by Tracie Cone from the *Winston-Salem Journal*, published just three days after this second attack, which raised questions about a possible link between the two crimes.[2] According to the article, after the Sykes murder, Integon had taken security steps to prevent something similar from happening to one of its employees, steps that hadn't helped Kellar.

It was clear from the article[3] that police were saying that the crimes were unrelated. The victim of this recent attack told them that the man who raped her was about five feet four, while the original descriptions of suspects in the Sykes case had the killer at six feet or taller. So in spite of the many other similarities, the police didn't question, at least in public, whether the descriptions the witnesses gave were accurate. It didn't seem to occur to them that witnesses, even victims themselves, could be wrong, that memory could be fallible. Hunt was in jail, and that's what mattered to police. As the story about this new rape case noted about Sykes' case, "Police made one arrest in that case and have said that the investigation is closed."[4]

Rabil, though, wondered how the police could say that the case against Hunt was closed when here was another young woman attacked within sight of where Sykes had been murdered. The time of day, the rape, the multiple stab wounds were all so similar. Gray lived out by the Flamingo Drive-In. Coincidence or a clue? What did the attacker in this second rape look like? What did he say?

Would the victim recognize him? If only Rabil could talk to her,
but he didn't know her name. Normally, the newspaper published
the names of rape victims, a practice that the police decried and
that seemed, even to Rabil, inhumane. But this time, the victim's
name was left out. Like so much else in Hunt's case, it seemed that
everything was stacked against him and his defense.[5]

They sent Slick Poteat to the police department for the incident
report in the Integon rape case. He was refused. He tried to sweet-
talk the security officer at the Integon building into giving up the
victim's name. Another dead end. Hunt's lawyers asked Little to ask
around with his police sources, but police were under strict orders
by then not to talk to him. Rabil thought about Johnny Gray, but
by then, Gray was in jail on an unrelated robbery charge and out of
reach. Hunt passed along rumors he heard in jail. The chief suspect
in the Integon rape was rumored to be a man nicknamed "Billy Boy,"
who was in jail on another charge. Someone said he was talking in
his sleep about murder, saying, "I didn't mean to do it . . . I didn't
mean to do it . . . I didn't mean to kill that woman." It wasn't hard to
track down Billy Boy's full name. Jail records showed that Billy Boy
had been in and out of jail all year, but he was out the day Sykes was
murdered and the day of the Integon rape. All through the spring,
Rabil waited for an arrest and, with it, more information. But there
was so much to do to prepare for a capital murder case and, with
the trial approaching in May, time was running out. He added the
Integon rape to a long list of possible leads and moved on.[6]

～

Early on, before they even had a chance to talk with Hunt, both lawyers had reason to think of him as something other than a depraved
killer. By coincidence, their firm had managed the estate of Hunt's
grandfather, and they recognized Hunt as the young man who
turned up at their law office once a month to collect money from
the estate. He always wore the same black ball cap emblazoned with

the Playboy bunny logo. And he was always polite.[7] In spite of that, Rabil and Jenkins had both initially assumed Hunt was guilty, or at least had something to do with the crime. Clients in a criminal practice were rarely innocent. Jenkins went to see Hunt first and was impressed by his demeanor.

Not until October did Rabil have time to visit Hunt in jail. The brutality of the crime still haunted him. He and his wife, Pam, lived in the West End neighborhood, within walking distance of downtown and the Crystal Towers neighborhood where Sykes was killed. Like Crystal Towers, West End was a neighborhood of Victorian houses that had been neglected all through the '60s and '70s and was just beginning to come around. He and Pam had moved into a ground-floor apartment in an old house only because the rent, at $150 a month, was cheap. With Pam pregnant with their first child, they were trying to save money. Still, Rabil feared for his wife's safety. Earlier in the summer, a woman had been raped near their apartment, and he often saw vagrants hanging around their street, once even urinating outside the front door. Sykes' murder made the neighborhood feel even more threatening. By October, they were making plans to buy a small house in a safer neighborhood, but that visceral fear he felt any time he thought of Sykes lingered.[8] He would do his best to defend Hunt, that was his job, but he assumed he would be meeting with a man capable of harming Pam.

Rabil and Hunt met in the visitation room on the first floor of the county jail, where Hunt was still being held, segregated from the rest of those imprisoned with him who were held upstairs. They sat on metal stools, face to face, one a slender teenager taller than his lawyer, the other a lawyer young enough to be his client's older brother. Rabil would later remember the questions he asked and the answers Hunt gave, word for word.

"Did you have anything to do with this crime?"

"No."

"Do you know who did it?"

"No. They tried to get me to say that Sammy did it, but he didn't have nothin' to do with it, so I didn't put it on him."

"What do you mean?"

"They took me to Mr. Tisdale office. Little Bit was sittin' there in a chair. Tisdale told me they knew that Sammy Mitchell killed that woman and that I was there as the lookout. He went over to a closet behind his desk and pulled out a stick. He said that Sammy had tried to kill somebody with that stick and that he had been found not guilty of that, but he was not going to let Sammy get away with this one. Tisdale told me that I could tell them Sam did it and I could go free. If I wouldn't testify, then they was goin' for the death penalty against me. He also told me that I could get the $12,000 in reward money if I said Sam did it. I told him Sam didn't do it and I didn't have nothin' to do with it. He got Little Bit to tell me to say Sam did it. She begged me to say it, and she started crying. I just didn't say anything else. Tisdale got mad, and he told Daulton to draw up a warrant for first-degree murder and put me in a lineup. And if they identified me from the lineup, he was going after the death penalty for me, and there was no goin' back. And so they took me to the jail and put me in a lineup. Then they took me to the magistrate's office and charged me with first-degree murder."[9]

Hunt told him about spending the night before the murder at the McKeys' home and watching *The Beverly Hillbillies* on television the next morning, as he always did. The detail seemed important to Rabil. How could anyone who watched the show, a light-hearted comedy about an Ozark mountain family whose members strike oil and move out to California, commit the brutal murder Hunt had been accused of? Hunt explained how after the show was over, he'd gone to the courthouse with Mitchell and Mitchell's mother for one of his friend's many court dates that summer. The case was continued to a later date, a fact that checked out. The more Hunt talked, in a slow, steady voice, the more Rabil came to believe him.

Why on earth would two men who just stabbed a woman to death show up in court?[10]

Hunt told Rabil how the police kept hounding them, all through August and into September, and about everything he and Mitchell had done to cooperate. Rabil even lied to his client, telling Hunt that there was something called DNA testing (which hadn't yet been invented) that could tell with certainty whether Hunt had raped the woman or not. Hunt agreed to the testing without hesitation. Finally, Rabil asked Hunt if he was angry.

"No," Hunt replied. "Anybody can make a mistake."[11]

As the interview came to an end, Rabil realized he no longer presumed guilt. His client was innocent. Worse than that, he was a Black man accused of raping and murdering a white woman, in a region where not that long ago, a Black teenager like Hunt accused of such a crime could be lynched. The weight of Hunt's plight sunk in. Maybe Hunt wasn't angry, but Rabil sure was. And deep down, he was afraid.

Rabil grew up in Winston-Salem and understood his home-town well. He loved the smell of cured tobacco that hung in the air downtown, especially on humid summer nights, and the way the city quickly gave way to countryside on long bike rides he took on weekends, with Pilot Mountain emerging in the distance, beyond the fields of ripening tobacco. As a kid, Rabil liked to hang around his father's drugstore, Bobbit's Pharmacy, on the ground floor of the Reynolds Building, with its art deco tobacco motifs in gold and silver leaf and brass elevator doors. Jake, the building's janitor, would tell him of his double life as a pool shark at night and a janitor by day. Cleaning work was a typical role for a Black person in Rabil's child-hood, as Rabil's family lived the privileged life of a well-off white family. At home, his mother had a Black maid. But even as a child, Rabil felt the hint of an outsider's status. His family was Catholic, which opened him up to ridicule in the Baptist South. What's more, his darker skin, inherited from Lebanese grandparents on his father's side, turned a deep brown in the summer, such that one summer a kid at camp asked if he was a "nigger."[12]

By the time Rabil went away to Davidson College, an elite liberal arts school about an hour away from home, he was just beginning to understand the depth of the region's racism. He studied English literature and spent a semester in Spain before law school at UNC Chapel Hill, the state system's flagship university. He and Pam met in law school, and both found jobs back in Rabil's hometown. Rabil's education prepared him to join a large firm, but his plan was to become a solo practitioner. He knew he wouldn't make a lot of money, but he wanted the independence. In his first years with Jenkins' firm, Rabil went to the monthly meetings of the local criminal defense lawyers association, at the Sir Winston restaurant across the street from his downtown office. Most of the others in the association were older men, heavy drinkers who bragged of their back-room deals. The district attorney, Don Tisdale, was invited to give a guest talk one month and delivered a warning. "You can't out-son-of-a-bitch the D.A.,"[13] Tisdale told the group. Rabil was surprised by his candor. The others were not. Rabil also witnessed the casual racism around the courthouse. In law school, he had read old North Carolina case law on property disputes over enslaved Black people and about laws banning miscegenation, relationships between Blacks and whites. Rabil's mother had banned the n-word at home, and from her he learned to treat everyone with respect, regardless of race.[14] Still, he found himself laughing at racist jokes others told around the courthouse. He didn't want to rock the boat. But now, people he knew around town, white people, would stop him and chastise him for representing the man who'd killed that lovely young woman from the newspaper. "How can you represent that man?"[15] they would ask. Like it or not, if he was going to continue with this case, it was time to rock the boat.

Hunt liked Rabil immediately. Although Hunt appreciated Jenkins' hard work, Rabil spoke to him from the heart. When they met, Hunt was still worried about the guards who were rumored to be KKK members, in spite of reassurances from the Black sergeant he trusted that the white guards were all talk. A man imprisoned upstairs, named Woods, had been given the status of "trustee" with special privileges, and he checked on Hunt many times a day. That helped him feel less alone. Hunt wrote long love letters to one of his summer girlfriends, a woman named Rhonda. She would come on visiting days, as would Mitchell's mother. During the rest of the week, Rhonda or her mother would drop by the jail, find Woods, and give him money and letters to deliver to Hunt. "We love you and we are here for you," they would write. "We know you're innocent."[16] These cheered him up. Outside, summer was giving way to fall, but inside, the first floor was hot as hell. Hunt's clothes were always drenched in sweat, the kind of heavy sweat he would break into playing basketball at the Y. Some days Rhonda would stand on the street outside a window and wave. Hunt couldn't see her, but the others would watch for her and yell to Hunt that his girl was outside.[17]

In November, jailers moved him to the third floor with the other men but still kept him in a single cell. At first, Hunt was lonely, but he came to like the solitude. Rabil and Little brought him books to read, books like *The Autobiography of Malcolm X*, *Revolutionary Suicide* by Black Panther founder Huey Newton, and *Soul on Ice* by Eldridge Cleaver. Little also gave him a dictionary. Never much of a reader before, he started to keep index cards, noting words he didn't know, their definitions, and the way the author used them.[18] The language of Black power and liberation resonated with him and gave him courage. He stored the books in between the bars of his cell, and soon there were so many that he had to take them down each night so jailers could see him when they made their evening rounds. When Rabil came to visit, they'd talk case strategy and books. Rabil had a positive way of seeing things, which made Hunt feel that no matter what happened, he could count on Rabil the way he would count on a brother.[19]

With no experience defending a client on trial for his life, Rabil and Jenkins knew they were in over their heads and scrambled to learn all they could about capital murder cases. There weren't many lawyers in the state to turn to because the death penalty had just been reinstated in 1981 by the state legislature.[20] A friend who had recently defended a murder case gave them copies of the motions he had filed for them to use in Hunt's case. They drove to Durham to meet with one of the state's leading lawyers in the new death penalty statute, a man named David Rudolf.[21]

They learned that death penalty work was different from other defense work because of the way the trial would be structured. The first phase worked much the way other felony cases worked. The DA would present his case for guilt, with a series of witnesses including crime lab technicians, detectives, and eyewitnesses. Then Hunt's lawyers would have a chance to cross-examine, poking holes and sowing doubt. When it was their turn, they would be able to call alibi witnesses and anyone else to discredit the state's case. In theory, they didn't have to prove innocence. Their job in that first phase was to establish enough "reasonable doubt" for a jury to find Hunt not guilty. In practice, however, reasonable doubt was rarely enough, especially when a Black man's life was on the line. A generation ago, Clyde Brown, and dozens like him, died for allegedly attacking white women in cases where the evidence was even slimmer than in Hunt's. The sheer power of the prosecutor's office, the public demand for law and order, and widespread racism would make it next to impossible to persuade a jury to doubt the state's evidence. That's why Rabil and Jenkins felt they needed to find the real killer.

Other lawyers encouraged them to focus on the second phase, the sentencing phase, unique to death penalty cases, when the same jurors who had decided on guilt would decide whether Hunt would be sent to prison for life or executed. Legal jargon went with this phase. The DA would argue "aggravating" factors: the brutality of the crime, how Sykes had suffered in the moments before her death, and her family's bitter grief and loss. Rabil and Jenkins would argue "mitigating" factors, anything that would move jurors to show mercy. They brought in a psychologist, who diagnosed Hunt with a learning disability and a low IQ, bordering on cognitive impairment. To tell a sympathetic story about Hunt, they learned about his childhood, his paper route, his upstanding grandfather, his kindness to his sixth-grade teacher, and his mother's early death.

Rabil had sat through a death penalty case the previous year. It was one his wife, Pam, was assisting on. He'd gone to the sentencing phase for moral support and stayed while the jury deliberated. He couldn't forget the way one of the bailiffs looked over at Pam and her client, rolled up his shirt sleeve, and with his free hand pantomimed how to push a syringe that would plunge a needle into his arm.[22]

There were no state laws in North Carolina in 1984 requiring prosecutors to share their case file with the defense, even in capital cases. Prosecutors were only required to share statements by the defendant and lab reports (but not the underlying notes that might reveal questions or errors), and to give the defense access to physical evidence. In this case, the physical evidence was Sykes' bloody clothes, some of Hunt's clothes that police had seized from Mattie Mitchell's house, and crime scene photos. Prosecutors were also required to share witness statements, but they could wait until after the witness testified at trial, leaving the defense little time to study those statements for cross-examination. In theory, the 1963 Supreme Court case *Brady v. Maryland* should have given Rabil and Jenkins access to much of the state's case. *Brady* required prosecutors to share any witness statements, test results, and anything else that came up in the police investigation that supported the defendant's innocence or raised questions about the state's case. In legal terms, this is known as exculpatory evidence. But in practice, prosecutors interpreted *Brady* to suit themselves and they shared very little with defense attorneys.

Early on, Jenkins met with Tisdale in his fifth-floor office,[23] the same room where the DA weeks earlier had tried to bully Hunt into turning on Mitchell. This time, Tisdale was polite, but no less forceful. He told Jenkins that he had two witnesses who put Hunt at the scene. One was a white man he wouldn't name, "one of the best witnesses I have ever seen." The second was a Black man who had made the 911 call. Both men, he said, had identified Hunt from a lineup, though he did let on that the Black man had misidentified someone before Hunt. Tisdale also told Jenkins that Hunt had grass stains on his pants the morning of the murder and several days later told his prostitute friend that he and Mitchell had done it. But there were no reports. No names. Nothing for Rabil and Jenkins to go on.

They did have the search warrant for Mattie Mitchell's house.[24] It was dated September 13. To obtain it, Daulton had signed a sworn statement saying that a witness described the suspect as a Black man, about five feet ten inches tall, wearing a black T-shirt with a spiderweb design. For the witness's protection, Daulton didn't name him. Police did find a T-shirt with a spiderweb design among the belongings Hunt stored at Mattie Mitchell's place. It was such a specific detail that finding it helped the prosecution put Hunt at the scene. When Rabil talked with Hunt and Mitchell about this incriminating piece of evidence, they both insisted that they hadn't bought the shirt until August 20, ten days after the crime, at a place called the Soul Train on Trade Street. That checked out. The store owner confirmed those T-shirts weren't in the store until August 16, a week after Sykes' murder. He had the receipt to prove it. What's more, the owner insisted he hadn't unpacked the shirts until August 20.[25] There was no way a witness could have seen that spiderweb design at the crime scene. And if that was the case, how did police know they would find the T-shirt among Hunt's things? Someone was lying.

Rabil was certain that the "Black man" the DA had talked about, the one who made the 911 call, had something to do with the crime. Why else would he have used Mitchell's name when he called 911, if not to take the focus away from himself? Little was learning a lot about Gray from his own sources, including his history of violent crimes, such as sexual assault and armed robbery. He also found out that Gray hung around Recreation Billiards, a pool hall downtown. They sent Slick Poteat to wear a wire and see if he could get Gray to fess up to any role in the murder. The interview gave them a sense of what Gray would say at trial, beginning with what Gray saw when he peered through the bushes over the squat fence.

"Something told me to look. I looked over this way, I looked into the bushes right there the thing right there a little old pole through the bushes and the damn ... the telephone pole. Then I seen this dude was, now let me tell you I'm not gonna tell no lie on nobody, 'cause I don't want to see nobody get no time and no life sentence. You understand what I'm saying? This man was beating down on this woman."

"Was she on the ground?"

"Yes, she was on the ground."

"Was there just one man there?"

"One man. Look man, I've done told Mr. Daulton, I done took, like I said, I done took three, three lie detector tests. I ain't telling no lie. I, I walked in the department downtown on my own. On my own. I didn't have to do that, man. And I'm not tellin' no lie. Like I said though, but, I seen him hit this woman like I'm sayin' here ... He looked back at me, like I'm looking at you, right, I looked him dead in the face and I tell you how far he was from me, I say thirty–forty yards. He wasn't this far from here to the God damn wall. No he wasn't that far, a little closer than that. You know what I'm saying?"

The questioning continued, without much new information.

"Did that man say anything to you, that was doing the beatin'?"

"No, he didn't even see me."

"He didn't?"

"No, let me tell you what happened, you understand, when I heard the hollering, right, then I said I couldn't find where the hollerin' was comin' from, but I knew it was so close to me, you know what I'm saying . . . I looked over there, when I looked over there in the bushes I seen him beatin' down, beatin' that woman like he was straddling that woman, he was beatin' that lady . . . I couldn't tell if he had a knife in his hand, but evidently, he may have had one."

"Was she fighting him back?"

"Uh, no, I can't, no, I won't say she was fighting him back. What I was saying, it happened so fast when I looked I seen him doing this right here, right? His big Black hand right there, and I'll get on the witness stand and say that. And if Mr. Tisdale cares anything about me and himself and about his duty, he'll look out for me too. I'm catching hell. I'm not gonna get up on this God damn stand and put my God damn son and my God damn me and my son in jeopardy, now. I'm not going to do that. If I get on this God damn stand, I'm going to do it right. I feel like I deserve respect. God damn if I'm going get on that stand I deserve it. Now I'm not going to risk myself, I am not gonna, I, I am not going to cut that Darryl no slack at all. I'm not."[26]

Rabil and Jenkins pored over the tape Poteat gave them, listening for anything that they could use to pin the crime on Gray. There was a lot about what Gray had to say that didn't ring true, especially the fact that he kept insisting he didn't see a knife. How was that possible? Maybe Little, one Black man talking to another, could get more out of him than Poteat had. One Thursday in March, Little wore the same wire Poteat had used and drove out to Gray's apartment on the edge of town near the drive-in that showed porn flicks. Rabil and Poteat followed and listened. But the interview went much as the earlier one had gone.[27] They were certain Gray was lying, but that wouldn't be enough to help Hunt's defense.

In early April, with the trial date just weeks away, Gaither Jenkins, Gordon's father, called Rabil to his office, using the affectionate nickname he had given his young associate.

"Marcus Aurelius, I need to tell you something. It's been bothering me and I can't sleep because of it. I've been having this recurring vision. In my mind, I see Mr. Gray, standing beside a creek. He throws a bloody knife into the creek. Then he washes blood from his hands in the creek water and leaves."

Rabil was baffled. In his mind, this erudite, Harvard-educated attorney never struck him as the kind of man who would put any stock in dreams. But he was ready to try anything, and Poteat believed in premonitions. So the following Saturday, Rabil, Poteat, and Poteat's 16-year-old son and a friend went exploring. They started at the crime scene, then headed three blocks southwest, past the Hanes Dye and Finishing plant, and saw that the railroad tracks that brought freight to the factory would make an easy escape route from the crime scene. The tracks follow Peters Creek, which flows behind the factory toward Hanes Park, behind the apartment Rabil had lived in the previous summer. Poteat brought a metal detector, which they used to search the creek and the overgrown banks littered with trash. They found tires, rusty cans, grocery carts, and old clothes. They did not find a knife.[28]

As the May 28 trial date approached, Rabil and Jenkins decided that Hunt should testify. It was a risky move, one that violated conventional wisdom. The safe route was to attack the state's case one witness at a time. Gray was a criminal. A witness from a downtown hotel named Roger Weaver hadn't come forward until he saw Hunt's picture in the paper. Murphy was a Klansman. Crawford was an unstable runaway and a liar. But Rabil and Jenkins hadn't solved the crime and probably wouldn't, which meant that they couldn't provide an alternate story to explain Sykes' murder, one that would satisfy a jury's demand for justice. Putting Hunt on the stand would open him up to a brutal cross-examination by Tisdale. But Hunt had stood up to Tisdale once before. They would take the risk and give Hunt the chance to tell his story.

About a month before the trial, Rabil put a cassette recorder in his pocket and walked over to the jail. Rabil had a list of questions prepared, so that Hunt would know what to expect at trial and Rabil could study how Hunt would answer.

"Do you pray, Mr. Hunt?" he began.

"Yes. I pray every night."

"What do you pray for?"

"Justice."

"Do you pray for any particular result in this case?"

"Yes, I do."

"What is that?"

"That the police department would find the right person who did this crime."

"Do you pray for anything for yourself?"

"Yes."

"What do you pray for?"

"That I could live a decent life."[29]

Rabil believed his client. So did Jenkins. They hoped a jury would, too, especially if he and Jenkins picked well.

Chapter Six

A High-Stakes Game

Late May in North Carolina comes at the end of a Southern spring, a time of expectation, just before the oppressive heat of summer sets in. Out in the street, dozens of supporters marched from Patterson Avenue to the courthouse the Saturday before Hunt's trial was set to begin, carrying banners and chanting slogans. From his cell, Hunt couldn't hear them, but he read about them the following day and saw a picture of them carrying banners. "Free Darryl Hunt," one banner read. "Mr. Justice, Where Are You?" read another.[1] To think that all these people were marching for him, a skinny 20-year-old nobody from the streets, gave him courage. He was ready to be done, to clear up this mess of lies.[2]

That evening, Rabil came by the jail to coach him on how to conduct himself during the trial. Hunt had already been through interview sessions with a psychologist Rabil had brought in to help with the sentencing phase, if it came to that.[3] The psychologist had asked about his family history, then gave him an IQ test, part of a life story they would tell in the event they lost and Hunt was found guilty. Hunt knew they had to be prepared for a guilty verdict, but it shook him up nonetheless. The psychologist's findings made him feel worse. He scored a 70, borderline for mental retardation,[4] which would be useful as a "mitigating" factor at sentencing, but still made Hunt feel like a fool, or as he would say, "one ignorant Negro."[5] Prepping with Rabil was different. Rabil brought the legal pad that would sit on the table between them in court. If Hunt had any questions or thought of something during the proceedings, he could write it down for his lawyers to read and they would reply in writing. But he would need to keep his composure, regardless of how he felt. He couldn't shake his head when a witness said something too stupid to believe or shout out, "You're lying!" He would have to follow the rules of decorum.

His lawyer was someone he could really talk to. Their conversation might turn to the books Hunt had been reading, the people who visited him, and the things he was learning. Drinking Pepsis and snacking on peanut butter crackers from the vending machine, they talked until well past midnight. Later that weekend, Rabil returned with Jenkins and Little for a mock trial, so Hunt would know what to expect when he took the witness stand. Little and Jenkins played the DA; Rabil played himself. The cross-examination was so brutal that for a moment Hunt imagined that his friends had turned on him. That night, Little returned, to let him know once again about all the people who believed in his innocence and who planned to be there in the morning.[6] He wouldn't be alone in the courtroom. Little had made sure of that.

Hunt and his attorneys had lost track of the rape three months earlier of the woman who worked at the Integon building, across from the newspaper office. They didn't know that the victim had asked about a possible connection between her rape and the Sykes case or that just that week she had picked a picture out of a photo lineup of a man named Willard Brown. The newspaper hadn't followed up with any news of the police investigation either. Without an arrest, Brown's name and the victim's name were never made public.

In the days leading up to the trial, the news coverage of Hunt's case, however, was relentless. WXII, the NBC affiliate, would be broadcasting live, a first in Winston-Salem.[7] The afternoon paper, where Sykes had worked, had closed down that spring, but the *Winston-Salem Journal* kept up with the case, reporting on it in the style of the mainstream press, relying heavily on what the police and the DA were saying about the investigation. Those who read the *Journal* knew that Hunt was a young man with a record of misdemeanor offenses who ran with a rough crowd. They also read accusations of racism made by Hunt's supporters, who had been rallied to Hunt's defense by Little, the former Black Panther and city alderman, a man not just well known but feared by many white readers. Occasionally, the *Journal* wrote about some of the case's inconsistencies that Little was talking about, but always in the "he said, she said" style of what was considered objective journalism. Black residents who read the Black weekly, the *Winston-Salem Chronicle*, found a more nuanced story. A profile published in the *Chronicle*, three months before Hunt's trial, told of a young man with a sweet smile, who had been trying to follow in the footsteps of his hard-working grandfather. "Darryl Eugene Hunt is a soft-spoken, brown skinned man with a slim build, friendly eyes and mouth that slightly curves into a perpetual half smile,"[8] it began. It was a thorough piece of journalism, based on interviews with Little, Hunt's uncle, his sixth-grade teacher, even a jailer in the county jail. Included was a photograph of Hunt as a little boy, one he always hated, that showed him with thick glasses and a wide grin, as well as a photo of the grandfather who raised him, another of his uncle, who took him in when his grandfather died, and one of Hunt's mother, with her hair cut short, wearing a sleeveless blouse. "Jean Hunt: Taken in by another family just as Darryl was," the caption stated. The story explained that Hunt's mother had been abandoned as an infant in the house next door to his grandparents. They adopted her, and when her boys were born, they adopted them as well. The writer, Allen Johnson, made room for Hunt's voice. "I pray every night," Hunt was quoted as saying. "I ask that whoever did this thing would turn themselves in, or that the police would find something that shows people I ain't no murderer."

~

For all his bluster with the press, Tisdale didn't like much of anything about the case against Hunt. He didn't say so in public, but privately he made it clear to police that they had relied too heavily on unreliable witnesses. Tisdale hated having to tell Sykes' mother, Evelyn Jefferson, that he had such a lousy case against her daughter's killer. "Yesterday I had the unpleasant task of talking to the family of Deborah Sykes, only to find that they were optimistic about the case," he wrote the police chief in a letter dated October 19, 1984, just a month after Hunt's arrest. "They had been informed by the police that there were sperm found, that hair samples were found, and that there was significant blood evidence, and that the eyewitnesses were ideal. I did not find it appealing to lie to them, and my most encouraging words to them was that we were in trouble."[9] Tisdale was upset, too, that the lead detective on the most high-profile case of his career was an inexperienced investigator who had spent most of his career as a motorcycle cop. He was particularly troubled by Thomas Murphy, the former Klansman whose background the police had never checked, and by Johnny Gray, who clearly was not telling the complete truth. "It is as preposterous that Mr. Gray could pull Sammy Mitchell's name out of thin air without knowing him as Darryl Hunt could name the next police chief," he wrote in the same blistering letter. Before Hunt's arrest, when Gray was himself a suspect, he had passed a lie-detector test that was focused on whether he had killed and raped Sykes. The test found his denials truthful. But after Hunt's arrest, the police had Gray take a second lie-detector test. This time, the test found that he lied when he denied knowing Hunt or Mitchell. The result cut to Gray's credibility as a witness. If he knew Hunt, then why did it take him a month to identify him? And why did he misidentify Terry Thomas when he first came forward to police? Hunt's lawyers didn't know about the second polygraph results, but Tisdale did.[10]

Polygraph tests are not admissible in court, but police, and sometimes even defense attorneys, use them as an investigative tool. Tisdale, for example, could have dropped Gray from the list of witnesses once he knew that Gray had failed a polygraph. The DA's code of conduct requires a clear evaluation of the facts, which would include a prohibition against using witnesses they know to be lying.[11] But he kept Gray as a witness.

Hunt and his lawyers also thought having a polygraph done was worth a try. They chose a retired police officer from New Jersey living in North Carolina, someone who would not be accused of being soft on crime, to administer the test. Robert Peterson kept the test simple, asking whether Hunt had murdered Sykes or seen the attack. Hunt passed the test, answering no to each question.[12] They shared the results with Tisdale,[13] who could have dropped the charges or delayed the trial. A district attorney has that leeway. Some would call it that duty. But he pressed on with the case against Hunt. In a letter to the police chief dated February 6, 1985, Tisdale complained of the shoddy police work and the leaks to the media. "Contrary to what has been expressed publicly, we do not have a solid prosecution of any kind," he wrote.[14] But in spite of the weaknesses in the case, and Hunt's truthful responses to a lie detector test, Tisdale didn't back off. The trial would start as planned, with the death penalty still on the table.

~

Hunt was up before six the morning of the trial. He was too nervous to eat, so he showered and waited for the jailer to bring him a clean suit of clothes,[15] the first time in months he wore something other than a jail-issued T-shirt and trousers. He had asked Mitchell to pick out a suit for him. If they had been planning a night on the town, the clothes Mitchell chose would have been fine, but the high-wasted, wide-legged pants, tuxedo jacket, and ruffled shirt made Hunt look like a pimp. He felt ridiculous. O,n the way to the van, which would take him the two blocks to the courthouse, anyone who saw him burst out laughing. At the courthouse, he tried to get a message to Rabil from the cell where defendants waited for court, asking that he find him another suit.[16] With other things on his mind, Rabil ignored the note, the first of many mistakes that would dog him throughout the trial. The courtroom was full by the time Hunt was brought in. Sykes' family sat behind the prosecution, with police and other witnesses seated behind them. Hunt's supporters sat on the other side of the central aisle and in the rear of the courtroom, a sea of Black faces. "Who brought you those clothes?" Rabil asked when Hunt was seated beside him. "Sam did." A note was passed to Little to find another suit for Hunt to change into, but that would have to wait until the lunch recess. It was time to pick a jury.

Compared to the rest of a criminal trial, there's little drama in jury selection, but as Rabil and Jenkins well understood, Hunt's freedom rested on them picking jurors biased in Hunt's favor. In January, they had hired a psychologist from North Carolina State University to help. First, they wanted to test their hunch that the biases jurors would bring to the case would fall along racial lines. With permission from the court clerk, they surveyed potential jurors who were called to the courthouse for other cases that spring. These randomly selected jurors would serve as proxies for those who would be called for jury duty for Hunt. The questionnaire was designed to test the demographic factors tied to whether someone thought Hunt was presumed guilty or innocent. It began with basic demographic information, then moved on to questions Rabil and Jenkins might use for potential jurors at Hunt's trial. Is crime a big problem? What do you think of women out in the streets early in the morning? Can there be a fair trial in this community when the victim is white and the defendant Black? Is it OK to convict based on eyewitness testimony alone? The survey ended with the question of Hunt's guilt, and finally, whether he deserved life in prison or death. Altogether, they surveyed 183 jurors.[17]

With all the media coverage, almost everyone had heard about the case. As they expected, opinion fell clearly along racial lines, with more than 90 percent of potential Black jurors believing Hunt was not guilty while 70 percent of white jurors said they thought he was guilty. The conclusion was obvious. "You want Blacks on the jury (as if you didn't know)," the psychologist James Luginbuhl wrote in April 1985.[18] Tisdale didn't need a survey to reach the same conclusion. As an elected DA, he understood the voters of the county well. In general, white people were crying out for justice in Sykes' murder, while Black people wanted justice for Hunt. If Tisdale wanted to remain an elected DA, he would need to win this trial. To do that, he needed white jurors just as badly as Hunt needed Black jurors.

Lawyers on both sides had many grounds they could use to excuse a juror for cause. If they didn't believe in the death penalty, the DA could excuse them. Jurors could also be excused if they knew any of the witnesses in the case. These were clearly biases that would interfere with a fair trial. Each side also had 14 peremptory challenges, which meant that they could excuse a potential juror without stating a reason. Another year would pass before the US Supreme Court ruled in *Batson v. Kentucky* that lawyers could not use race as one of those unspoken reasons.

Jury selection began with the clerk calling the first 12 jurors to the jury box for questioning. In the 1980s, Black residents made up nearly 33 percent of the population of Winston-Salem and 24 percent of Forsyth County.[19] If things worked out the way Hunt's defense wanted, they would get at least three Black jurors for a jury of Hunt's peers. Still, they were worried about Tisdale, who they knew had a habit of using his peremptory challenges to strike Black jurors. Such discrimination was theoretically unconstitutional, but the standard for proving it was nearly impossible to meet. Rabil and Jenkins introduced affidavits from two other defense attorneys who said that Tisdale had used his challenges in previous cases to excuse Black jurors, hoping the judge would intervene. As expected, Judge Preston Cornelius denied their motion.

Rabil kept careful notes on a yellow legal pad, keeping track of each juror's race, age, occupation, and other relevant facts. Tisdale focused his questions on Black jurors, such as a telephone operator named Dawn Houston.[20] Like most of the other men and women called for jury duty that week, she remembered hearing about the murder of Deborah Sykes. It would be hard to forget a rape and stabbing right in downtown Winston-Salem. And she had read about the case against the defendant, Darryl Hunt. She believed in the death penalty, but conceded it would be "an awful hard decision" to make.

"It should be," Tisdale replied.

Then Tisdale asked Houston some questions that he used for only the Black jurors in the pool, one of which was a question that cut to the core of a case about a Black man accused in the rape and murder of a white woman.

"If it came out in the evidence that the victim of this crime was a young white female, the defendant being a Black male, would that interfere in your verdict in the case?"

"No," Houston answered.

"Miss Houston, I'll ask you if you decided this defendant was guilty of first-degree murder, and if you returned a verdict at the second phase of the trial which involved the death penalty, would it be hard for you to go back and live in the community you live in?"

"No," she said.

"You could withstand any pressure or intimidation from your community?"

"Yes."

"And you could live with your verdict?"

"Yes."[21]

In spite of her testimony, Tisdale wasn't taking any chances. Houston was out.

Of the 66 potential jurors called for duty that week, only 11 were Black.[22] According to Rabil's notes, by the end of the week, Tisdale excused six jurors without cause—three more Black women, a Black man, and two white women. Tisdale also excused five Black jurors for cause, because either they were opposed to the death penalty, they knew Hunt, or they had some other connection to the case. "I'm a prosecutor and I've got a little common sense and I do my own mental survey, and 90 percent of Blacks believe Hunt is innocent and 70 percent of whites believe he's guilty. It's not a tough math question. Who do I want as a juror?" Tisdale said years later.[23]

Rabil and Jenkins were equally strategic about race, using the jury-selection process to probe white jurors for hidden prejudice. They didn't want people bent on vengeance, who might believe that a death sentence was the only punishment for murder. So they asked white jurors about their views on interracial dating. Had they been victims of a crime? Did they have Black colleagues? Neighbors? By the end of the week, they excused 13 jurors without cause. All of them were white.

Only one Black juror, a tobacco company worker named Joel Cole,[24] escaped Tisdale's challenges and made the final panel of 12 who would decide on Hunt's guilt or innocence. None of the three alternate seats were filled by Black jurors, either. Thus, before a single witness took the stand and anyone swore to tell the truth, Hunt's chance of freedom was slipping away.

There was nothing unusual in the way both sides used their peremptory challenges. The strategies they used were used by lawyers in every courthouse in North Carolina and beyond, even after *Batson v. Kentucky* prohibited race as a factor in choosing jury members. The rules against racial discrimination were one thing, but the biases Black and white jurors brought with them were so strong that lawyers on both sides routinely used those biases to their own benefit. Years later, a study of 1,300 felony cases in North Carolina from 2011 found that defense lawyers and prosecutors routinely used their challenges to try for the racial makeup, and with it the bias, they wanted. That year, prosecutors removed about 20 percent of available Black jurors compared to 10 percent of white jurors, defense attorneys the reverse.[25] Hunt watched his lawyers and the prosecution play this game. Everyone, even the jurors, knew the rules, if only instinctively. Lawyers used race to pick a jury. And jurors who wanted to be seated simply gave the answers the lawyers wanted to hear. This was no jury of Hunt's peers, as the law promised. Now that he saw how it all played out, jury selection struck Hunt as a high-stakes game of chess.[26] As Tisdale would say years later: "They miscalculated that they could get the jury they wanted."[27]

Chapter Seven

We Were Not Absolutely Sure

Hunt had been waiting to tell his story for nine months now, ever since they'd dragged him down those stairs from Tisdale's office and charged him with murder. He hadn't killed Deborah Sykes. He hadn't raped her. And he had no idea who had or why all these people had spent the two weeks since the jury was seated telling lies about him. On the stand, Little Bit, at least, had recanted. But all those others who testified for the state and claimed to have seen him on West End Boulevard that terrible morning, all of them were wrong. Now it was his turn to speak, if only someone on the jury would listen.

Up until now, he'd been sitting with his back to the audience. Now in the witness box beside the judge, he could see the audience in front of him and, to his left, the jury and three alternates—14 white faces and the lone Black man. Hunt's supporters were all there, filling up the benches behind the defense table. It was nice to be able to see them without having to twist around in his chair. Sykes' family and the police officers who had railroaded him sat behind the prosecutor's table. He'd find no sympathy there, especially after all the tension of the past days.

The defense committee had tried to enforce decorum inside the courthouse, but with emotions running high, that didn't always work. Early on, Sykes' mother complained of hostile looks and jeers, with someone even calling her "white trash" during recess outside the courtroom. After that, the judge set aside a room for Sykes' family to spend time during the recesses. There was a metal detector at the courtroom door and extra bailiffs assigned to watch for witness intimidation. The head of the local chapter of the Ku Klux Klan had told reporters before the trial began that someone from the chapter would attend.[1] Murphy and Tisdale both received death threats. [2] Hunt's sixth-grade teacher, Jo Anne North, found a note on her windshield the day she testified, with the words "Go home nigger lover" scrawled in red ink.[3] On the trial's seventh day, the judge cleared the courtroom after a bomb scare.[4] And just that morning, one of the jurors told the court how she'd been harassed in a gas station over the weekend by a Black man who recognized her from the trial's news coverage. He'd warned her that she could end up dead like Sykes if the jury came back with the wrong decision. In spite of the threat, she wanted to stay on the jury and hear the case to the end.[5]

With the morning break over, it was time to begin. Hunt placed his left hand on the Bible and raised his right.

"Do you swear to tell the truth, the whole truth, and nothing but the truth, so help you God?"

"I do."

Rabil, reassuring as always, began.

"Are you nervous, Mr. Hunt?" Rabil asked, getting straight to the point.

"Yes."

"Mr. Hunt, did you have anything to do with the murder of Deborah Sykes?"

"No, I didn't."

"Do you have any knowledge of who did it?"

"No."[6]

Rabil's questions took Hunt through his life story, how he had been raised by his grandfather, how he helped him count out cash to pay the monthly bills, and how his mother had been murdered when he was nine. He testified about living with an aunt and uncle after his grandfather's death and moving to California to live with a cousin, where he worked and babysat. These details were designed to portray him as an everyman, down on his luck, but at his core an honest, non-violent person.

Hunt shared his record of misdemeanors and his relationship with Little Bit, which had landed him in jail in the first place, and talked a lot about his hairstyle, which seemed silly but mattered because of the lies the witnesses had told about him. Tisdale kept objecting, which made it hard for Hunt to keep his thoughts straight. He wanted to talk about his prayers for justice, but for some reason, the judge wouldn't allow that. He was determined to keep his cool, even when the simplest questions were objected to.

"Are you angry with police for charging you with this crime?" Rabil asked.

"Objection."

"Overruled."

"No," Hunt replied.

"Why not?"

"Well, everybody makes mistakes."[7]

~

The case the state had laid out against Hunt over the previous two weeks was so riddled with mistakes it was hard to imagine that anyone would believe it. Jurors had heard first from Evelyn Jefferson, Sykes' mother, whose tearful testimony set the emotional tone for the trial. The officers who'd first arrived at the scene came next, followed by technicians and the medical examiner. These early witnesses had to deal with a glaring weakness in the case, and that was the lack of physical evidence to tie Hunt to the rape or murder. The blood found at the scene was all Sykes'. So were the hairs. A handprint on Sykes' car didn't match Hunt. Even the semen collected from her body didn't match Hunt. In the early 1980s, ten years before DNA testing became available, crime labs used blood-typing proteins to identify semen samples. The semen sample at the scene tested type O, no match to Hunt's B blood type. A technician from the state crime lab had a ready explanation for that. The sample, she said, contained a mixture of semen and Sykes' cells, so that her blood type, which was O, masked the semen's blood type. In other words, the testing had simply failed to detect Hunt's B blood type.[8] This was spurious science at best. Yet even on cross-examination she stuck to her testimony and insisted that although the physical evidence didn't implicate Hunt, it didn't rule him out.

Thomas Murphy, the former Klansman, was the first to identify Hunt in court.

"Mr. Murphy, I'll ask you if the individual that you saw on the street on that morning of August 10, 1984, is in the courtroom today?"[9] the DA asked.

Murphy pointed straight at Hunt, a moment captured by a newspaper photographer, and never wavered, even under cross-examination. He also insisted that his Klan affiliation was nothing more than a youthful mistake fueled by alcoholism.[10]

"I've got some of the best Black friends that there is in this city and I think as much of them as I do my white friends,"[11] he testified.

Johnny Gray, the only witness to the actual attack who could identify Hunt, came next. Like Murphy, Gray pointed right at Hunt. Rabil was prepared for Gray, though many of the police reports that revealed the discrepancies in Gray's story had been kept from the defense team. Rabil didn't know about Gray's failed second polygraph or problems with Gray's identification of Hunt in the lineup, which he wouldn't learn of until later in the trial, or even much detail about the mistaken identification weeks before Hunt's arrest. In spite of these disadvantages, Rabil used his cross-examination to bring up Gray's initial identification of Terry Thomas as the man he saw on the street the morning of the attack, as well as to hone in on Gray's criminal record and on the fact that Gray may have received reward money from the police.

After Gray, the state had called a witness who came up later in the investigation, a clerk at the downtown Hyatt House hotel named Roger Weaver, who had identified Hunt only after his arrest and after his picture was in the newspaper.[12] He had been working the reception desk the morning of the murder and testified that he saw a man with Jheri curls come into the lobby through the revolving door and turn left for the men's room. After he left, Weaver checked the bathroom, where he found bloody towels in the trash and drops of pink liquid, which he took to be blood, in the sink.

The police had waited until three weeks before the trial to take Weaver up the elevator in the county jail for a lineup, where he easily picked out Hunt.[13] By then, of course, Hunt's picture, with his hair in cornrows, had been in the newspaper and all over the local TV news dozens of times. Jenkins, who took this cross-examination, was ready for Weaver, especially the point about the Jheri curls, a style of loose curls made famous by Michael Jackson on the 1982 cover of *Thriller*, which looked nothing like the tight cornrows Hunt wore during the summer of 1984.[14]

"How was his hair?" Jenkins asked.

"It was—it had the appearance of being greasy or wet. It was in a straight-type Jheri-curl," Weaver replied.

"It was not plaited?"

"No, it was not in cornrows or braids."

"Not in cornrows?"

"Not in braids."

"Not in braids. Like Michael Jackson, you said?"[15]

Hunt's supporters laughed at the absurdity of Weaver's testimony. Clearly the witness had mistaken Hunt for a man with a completely different hairstyle.[16] It was obvious to them that Weaver had no credibility, but whether the jury understood the significance of the mix-up was another question.

Things had gone even better for Hunt's defense with Marie "Little Bit" Crawford, whom Tisdale had saved for late in the trial. She was the only one who claimed Hunt had confessed. Tisdale didn't trust her, with good reason. She had disappeared early on in the investigation, landing in jail in Atlanta, Georgia, where Rabil, Jenkins, Little, and their investigator, Poteat, found her. When she took the stand, Tisdale wasn't sure what she would say. At 15, she looked older, with high cheekbones and a defiant scowl.

"Did you make the following statement to Officer Daulton? 'On August 10th, me, Darryl and Sammy were at the Motel 6 and Darryl Hunt and Sammy Mitchell left the room at 6:00 o'clock am and they were both wearing black shirts and black pants and Darryl told me he was going to call a cab. The next time I saw Darryl was about 9:30 am, and he was nervous when he came back to the motel room and he said he needed a drink. Darryl had mud or grass stains on his knee.' Did you make that statement?" Tisdale asked.

"No, sir, I did not," she replied.

"You deny making the statement?"

"Yes, sir."

"But this is your signature?"

"Yes, sir."

"Now this is not your handwriting, is it?"

"No, sir, it is not."

"That's officer Daulton's handwriting, isn't it?"

"I don't know. I don't know what he writes like."

"Did he write it in your presence?"

"I said, I don't remember."[17]

She denied her later statement, too, about Hunt telling her "that Sammy did it and fucked her, too."[18] In spite of the denials, Tisdale entered the statements into evidence, which would later provide grounds for Hunt's appeal.[19]

Things seemed to get even worse for the state when Detective Daulton took the stand for the second time to rebut Crawford. During the trial, Little had learned from a friend of Johnny Gray's of a strange notation Gray made when he first picked Hunt out of a police lineup,[20] one that should have been shared with Hunt's team by the prosecutor as exculpatory evidence. Rather than write the number Hunt wore on his chest (4), Gray wrote two numbers, separated by a hyphen: 1-4. Daulton explained that, like the other witnesses, Gray rode the elevator up to the third floor of the county jail, which is where Daulton asked him to write the number of the man he saw on the scrap of paper. Rabil pressed hard.

"And did he write down on a piece of paper the number of a subject?"

"Yes he did."

"And how many numbers did he write down?"

"On the sheet of paper?"

"Yes, sir."

"He wrote two numbers down."

"Which two numbers did he identify?"

"He didn't identify two numbers. He wrote two numbers on the piece of paper indicating to me that Number One was Number Four."

"I'm sorry, I don't understand. Can you explain that?"

"He indicated to me that the number one suspect was the number four that he identified."[21]

Rabil hoped the explanation would seem as ludicrous to jurors as it did to him. Did Gray identify Hunt? Or did he identify two men? Or was Gray simply deflecting attention from himself?

Hunt's supporters were relieved when they overheard the assistant district attorney cursing Daulton, in an exchange reported by the *Chronicle*: "You blew it. We been schooling you for months and you blew the whole damn thing in front of everybody."[22]

∼

With Hunt on the stand, Rabil made sure to show how his client had cooperated with Daulton from the beginning and to make it clear to the jurors that he had nothing to hide—not his drinking, not even his unsavory relationship with the young prostitute. Hunt also testified, without any objection from the state, about Tisdale's attempt to bribe him into turning on Mitchell.

"They told me I was lying and that to tell them that Sammy Mitchell did it and that they'll let me go."

"What did you tell them?"

"I didn't know nothing about it."

"Did anybody in the office offer you anything if you would say Sammy Mitchell did it?"

"Yes. Mr. Tisdale exact words [were] we can get—you can get the $12,000 if you just say that Sammy did it and he looked at Daulton and said, 'Ain't that right,' and Daulton shook his head yeah."

"What did you say in response to that?"

"That I would tell no lie for nobody or against nobody for $12,000."[23]

It was a good thing Hunt had practiced for the cross-examination. Tisdale left that task to Richard Lyle, an assistant DA with a reputation for tenacity, who badgered Hunt, trying to trip him up on his alibi, with a series of confusing questions about a bicycle and multiple questions about his hairstyle, his drinking, and his alibi, then more about his relationship with Little Bit. As much as he tried, Lyle was unable to shake Hunt from his account of how he'd spent the morning of the murder, but the detailed questioning was enough to confuse anyone.

A few things hounded Hunt and his defense throughout the trial. The first was that he had pleaded guilty to contributing to the delinquency of a minor for his relationship with Little Bit. The plea deal used August 10 as the date Hunt and Little Bit had sex, which contradicted his alibi. Even though the attorney who handled that charge explained that the date hadn't been important to the plea deal, the confusion undermined Hunt's credibility. Testimony from his alibi witness, Cynthia McKey, wasn't solid, especially when she was confronted with an article in the *Chronicle*, which quoted her saying she was asleep when Hunt left her house the morning of the murder. The DAs also attacked Little, alleging that he had posed as a lawyer to visit Little Bit in jail and as a police officer to gain access to taxi records.[24] This happened during recess, out of earshot from jurors, but was widely covered by reporters in stories that undermined the defense team's credibility, especially with white readers, by making it seem as though Little and the defense had violated ethical standards.

Jury deliberations began on a Wednesday. Jurors chose an engineer named Malcolm Ryan as the foreman, who kept meticulous notes in a pocket-sized yellow spiral notebook.[25] At night, a bailiff brought Hunt back to jail. Supporters gathered in the street along the two-block route, waving and chanting his name. Their presence gave him comfort.[26] In the morning, bailiffs would return him to the "bullpen," a cell that reeked of urine from the open toilet in the corner and smelled to Rabil of desperation. For three long days, he kept his client company there, talking about books, anything to try to keep Hunt's spirits up. When they ran out of things to talk about, they pitched pennies.[27] On the second day, the judge kept the jury into the night, hoping they could break their deadlock. At nine, the foreman said they were still divided, 10-2, and the judge recessed until the morning. Even at that late hour, Hunt's supporters were still in court and out in the street, buoying his confidence. There was no way those jurors believed the mess of lies, he thought. It must be ten votes for innocence, two for guilt.[28]

The amount of time jurors were taking to decide also gave Rabil reason for optimism. Some of them must have their doubts, he

thought. Even Tisdale was getting nervous. By the second day, he
had begun chatting with Rabil and Jenkins outside the courtroom,
wondering where they could hold a second trial if the jury hung. The
following day, a Friday, Rabil brought his infant daughter, Sarah,
to court so Hunt could see her. The bullpen itself was no place for
babies, but there was a window in the door that looked out on the
corridor leading to the bullpen. The door to the cell also had a window. Rabil held his blue-eyed baby at the window height. From his
window in the bullpen, Hunt could see her, gazing in his direction.
He waved and smiled, then waved again. Holding his daughter close,
Rabil thought about the decent life his client wanted.[29]

At 11:35 a.m., the foreman, Ryan, summoned the court clerk,
and the jury returned to the courtroom, where he handed the
formal verdict sheet to the clerk to read aloud. They had found
Hunt guilty.

Seated at the defense table with Rabil to his right and Jenkins
to his left, Hunt stared straight ahead at the state seal hanging from
the front of the judge's bench. Jenkins asked that the jury be polled.

One by one, each juror, including the lone Black juror, stood
when their name was called to give their verbal consent to the guilty
verdict.

"Is this your verdict?" the clerk asked.

"Yes."

"Do you still assent thereto?"

"Yes."

Twelve times the clerk repeated the guilty verdict. Hunt could
hear people crying behind him.

"Is this your verdict?"

"Yes."

"Do you still assent thereto?"

"Yes."

Rabil put his arm around Hunt's shoulder.

"I'm sorry," he said.

It was Ryan and one woman who had held out against guilt. For three days, he had struggled over the difference between the legal standard for guilt "beyond a reasonable doubt" and "beyond a shadow of a doubt." As Ryan understood the two phrases, he could have some lingering doubt and still find Hunt guilty. "It was very, very murky," he would later say.[30]

The next phase of the trial, when the same jury would decide whether he should be executed, hardly mattered to Hunt. Inside, Hunt already was dying.[31] He kept his gaze fixed on the state seal. There was no way he would let these hateful, lying people see him cry. Rabil walked with him back to the bullpen. The bailiff locked the metal door behind them. Only then did Hunt give in to tears.[32]

~

Unable to bear the tension in the courtroom, Little had been waiting for the verdict in the lobby. The story he'd heard growing up, of the Black man who'd been executed a generation earlier in the rape of a white teenager, weighed on him throughout the trial, as it did on the older members of the defense committee. During the first week of the trial, the *Chronicle* had published Little's guest column titled "Hunt: Will He Die Like Clyde Brown?" "We must earnestly do all that we can, and by all means, we must continue to pray,"[33] Little had written. "Then, by the grace of God, justice will flow and Darryl Hunt will not die like Clyde Brown."

If there was ever a time to pray, it was now, he said, calling on supporters to join him at the Lloyd Presbyterian Church. About one hundred protesters met him at the church, just around the corner from where police first questioned Hunt and his ordeal had begun. Little spoke from the heart, invoking civil rights icons from a generation ago.

This system has decided to spit on us, to step on us, to stomp on us again. I guess we shouldn't be surprised. I guess we know

America by now. When it comes to justice in America, there is still a double standard. White people who are in power do not intend to treat us fairly.

I'm hurt now. I'll go home and cry for a while. But I won't give up because I know Martin didn't give up. Malcolm didn't give up. Medgar didn't give up. I'm going to collect myself. I'm going to get back on my feet. I'm going to do more battles. I'm not letting Darryl go.[34]

Hunt's lawyers skipped the rally. With court recessed until after lunch, Rabil and Jenkins had just two hours to prepare for the heaviest burden of all, and that was keeping Hunt off death row. History gave them ample reason to be afraid.

North Carolina has a long and brutal history of retribution against Black men, especially when a white woman's honor is perceived to be at stake. During the late nineteenth century and early twentieth century, 86 Black men—compared to 15 white men—were lynched,[35] often when only the whisper of a crime had occurred. The same pattern applied in the way legal public hangings were carried out. Between 1726 and 1910, 72 percent of those executed were Black. The state government assumed responsibility from the counties for executions early in the twentieth century, and the pattern of retribution against Black men continued, though now it was legitimized as state-sanctioned justice. In the first half of the twentieth century, North Carolina executed 283 Black men, which came to 78 percent of 362 total executions, far in excess of the percentage of Black men in the general population. Executions for the crime of rape fell even more disproportionately on Black men. Burglary was also a capital crime, but the punishment was applied exclusively to Black men, as though there was something more loathsome about a Black man breaking into the privacy of a white home. Of the 12 men executed for burglary during this period, all were Black.[36]

The race of the victims also determined the punishment. Not surprisingly, overwhelmingly the cases with white victims were punished by death. The loss of white life, the rape of white women, the threats against white families in their homes demanded justice, while the same threats against Black life did not.[37] When executions resumed in 1984, the first two defendants executed were a white man convicted of killing three state troopers and a white woman convicted of poisoning her boyfriend and suspected in five other deaths,[38] but they were small comfort when the weight of history was stacked against them.

Rabil and Jenkins had lined up a host of witnesses who could help jurors see that the man they had come to know, a man who aspired to follow his grandfather's example and lead a decent life, was something other than the beast of their imagination. Juanita Johnson, the cousin Hunt thought of as a sister, who had invited him to California where he cared for her children and helped with expenses from his restaurant work, testified, as did Ellsworth Boston, who gave Hunt a job in his construction company and admired his gentle ways. Hunt hated to see Johnson testify because of the pain it caused her. He hated the picture she brought of him as a little kid, the one that ran in the *Chronicle*. And he wept when Boston, now sick with throat cancer, spoke.[39]

The law governing the death penalty asks jurors to consider a series of sanitized questions, as though the taking of a life can be reduced to formula. Sentencing is supposed to be separate from the verdict, with the evidence of guilt the standard for the verdict, and the weight of Hunt's life story measured against the crime the standard for sentencing. Despite the way the system sets up the verdict and sentencing phases, behind closed doors, jurors often do what they want. That's how it was in Hunt's case. For despite the fact that the jury deliberated over the 25 death-penalty questions for hours on Friday afternoon and Monday morning, after the weekend recess, its members had decided on the sentence of life without parole before

the phase had even begun. Jury foreman Ryan later told Rabil that
he and the other holdout would agree to a guilty verdict only if the
others would agree to spare Hunt's life,[40] a compromise outside the
law but one defense attorneys often count on.

"It's a wrenching experience, especially in a case like this that
was all circumstantial. There was very little evidence," Ryan would
say years later. "Overall, it was beyond a reasonable doubt, but it
was not absolute. None of us were willing to sentence somebody to
death if we were not absolutely sure."[41]

Chapter Eight

A Chamber of Horrors

The ride from Winston-Salem to Polk Youth Institution took Hunt due east on the interstate to the state capital of Raleigh, about two hours away. Polk was built in the 1920s on a former World War I army base and by 1985 was a processing center for every male aged 19 to 21 sentenced to prison. Of the state's 97 prisons, Polk was the most overcrowded, incarcerating twice as many prisoners as the 340 it was built to hold.[1] It was cramped, violent, and outdated. By the 1980s, the Department of Correction had moved to a system of single cells for its most secure adult prisons as a way to control violence. But at Polk and 48 other medium-security camps across the state, men slept in open dorms with dozens of other men, in triple-level bunks, with little if any space between them.[2] Reformers had been warning about the conditions for years. In 1976, for example, a member of an advisory committee to the US Commission on Human Rights testified about widespread sexual violence in the open dorms once guards locked the men inside for the night. "There have been attempts to just build a cage around the individual bunk in some units so a man can secure himself in there at night," Judge Frank Snepp testified. "The dormitories at night are no-man's land. A guard would not dare go in there—except in force."[3] The violence created by these conditions persisted, dutifully tracked by the North Carolina Department of Correction, with the rate of disciplinary actions at Polk twice as high as those even at Central Prison, the state's maximum-security prison on the other side of town, where adult men were processed. A newspaper editorial calling for Polk's closure referred to it as a "chamber of horrors."[4]

~

Hunt knew how to defend himself around a tough crowd, but he wasn't so sure about prison. Maybe he could handle men who'd grown up as he had, in tough Black neighborhoods in cities and towns around the state, but the prospect of being confined in such close quarters with men who carried the same kind of hatred in their hearts as the "crackers" who had told all those lies about him was something else. He didn't just fear those imprisoned with him but also his captors, whom he had learned to fear when he was first charged with murder, alone in a single cell at the end of a dark hallway of the county jail. Their taunts haunted him: "The last nigger we had in here we found hanging the next morning."[5] But at least in jail, guards he knew from the neighborhood looked out for him. In prison, he would be alone.

Hunt had spent the first days of his life sentence in the county jail, on familiar ground. After his sentencing, Little had been able to arrange a prayer meeting with members of the defense committee, just Hunt and the people who supported him in a room together. "We'll keep up the fight," they promised him.

The delay in transferring him to prison also gave Hunt time to catch up with friends. North, his sixth-grade teacher, came to see him. Hunt promised her he would get an education in prison. Griggs, the imam at the local mosque, gave him a copy of the Quran. Mattie Mitchell, Sammy's mother and a surrogate mother to him, visited. So did his girlfriend, Rhonda, whom he loved more than ever. Even some of the bailiffs were on his side. One female guard wept, holding him in a hug, and promised she would pray for him. Another female guard gave him a poem she wrote for him.[6] He had no expectation of such kindness from the guards in prison.

Little had suggested Hunt keep a journal as a way to make up for all his missed schooling. Nothing about writing came easily to Hunt, but he was determined to make Little proud. In the days before they shipped him off to state prison, Hunt began to fill the pages of a spiral-bound notebook with a jumble of anger, yearning, and despair, feelings he'd hidden all through his trial. In truth, he was mad as hell.

People ask me why them white people got up there and lied on me, I wish I know, but don't take, nothing for a white man to lie on a nigger. And then they had this black Punk to say he seen me beating some white woman I have never seen In my life, except in the Picture's they showed in court and in the paper. I still say he did it, cause who knows going to see some shit like that and don't do nothing to help. But the Police didn't want to look at him They want Sammy, and when they couldn't get Sam they said they would get the next thing to him, Me. And they charge me with this because I went with a white girl. So they railroad me, they had the Police to lie in court, they had Johnny Gary, or what every his name is. To lie, they give me a all white Jury, I'm talking about the Black to, he was just as white as the rest of them divel's, the hole court Prosising was Riged. The Judge wasn't shit either he probly told the Jury to find me guilty cause I was (black) if he did they did it anyway. Cause they knew I was innocent, but they had to convict some body, and that some body was (me.)

I know I will never get over this, but I won't let it get to me, I'm glad the Lord give me the strength for these 10 months, and I know he will give me the strength for the rest of my life, I also

know he will see that justice be done, it might tak some time
but evently he will see jutis is done for me and that woman.[7]

~

Prison is meant as a punishment for crime, a cruel justice but justice
nonetheless. For an innocent man, there is no crime, only a tangle of
lies and errors and a shattered truth at odds with any social order the
justice system is meant to uphold. Wrongful conviction violates the
trust in that system completely. From the outside, Hunt's life before
his conviction may have seemed indolent to some, even lawless, but
inside he was guided by a deeply felt moral code. His grandfather
had taught him responsibility with a paper route, chores at home,
and a swift beating when he messed up. Family meant everything
to Hunt. Even in his life on the streets, he stood for loyalty and
honor. That's why he wouldn't betray Mitchell, even for $12,000
in reward money. When police wanted to talk with him about the
Sykes murder, he cooperated freely, and he told the truth. That was
part of his moral code. He had spent time in jail before, six months, a
long time for a brawl, but at least he had committed the crime. That
made a kind of moral sense. But this mess of lies he was trapped in
violated everything he'd ever learned about right and wrong.

It's hard to find the words for the trauma of such betrayal. Saundra Westervelt, a sociologist who has studied the impact of wrongful
conviction, has observed how, years after an exoneration, the men
and women she has spoken with are still trying to reclaim their
innocence, as though the conviction itself had torn into the very
core of their being. Worse than the trauma of prison is knowing
that people think of them as something other than who they are, an
experience Westervelt calls the "crippling stigma" of a false accusa-
tion.[8] She uses a phrase borrowed from the sociology of disasters,
"sustained catastrophe,"[9] to name a betrayal that is beyond words.

Another researcher, Zieva Konvisser, calls wrongful conviction
a "moral injury,"[10] when the very foundation of what we know as

right and wrong crumbles. Soldiers face this kind of betrayal on the battlefield, especially when discipline breaks down and the structure of their platoon collapses. Children abandoned by the families they once trusted are damaged in this way. So are citizens of police states, where the very fabric of a social order falls apart. For all its chaos and loss, Hunt's upbringing gave him a sense of a social order. Tell the truth. Face the consequences of your actions. You are innocent until proven guilty, judged by a jury of your peers. All that had failed Hunt, as it had failed generations of Black men, because the truth is the system was never meant for them. It was enough to make him scream or weep. But there was no place for either in prison. Any sign of weakness would be punished.

~

As the car approached Polk, Hunt could see the chain-link fencing, the coils of concertina wire, and the red-brick guard towers.[11] It was time for strength and self-control. He managed to hold back tears, but his trembling hands betrayed him. Inside, he was stripped naked, all 145 pounds of him,[12] searched, and given a number. He had heard about the rapes and murders at Polk and brutality by the guards. "If they're gonna kill me, this is the time," he thought.[13] They took away the books that would make him smart and other gifts from Little, Rabil, and other supporters. They also took most of his $300 in cash for his prison account, leaving him with $30. Once he was dressed in prison browns, another imprisoned man took him to the dorm, with its rows of bunk beds, then showed him the locker where he could store his things and the canteen where he could buy a lock.[14] His life as inmate #0197495 began.[15]

There were some familiar faces at Polk, brothers from home he'd gotten to know in jail in the "Tre 4," prison slang that referred to the 34th district, which included Winston-Salem. And because of the publicity in the case, just about everyone knew his face. In fact, the injustice he suffered gave him a certain status, one he felt offered some protection. That first day, he wrote a letter to Rhonda, to let her know the visiting schedule. And he wrote in his journal, determined not to let Little down: "It's the first time I been in prison. But I can make it. If Larry got confidence in me, I got confidence in myself."[16]

~

Imam Khalid Griggs visited Hunt almost every weekend, following him from Polk to a wretched place called Blanch, about an hour east of Winston-Salem, in Caswell County,[17] red clay country where the Ku Klux Klan took hold at the end of the nineteenth century and never left.[18] From there he'd be transferred to Southern Correctional Facility, also hidden away in a rural county, this one about a 90-minute drive south. Often, Griggs brought his two daughters, then eight and ten, whom he'd dragged to rallies and protests back before Hunt's conviction.[19]

Griggs had seen how Islam helped so many others in prison. He had started ministering to Muslims in federal prison soon after he graduated from Howard. And ever since moving back to his hometown, he had volunteered at prisons across the state. From what he'd seen with other incarcerated men, he felt sure that the discipline of Islam, with prayer five times a day, dietary restrictions, and prohibitions against alcohol and drugs, would help Hunt endure incarceration, maybe even give him a new moral structure to replace the one he had lost. Griggs especially loved verses from the fourth chapter of the Quran, with its message of justice and equality. He hoped the message would speak to Hunt and felt the religion would provide Hunt with a community in prison, and with that, protection. Although traditional Islam wasn't as prevalent in prison as the Nation of Islam, Muslim men still commanded respect and looked out for one another. All through the summer of 1985 and into the fall, Griggs made the weekly drive, bringing with him news of home and literature on Islam. Hunt was always polite, but it was hard for Griggs to tell whether the books he brought him resonated.

During the early weeks of his life in prison, Hunt kept the promise he'd made to himself to keep a journal. Sometimes he wrote about the mundane—the boredom, the food, his time lifting weights on the yard. He missed his girlfriend, Rhonda, and daydreamed about life after prison, returning to his fantasy of a family of five, with the eldest being Tahara, the baby girl whose diapers he had changed while his former girlfriend Renee went out. The other children he dreamed of were still to come. He wrote about the daily indignities and the breaks white men imprisoned with him received at the expense of Black men. Always, there was the pain few could understand, the pain of enduring all this for someone else's crime. In early July, he wrote:

> Everyday I walk out side, and feel free, and then realize that I'm not. That really hurt's but one day they will not be able to hold me and talk shit to me, cause I will be a free man. Some times I feel like I'm going to explode but I say to myself, That's what the white man want me to do, then when I heart some body, they will have something to (s)ay I did. That's just some of the side shit they do, to put pressure on some one, so they can explode but I'm not, I've been strong this long I will make it a little longer.[20]

There also was an ever-present sense of danger. At night, the guards locked the door to the dormitory, leaving him and dozens of other young men to fend for themselves. Hunt didn't write about what he witnessed, but others who spent time at Polk during this period reported rapes and other attacks and they learned to turn away.[21] Prison life requires a code of silence, for the perpetrators of violence, for its victims, and for its witnesses.

On the Fourth of July, Hunt woke up to rumors that the guards had a picture of him posted in the guard tower, which meant they were prepared to shoot if he fled. As he wrote in his journal:

They think I want to run. I'm not a fool. I might not look like I
have sense, but I do.[22]

Death threats came next, anonymous notes left on his bunk.

This morning I woke up at one o'clock, just to find a note on my
bed, that say's 3 niggers are going to be stabbed. This morning
and by noon, 3 more. I don't know how the rest of the day is
going to go, but I sure hop it's better.[23]

Blanch was worse than Polk. The prison covered 23 acres off a
dead-end road in Caswell County, just south of the Virginia line,
in the community of Hamer, where the lone store is now closed.
Built for security, with steel walls and doors and a concrete floor,
Blanch was known as North Carolina's "Little Alcatraz" but was then
another prison for young men.[24] To the guards who worked there
in the 1980s, the long corridors of single cells still remind them of
pictures they'd seen of the infamous Alcatraz.[25] Hunt wrote very
little about the place. Knowing that his notebook could be taken
from him at any time, Hunt was leery of putting too much in writing. There was no telling what these guards would do if they knew
what was in his heart. He didn't belong there, he reminded himself,
but no one, even men punished for crimes they actually committed,
should have to endure such conditions.

How they treat us, I know some of the brother's here have done
there crime's. But, that doesn't mean they have to be treated like
dog's. Each person here is a human being and deserves to be
treated like one. But if a person can imagine what hell is like,
he can imagine what I am going through right now. I know its
about 98 degrees in this cell, we have no cold water. The water
that comes out is so hot and nasty.[26]

All through this miserable time, Hunt began to learn Salat, the daily Muslim prayer. "O Allah, how perfect You are and praise be to You. Blessed is Your name, and exalted is Your majesty. There is no god but You." The prison bureaucracy set the rules for meal time, shower time, yard time, visiting time, and bedtime, and the guards enforced those rules. Islam gave Hunt a set of rules that came from beyond the prison walls. Five times a day he prayed, on a schedule set by the Earth's rotation around the sun. The words, too, came from beyond. "I seek shelter in Allah from the rejected Satan," he said, repeating the second line of the Salat.

In September, he was moved again, this time to Southern Correctional, a medium-security prison with space for 664 men, in Montgomery County, in the foothills of the Uwharries, an ancient mountain range once taller than the Rockies. There, Hunt found other Muslims, a brotherhood of men he prayed with, ate with, and watched out for. Griggs was right about the sense of community and the protection Islam would give him.

The rules at Southern Correctional were more relaxed than at Blanch. Griggs could now bring Hunt the things he would need to lead a Muslim life—a prayer rug, prayer beads, and a white knit skullcap he wore with pride.[27] Hunt learned the rhythm of the five daily prayers, when to kneel and bow his head, and when to rise up. The dawn prayer was before sunrise, the second prayer just after noon, the third prayer later in the afternoon, then one at sunset, followed by the final prayer of the day at night. Soon he knew the words to the Salat in Arabic. "All praises and thanks be to Allah, the Lord of the worlds, the most Gracious, the most Merciful; Master of the Day of Judgment. You alone we worship, from You alone we seek help. Guide us along the straight path—the path of those whom You favored, not of those who earned Your anger or went astray." His official conversion ceremony on November 5 brought him happiness he would remember as more intense than any high from weed or alcohol.[28] Soon, the 25 or so other Muslim men in the prison selected Hunt to be their imam.[29]

~

North Carolina's prison system in the 1980s was made up of 97 facilities, half of them medium-security camps in rural parts of the state. These were left over from the era of county road crews, when imprisoned men were housed in barracks in each of North Carolina's 100 counties and transported to worksites in cages mounted on wheels, each measuring, at most, 20 by 8 feet. Until the practice ended in the 1920s, as many as 18 men would spend the night in one of these cages, with a stove, a lamp, and a single bucket for a toilet.[30] Pictures in the local public library from that era show a group of Black men in striped jumpsuits[31] posed in a field beside one of these wagons. If there were white men working on these road-gangs, they weren't pictured.

For generations, Black people made up half of the state's prisoners, far outstripping their portion of the general population.[32] By the mid-1980s, the rate of Black admissions to prisons in the state was 342 per 100,000; for whites it was 63 per 100,000.[33] In other words, a Black man was more than five times more likely to end up in prison than a white man. Black men most dreaded a transfer to one of the mountain camps, where they were outnumbered by white men.[34] The 1976 report to the Civil Rights Commission on prison conditions noted another statistic that would add to the pattern of institutional racism Hunt faced in prison. Although the majority of the total imprisoned in North Carolina were Black, the overwhelming majority of men assigned to guard them were white.[35]

As the War on Drugs and other tough-on-crime policies took off during the 1980s and 1990s, the disparity between white and Black imprisonment rates worsened. This was no accident. In 1980, four years before Hunt's arrest, Ronald Reagan won the presidency by adhering to the Republican Party strategy of pandering to racism with rhetoric about crime and welfare fraud that had begun with Richard Nixon's "Southern Strategy." By 1982, Reagan turned that election strategy into policy with his declaration of a War on Drugs, which without explicit mention of race would nonetheless target Black drug offenders. In 1985, an article in the *Washington Post* reported on the biggest prison expansion in the country's history, with 100 prisons under construction at a cost of $3.5 billion.[36] The following year, Congress passed the Anti-Drug Abuse Act, which set mandatory minimum sentences for drug offenses, with the longest sentences reserved for crack, a form of cheap cocaine that had taken hold in Black communities. As the War on Drugs picked up, prison numbers across the country swelled and the disparity between Black and white incarceration rates widened. By the mid-1990s, the rate of Black imprisonment exceeded the rate for whites by a ratio of seven to one.[37]

A generation passed before critics started to refer to the "carceral state," but even in the 1980s, reformers understood that high rates of imprisonment did little to reduce crime. It was the cost, rather than the futility, of mass incarceration that caught the attention of North Carolina lawmakers. At first, legislators tried to control the growth in prison spending by setting a prison cap of 18,000 people. In 1990, for example, the state released more than 500 imprisoned men and women to comply with the cap.[38] But even with these releases, lawmakers were unable to control spending. From 1985 to 1995, North Carolina would spend $550 million to add 16,600 prison beds.[39] During that period, prison admissions nearly doubled, from 17,500 in 1986 to 30,800 in 1992.[40] In 1994, North Carolina tried a different approach that was gaining popularity around the country as a way to control prison spending. Rather than leave sentencing to the discretion of judges, lawmakers passed the Structured Sentencing Act, which set strict guidelines on prison terms. Sentences for those convicted of violent crimes increased, while those for low-level crimes went down by as much as 80 percent.

Like so much of public policy, these laws were driven by concerns over money. It took a federal lawsuit, filed by prisoners in North Carolina the year of Hunt's conviction, to force a reckoning with the violence and overcrowding Hunt would have experienced. The lawsuit, *Small v. Martin*, focused on conditions in the medium-security camps that housed people in open dormitories and demanded that the state reduce crowding by replacing triple-decker bunks with double-deckers, allot 50 square feet of space for each imprisoned person, and require guards to patrol inside the dorms at night rather than leave the most vulnerable to the mercy of the others. As the federal court orders in the case noted: "There was extensive testimony about assaults and homosexual rape carried out behind bunks draped with blankets, thus preventing observation by security officers."[41] The court took four years to negotiate an agreement to the modest demands made by the plaintiffs, and the state took ten years to fully comply. As one man would tell a National Public Radio reporter nine years into the case:

Sometimes it can be, you know, total chaos, you know, mass confusion, and it's crowded and tensions flare and to the point at times you step on somebody's feet, it's like you ready to fight, you know what I'm saying?[42]

As for the question of wrongful conviction, Hunt was ten years into his sentence before DNA evidence spawned the innocence movement. If other innocent men were locked up with Hunt, their particular anguish was a hidden one.

~

In Winston-Salem, Hunt's supporters got busy raising money. They would need it to hire attorneys to appeal the conviction and get Hunt freed. With all the publicity over the trial, support for Hunt was growing among Black people. White people, for the most part, accepted the conviction in the belief that once a jury had heard the evidence and reached its verdict, justice was achieved. But for many Black observers, the trial reinforced their earlier belief that Hunt was railroaded. The lone Black juror had let them down. Hunt's defense committee could hold rallies now at some of the larger Black churches in town, filling sanctuaries at places such as First Baptist Church on Highland Avenue and Emmanuel Baptist Church way out on Reynolds Park Road, places where doctors and lawyers and teachers worshiped. The offering tray would fill, too, with five-, ten-, and twenty-dollar bills,[43] much more than the smaller offerings collected in the tiny sanctuary of Lloyd Presbyterian.

The publicity didn't stop with Hunt's conviction. District Attorney Tisdale kept making allegations against Little about his conduct leading up to the trial, threatening an investigation by the State Bureau of Investigation. Little had gone to the county jail in Atlanta with Hunt's lawyers and the private investigator a few weeks before the trial to interview Little Bit about her initially damning statement about Hunt, which she gave to police and recanted at trial. Tisdale accused Little of deceit for signing in on the visitor's log as an attorney. Tisdale also insisted Little had deceived Johnny Gray when he secretly recorded an interview with him, saying Little had flashed some sort of badge that looked like police ID. Finally, Tisdale questioned Hunt's eligibility as an indigent defendant. By the time of Hunt's trial, the defense committee had spent $4,928, mostly to pay for the private detective and the psychological evaluation, costs that today would be covered by the state. Tisdale even filed suit to gain access to the committee's accounting books to show that Hunt was no longer indigent and therefore no longer eligible for the court to pay his legal fees.[44]

The *Journal* dutifully covered these stories, keeping Little's and Hunt's names in the news. For white readers, these allegations suggested that there was something fishy about the defense committee, a suspicion that only reinforced Hunt's guilt. But for Black readers, the allegations added to the belief that Hunt had been railroaded by a racist system now out to get those who supported him. Hunt's legal case was no longer his alone. If he could be railroaded, so could any Black man. Ministers who had held back early on joined the fight. And so did the writer Maya Angelou, known around the world for her autobiography *I Know Why the Caged Bird Sings*. She'd been living in Winston-Salem since 1982, teaching at Wake Forest University, and had become a loyal member of Mount Zion Baptist Church. She spoke at a rally at Dellabrook Presbyterian Church, where Eversley was pastor, the familiar timbre of her voice carrying strength. "We must remember that Winston-Salem is down South, but New York City is up South. Darryl Hunt exists in San Francisco, in Paris, in London, and you know how many there are in South Africa. A case can be built here on any person founded on lies and hate that can send us to the gas chamber or the electric chair."[45]

Emboldened, the defense committee turned to the state's top civil rights lawyers for help. Jim Ferguson and Adam Stein had founded their firm in 1968, the first integrated law firm in the state, and since then they had led just about every significant civil rights action in North Carolina. They also had a connection to Little from his days in the Panthers. Stein, raised in an activist Jewish family in Washington, DC, headed south after law school to fight for justice; Ferguson, a Black lawyer raised in Asheville, North Carolina, believed in using the law to force his home state to do what was right. Throughout the 1970s and 1980s, they won case after case, from those involving school desegregation to those involving voting rights, and on the side had a thriving personal injury practice.[46] If anyone could stand up to the likes of Tisdale and the Winston-Salem police, Hunt's defenders believed they could.

The outcry in Winston-Salem led the State Bureau of Investigation to conduct its own probe. Two bureau agents spent most of 1986 working with two Winston-Salem detectives reviewing the police reports in Hunt's case, reinterviewing the witnesses who had testified at the 1985 trial and interrogating new ones. Much of their work focused on witnesses who told agents that Johnny Gray, the man who made the 911 call, had confessed to stabbing Sykes himself. Their reports filled more than 3,000 pages, yet the state agency never discussed its findings with local district attorneys and certainly not with Hunt's lawyers. Unable to produce what it saw as any new evidence for or against Hunt, the State Bureau of Investigation closed its joint investigation with city police in November 1986.[47] That month, the city manager came out with a report that offered a stinging rebuke of his own police department and the Sykes murder investigation. Daulton, the lead detective, was demoted to the department's radio room, two supervisors were suspended, and the chief was reprimanded.[48]

It was clear that the case against Hunt was riddled with errors. But the appeal Ferguson and Stein were working on could not be based on the flaws in the investigation, on whether, for example, Gray lied or Weaver knew the difference between cornrows and a Jheri curl. A jury had heard the evidence and found the witnesses credible. The appeal could only be based on procedure, on errors in the law, of which there were many. For example, it was clear to Stein and Ferguson that Tisdale had, in fact, relied on race to remove potential jurors. That was a violation of due process. When the hotel clerk identified Hunt in a lineup, neither of Hunt's lawyers had been present. That, too, could be grounds for appeal. And finally, introducing Crawford's police statements into evidence when she had already recanted them broke rules meant to provide for a fair trial.

In January 1986, the defense committee made plans to celebrate the first Martin Luther King Day holiday in the country. King had spoken in Winston-Salem—in 1962 in the chapel at Wake Forest University and in 1964 at Goler Metropolitan AME Zion Church, on East Third Street. Some of the defense committee organizers had heard him speak, squeezing into the hot sanctuary to hear the young minister from Atlanta. Now there was a national holiday in his honor and a local case in need of his spirit. There would be a parade for King, from Mount Zion Baptist Church on the east side of town down Fifth Street to the city's convention center. Organizers with Hunt's defense committee passed a hat in the convention center and raised $10,000 for the appeal.[49] The following month, Angelou spoke at another rally for Hunt. "I have no independent knowledge of Darryl Hunt," she told the congregation. "But they say in the beauty parlor he got a raw deal."[50]

The nobody from the streets was now a cause.

Chapter Nine

What in the Fuck Is Going On?

In April 1986, Winston-Salem police announced that they were reopening a handful of cold cases with Black victims,[1] among them the death of Arthur Wilson, whose body had been found down the street from a liquor house on Claremont Avenue run by Ezelle Clowers. Merritt Drayton Williams, in jail on a charge that he'd killed a white woman, saw his chance and called the police department ready to deal.

Williams figured if he helped police with these old murders, maybe they would go easy on him. He hadn't meant to kill Mary Smith. She was drunk and getting out of hand. And his girlfriend, Mattie Mae Davis, wanted her out of her apartment. He shouldn't have pushed her. But he did. She must have hit her head hard on the concrete when she fell down the stairs, because she didn't move after she'd fallen. And now he was sitting in the county jail charged with killing a white woman.[2] He knew what that meant. Williams was 28 and had once felt destined for something larger than the life he was leading. He had wanted to be an architect, but now he did odd jobs. Back home in Walterboro, South Carolina, he had trouble making friends. As an adult, he was diagnosed with mental illnesses—depression, schizophrenia, personality disorder. He always felt cut off. Alone. And there was no one more alone than a Black man who killed a white woman. But if he worked with the police, maybe they would work with him.[3]

Teresa Hicks and Randy Weavil, both veteran detectives, took Williams' call and went to see him in jail. Hicks, with straight brown hair and fine features, was one of the few female detectives on the force but could hold her own in a man's world. Weavil, a former baseball player in the minor leagues, still had his boyish good looks and enthusiasm. Williams started off easy, telling Weavil and Hicks he knew something about the Wilson case. Known around the liquor house by one of several nicknames—"Jutt Holiday," "Doc Holiday," or simply "Holiday," Wilson was known to carry a wad of cash with him on payday, a "fool's knot," with a $50 bill wrapped around a stack of ones.[4] As Williams' story unfolded, he said he'd been there when Wilson was killed and offered up two familiar names, Darryl Hunt and Sammy Mitchell, who he said had argued with Wilson at the liquor house, then hatched a plan to rob him. Wilson's money would pay for quite a party, Williams said.

Two days after the initial call, the detectives went to see him again in jail. Were you there with Hunt and Mitchell when they killed Wilson? What about a weapon?[5] That's when Williams told them about the ax handle they'd used. It was in the closet in his house. The detectives took Williams from the jail to his apartment, and sure enough, they found an ax handle. Williams also offered to help with another unsolved murder, this time the case of Blanche Bryson, a retired cafeteria worker whose son was a rising lawyer. She'd been found strangled with a lamp cord in her house in December 1985. The police had a brown toboggan hat, found in her house, but after following up on leads and tips that came in all year, there had been no break in the case. Now, Williams was saying he had killed her. That made for two killings solved,[6] including the one in which he provided a weapon and named Hunt and Mitchell. To Weavil and Hicks, it was too good to be true.

With all the criticism the police department had taken over Darryl Hunt, Weavil and Hicks knew they had to be careful with the Wilson case. Lawyers were always able to find a legal loophole to upend good police work. In the Sykes case, the Crawford girl who recanted her statement gave Hunt's lawyers grounds for appeal. The evidence against Hunt and Mitchell in any Wilson case would have to stick. And Weavil and Hicks would have to move quickly before witnesses clammed up again. Liquor house crimes were always hard to solve. Witnesses were drunk and didn't want to get involved.[7] In 1983, when police had first looked into Wilson's death, two witnesses driving by in a car had said they saw three men attacking Wilson in the street, about a block down the hill from the liquor house. When they saw the car, the men ran. At 2 a.m., the dark street was lit by a single overhead light, but the witnesses had gotten a good look at one of the men. The witnesses were shown hundreds of mug shots but were never able to identify the one person they had seen. At the end of the year, police stopped working the case.

With Williams' statement and the weapon, the detectives tracked down others in the neighborhood who had been drinking at Clowers' place the night Wilson died. Some said they overheard Mitchell arguing with Wilson. Some remembered that he had a stick. Maybe it was the ax handle. Finally, two women from the liquor house crowd confirmed Williams' story, that they saw Hunt and Mitchell attack Wilson in the street. Williams' girlfriend, Mattie Mae Davis, confirmed it, too.[8] There were numerous red flags in the case, all ignored. The witness accounts were inconsistent. What's more, the autopsy didn't support the vicious beating they described. Instead of finding numerous bruises, the autopsy found a single wound at the back of Wilson's head. Investigators never considered other possible explanations. As drunk as he was, Wilson could easily have fallen and hit his head on the pavement, lying there unconscious until he died of alcohol poisoning, an easy mark to robbers.[9] But with Williams' statement and the statements from the three women, police had plenty of evidence to charge Hunt, Mitchell, and Williams.

~

The spring of 1986 was a lonely time for Hunt. In February, he turned 21, locked up in Southern Correctional as his appeal dragged on. He obtained his GED, but even that made him feel a fool for waiting so long. Then in March, Rhonda broke up with him. He had seen it coming, but the breakup hurt.

> I have to go through hell for being incarcerated for something I didn't do. Saturday, Sunday and Monday I went to the other hell of being without the one I truly (love) and I'm tired of being hurt for no reason at all. I'm human also and have feelings just like everyone else.[10]

Then on April 18, 1986, the warden called Hunt to the office. He had a message from his lawyer to call. It was only 8 a.m., so Hunt called Rabil at home.

"Are you standing?" Rabil asked.

"Yes," Hunt replied.

"You need to sit down."[11]

Rabil was devastated by the new charges of murder about to be filed against Hunt in the Wilson case, but he was determined to protect Hunt from his fears. He explained simply that the police were going to charge him with another murder, a cold case from 1983. Did he know a man named Arthur Wilson who'd been beaten to death outside a liquor house? Police had charged Mitchell the night before and were headed down to Troy that day to talk to Hunt. Stein and another lawyer were headed his way, too. In the meantime, Hunt shouldn't say a word.

"Why are these people doing this crap?" Hunt asked.

"Try not to worry too much. It's just a political move, to try to kill the publicity and your support."[12]

Half an hour later, three cops showed up. Hunt wouldn't make the same mistake he'd made in 1984. He wouldn't talk, not until his lawyers showed up, no matter what these cops said, how many times they called him a "nigger." A half hour passed, 40 minutes. It took that long for the lawyers to talk their way into the interrogation room. With them in the room, Hunt answered a few simple questions. He didn't know Arthur Wilson. He hadn't killed him. And he didn't know who had. That was it.

The police left, headed back to Winston-Salem to prepare a warrant for his arrest. Alone with his lawyers, it was time to prepare for another trumped-up murder charge. As always, Hunt had an uncanny knack for detail, and the night in September 1983 came back to him clear as ever. He'd been staying with a friend then to help him run a liquor house while the friend went to jail for the weekend on a DUI. He had been wearing jeans, as always, and a borrowed pair of cowboy boots. He remembered being at Clowers' place and leaving by 11 p.m. to be back at his friend's liquor house in time to collect the night's tabs. He heard about Wilson's death the following day.

Hunt had been in prison for a year now, and he couldn't do anything about these new accusations except keep his mouth shut. He spent a week back in the Forsyth County Jail for his arraignment. Then they shipped him back to Southern Correctional to wait. Hunt trusted Adam and Fergie, nicknames for the two acclaimed lawyers trying to get him a new trial in the Sykes case. He hoped they could protect him against these new charges in the Wilson case. But no one could explain why the police abused him so much.

Well in a couple of hours it will be one year since I've been convicted and one year since I've been in prison. I was just thinking about some of the questions people ask me, about it seems strange that they pick you. Well I don't know why they pick me and I ask myself over and over again, it's not because I did anything because I haven't and it's not because of Sammy or that I'm Black but it's something that God knows and he only but I wish like hell I knew everyday, now since I've been charged with another murder, I didn't do. I think about not getting out, not being alive to have a child of my own. What have I done in my life that's causing me to go through so much pain!! I haven't killed anyone. Why does it seem that all the bad shit happens to me? I want to talk with people about how I feel but I know they will get the wrong impression, some will think I'm going crazy and why not? And some will think I have a lot of hate inside of me, why not? And some will think I'm guilty, which I'm not. I can't talk to Larry or Khalid about how I feel because they have too much to worry or think about without me telling them how lonely and scared I am. How I want to be free to do what I want to do. I sit in my cell at night and dream about how nice it would be to be out there with Rhonda and have 5 or 6 kids and a big house with a dog and cat. Working everyday just being normal. But then I wake up and I be damn, here I am sitting in prison doing a life sentence now have another murder warrant. I just start to adjust to the fact that I'll probably have to lay in here 20 years, but now its like I'll never get out. I wish someone would tell me what in the fuck is going on.[13]

The answer was clear to those who believed in him. Part two of the frame-up had begun.

Chapter Ten

Larry, I Can't Do It

Hunt wasn't writing much in his journal anymore, but he did write long letters home, filled with frustration, loneliness, and despair. It was hard to fathom how a system of justice that claimed to protect had done the opposite, turning lies into truths and his truth into an unheard cry.

In 1987, a jury in Winston-Salem convicted him for a second murder, this time in the Wilson case, without a shred of credible evidence against him. Mitchell was also convicted in the Wilson case, so now the two Blues Brothers were both in prison, leaving Hunt to bear the weight of accumulated defeat as best he could. He prayed five times a day and worked at whatever job was available at whatever prison he was assigned to. At some prisons the Muslim community was stronger than at others. At Piedmont Correctional, where he spent ten months in 1987 and 1988, Muslims were assigned to jobs throughout the prison, which meant any time a Muslim went to the canteen, the cafeteria, or the gym there was another Muslim watching out for him. In spite of that support, the waiting was hard, making Hunt dependent on others, on his lawyers to draft his appeals, on the court to schedule hearings, on judges in Raleigh to take their sweet time deciding what should have been obvious to anyone.

He didn't belong in any of these prison camps.

Sometimes weeks passed before he got around to writing letters, knowing full well that on the outside life moved on and it could take weeks before an answer to his letters came. He kept these replies, cherishing them even when it was dangerous to cherish anything. One from Stein, speaking on the status of his appeals, all business, straight to the point, arrived at the end of March.

> Darryl, this case has taken longer to get decided by the North Carolina Supreme Court than any case I can remember in my 20 years of practice. However, I do hope to get a decision within a year from now. Also, I think we have a good chance of winning a new trial on appeal. If we were to lose on appeal, we still have the motion for further relief. I think our chances on that are even better. Don't give up.[1]

Hunt trusted Stein, but as the lawyer said, all Hunt could do was hope and not give up, even on a system that was never intended for him. In the meantime, Hunt tried to honor the promises he made to Little, to his sixth-grade teacher North, to all the others who believed in him that he would get an education, and with his GED finished, he was taking college business classes. Just before his 22nd birthday, when he was back at Southern Correctional, he wrote to North, a letter he'd been meaning to write for a long time, this time unable to hide the full measure of all he had lost.

> Well, Mrs. North, getting to why I am writing, I was just sitting here thinking about who I haven't wrote and you were the first person that came to mind when I really thought about how long it has been, it really made me feel bad, so I made up my mind not to put it off one more day. As I stated before, I hope and pray that you will forgive me. Mrs. North, I am still trying to

get used to this place. It's going on three years now and I still have trouble getting use to all this.[2]

Central, Piedmont, and Southern were all wretched places. But Caswell, just down the road from Blanch, that other hellhole from his first year in prison, was the worst. The prison is far from hidden. Anyone driving along County Home Road can see through the two rows of wire fencing that secure the place to men in their prison browns shooting hoops in the yard or lining up for chow. Most of the one-story brick buildings that hold the open dormitories, kitchen, laundry, and offices were built after Hunt left, during the expansion of the state's prison system of the 1990s, but the new buildings look much like the ones there in Hunt's time—made of brick or cinder-block. Inside, the dormitories are much the same as they were in 1988, open rooms, with rows of bunk beds and metal lockers. Four or five toilets, some with chest-high doors, some without, line one wall of the bathroom, with an open shower stall at the far end, in some cases beyond the line of sight of the guards on duty. By any measure, conditions are better today than they were in 1988, when men slept on bunks stacked three levels high, instead of two, and sometimes there was no floor space at all between bunks.

When Hunt arrived there in May 1988, the guards made no secret of what was in store for him.

"Nigger, I don't want you on my camp," the captain told him. "You will be gone before the sun comes up."[3]

The following morning, a Black man incarcerated with Hunt warned him of a plot he had overheard. The guards were planning to ask Hunt to empty a grease pail from the kitchen on the other side of the road, in the no-man's-land at the prison fence, and then shoot him in the back for trying to escape. Sure enough, later that morning, a guard asked him to do just that. For days, Hunt made excuses until the guard lost interest. Then came the death threats he found on his bed. Those didn't worry Hunt as much as the grease plot. He figured the threats came from a white man imprisoned with him, and he could beat any of them without too much trouble. But he had to be on alert, always. At night, he'd scatter crumpled-up paper or peanut shells on the floor around his bunk so that he could hear if anyone came near. He slept lightly, if at all.[4] After three months, he was finally moved to isolation,[5] a relief from the terrors of the open dorm.

Prison lingo has changed since the 1980s. Prison officials now call isolation by the more palatable term, "restrictive housing." The cells Hunt was held in are still in use today, in a low-slung brick building. When they arrive, men sent there leave their belongings on a table in a small lobby for inspection. Inside, another sally port leads to four corridors, each lined with four cells, measuring six feet by eight, and each furnished with a sink hanging over a metal toilet and a bunk. The men imprisoned here are fed three times a day on a tray passed through a slot on the gate. There's no table or chair, barely enough space for a grown man to do a push-up. The fifth cell on each corridor, half the size of the others, holds a shower. Once a day, the men get 15 minutes in the shower, their hands cuffed for the trip from their cell to the shower, then cuffed again for the return. They get 45 minutes a day on the yard, a fenced-in pen much like a dog run at a kennel, where they are led with their legs in irons, a chain around their waist, and their hands in cuffs until they are locked inside.

Altogether, Hunt spent more than four months at Caswell in isolation,[6] 23 hours a day in a six-by-eight-foot cell, eating from a tray delivered through a slot, and defecating in a metal toilet beside his bunk, with 45 minutes a day when he saw a sliver of the sky. In prison men call solitary confinement by a more accurate name—the hole.

The Department of Public Safety shows that Hunt spent nine months in solitary over the 19 years of his imprisonment. By Hunt's count, the months in solitary numbered far more, adding up to a total of four years. He often brought it on himself to avoid those he thought might snitch on him, or other dangers.[7] He told supporters that he would intentionally commit violations such as not showing up for work so he could be sent to solitary.

Hunt may have believed there were things worse than the hole, but weeks in solitary leave scars for many of the estimated 20 percent of imprisoned men and women confined in those conditions every year,[8] damage that has taken decades for researchers to document. For example, a 2018 study of 119 people who had served prison terms, published in the *Journal of Urban Health: Bulletin of the New York Academy of Medicine,* found that the 51 who had spent time in solitary were more likely than those who had not to be diagnosed with post-traumatic stress disorder. While the report stopped short of establishing causation, it concluded by pointing out the risks of these long-term psychiatric consequences for prisoners and the communities they would eventually return to: "If those experiencing solitary confinement are negatively affected by the exposure, it is society at large that bears the burden of 'resocializing' them."[9] Another more extensive study, conducted in North Carolina and published in 2019[10] in the *Journal of the American Medical Association,* tracked 229,274 formerly imprisoned people between 2000 and 2015. The researchers found that those who spent time in solitary were more likely to die after leaving prison than those who did not, especially of suicide, homicide, and overdose. While the study focused on North Carolina, its implications for the thousands of men and women who have spent time in solitary are clear. As the study notes, all those weeks and months—in some cases years—of idle time and isolation can make people lose their minds. In medical terms, the trauma manifests itself in such mental illnesses as reclusiveness, psychosis, and post-traumatic stress disorder. In other words, to avoid immediate danger, Hunt was forced to unwittingly subject himself to another form of trauma that could, and would, torment him the rest of his life.

Hunt kept most of the details of solitary and prison life to himself, only dropping hints of the darkness. One of many letters he wrote to Rabil, this one in December 1988 from Caswell, which he called "Caswell Concentration Camp," was so gracious and bereft of detail that it left the worst for Rabil to imagine.

> Dear Mark,
>
> May these few lines find you and your family in the very best of health and spirits.
>
> As for myself, I am doing okay under the circumstances. I am still held hostage in Caswell and the way things are going, I'll probably be here for Christmas. But whatever God willing, I will endure this injustice a little longer. One thing is for sure. I will not let them incarcerate my mind. God willing, I'll continue to educate myself, to be much better than I was before I was so unjustly arrested and convicted. Anyway, Mark, I want to apologize for the very long delay in my dead pen. I had intended to write you before now, but I was hoping to do it at Eastern Correctional Center, instead of Caswell Concentration Camp. Plus I missed placed your office address somewhere, but now I have it and it's wrote down in three places so hopefully I want misplace it again.[11]

Maybe there was no point in sharing news of the plots laid by racist guards or the sleepless nights or the way the walls of a six-by-eight-foot cell closed in around him. There was nothing Rabil or anyone else could do to free him from the camp, not until they got him out for good.

~

Stein was a master at appellate law, and in 1989, he won two appeals for Hunt, first in the Sykes case and then in the Wilson case. Little had raised $50,000 for bond from the National Council of Churches

in New York City, secured with his house on Okalina Avenue, just
north of downtown Winston-Salem, and thus in November 1989,
after five years in prison, Hunt left Moore Correctional Institution,
for home, to await the second trials in both the Wilson and the
Sykes cases.

Griggs provided him with a place to live in his tidy house on East
Third Street with his wife, Sofia, his stepdaughter, and her toddler.
As a condition of bond, Hunt had to be in by 11 p.m., but otherwise
he was free. A longtime activist and union organizer named Velma
Hopkins, who had also been involved in the movement to free
Clyde Brown in the 1950s,[12] gave him a job in the school cafeteria
she ran.[13] Hunt prayed at the Community Mosque and took classes
at Winston-Salem State University. One morning, Rabil took him
to see the park where Sykes had been stabbed to death. Hunt had
never been there.[14] Grown now from the skinny teenager in braids,
Hunt, with his easy manner and perhaps his image as the face of
injustice, soon attracted a girlfriend. Wherever he went, at least on
the Black side of town, he was greeted as a returning hero. Older
women would stop him on the street. "Hey baby, we're praying for
you,"[15] they would say. And strangers would ask him to autograph
whatever they had in hand, a Bible, even old hospital bills. He walked
for miles that winter simply because he could.

The Griggs household was always full of guests, so until she laid
eyes on Hunt, Griggs' stepdaughter, April Clark, didn't think much
about hosting another visitor. Too shy to say hello, she watched
Hunt on the other side of the room the day he moved in. She hadn't
expected such a fine-looking man. "Oh, my," she thought.[16] Clark
had never paid much attention to her stepfather's work on the case.
Only 16 when Hunt was first convicted, and now the mother of a
toddler, Chanté, with another baby on the way, she didn't have time
for her stepfather's activism. During the day, she and Hunt didn't
see much of each other. He was busy with work, with university,
and with meetings with his lawyers, first to deal with the murder of

the old man outside the liquor house, then to deal with the Sykes murder. What's more, Clark was still involved with her children's father, and Hunt with his new girlfriend. Chanté took to Hunt right away. "Darryl, Darryl," she would call out the moment he walked in the door. He still dreamed of a big family, five or six kids, and a house in the country.[17] Chanté, the smartest little girl he had ever met, could be part of that family, he thought.[18] Romance with Clark developed slowly, over long hours at home, over breakfast in the morning, and in front of the television in the evening. They did their best to keep it secret. A photograph of Hunt from this time of freedom reveals nothing of the weight of the coming trials. Rather, he is slouched against a pillow, hair cut close, with the look of a carefree 25-year-old, a man free for the moment to walk the streets until he tired, to throw his head back in laughter, and to lie down on clean sheets to sleep.

~

Winter turned to spring in 1990, with the red buds in bloom, their magenta bright against the pale green of new leaves all along the highway on the drive west to the Catawba County Courthouse. Stein and Ferguson had asked for a change of venue, hoping for another urban county where there would be a fighting chance of seating Black jurors. Instead, the judge moved both cases to Catawba County, a furniture-making region in the foothills of the Blue Ridge Mountains, with a Black population of barely 9 percent,[19] a far smaller percentage than the Black population in Forsyth County.

The second Wilson trial was scheduled first, in March. The state's case was much as it had been in 1987. The new DA in Winston-Salem was Warren Sparrow, who had beaten Tisdale in the Democratic primary in 1986 largely because of a backlash from Black voters over the Sykes case.[20] Ferguson, elegant in his well-cut suit, had deferred to Stein on the appeals but took the lead in the courtroom. He knew the Wilson case well, from the transcript in the first trial and hours spent at the scene, measuring the distance from Clowers' liquor house all the way down Claremont Avenue to the corner where Wilson's body was found. Each witness had sworn to tell the truth, and with the exception of two, a man and a woman who had cradled Wilson's head and swore it wasn't Hunt they'd seen attack him, the rest had pointed to Hunt as the man they saw beating "Doc Holiday" Wilson in the street after he left Clowers' place. It didn't matter that they had been puking drunk or that Wilson lay on the sidewalk nearly two blocks away, beyond the crest of a hill down a steep, dimly lit street at two in the morning. The first jury had believed them. It was up to Ferguson to make sure that the new jury did not.

Truthful storytelling relies on a record of events, either written or from recollections of those who were there. In the second Wilson trial, that record is difficult to piece together. There is no transcript because the verdict was never appealed. And the memories of those who were there have faded. But at some point during the trial, and no one remembers which point that was, something remarkable happened, so remarkable that the people who remembered it would speak of Hunt's integrity years later with awe and admiration. The district attorney—and it's not clear whether it was Sparrow alone or the DA who had been brought in to try the Sykes case, a man named Dean Bowman—offered Hunt an astonishing deal. He could plead guilty to both murders for time served and leave the Catawba County courthouse a free man. The state would count the six years Hunt had served as punishment enough for two murders. No more sleepless nights at "Caswell Concentration Camp." No more threats from "cracker" guards or racist prisoners. No more lonely days in isolation. He could walk free, that day, forever.

At any point in a trial, the state has the discretion to offer defendants a deal. In fact, the vast majority of felonies are resolved through plea negotiations, opening up time in overcrowded courts in jurisdictions throughout the country. Such deals also give the state a face-saving way out of a weak case. To offer a deal for time served, to have allowed Hunt to walk away a free man in a case over such a brutal crime, is almost unheard of. That prosecutors did so, without any public explanation, suggests that even as they were pressing ahead with two murder cases against Hunt, they did not believe they had strong cases and may even have suspected the truth, that the man on trial was innocent of all charges.

Only one of Hunt's advisers thought he should reject the deal, and that was Mendez, who argued for Hunt to model himself after the South African freedom fighter Nelson Mandela, who had been released from prison that year, to follow his conscience and turn the offer down. Little couldn't bear to think of Hunt going back to prison, which in spite of the brilliant lawyers on his side, seemed inevitable. Little pressed hard but Hunt pushed back, until finally the others asked Little to back off. On the ride back to Winston-Salem from court the day the offer was made, Little kept his word, joking around to keep the conversation light. It's a story Little relishes, telling it to his students at Winston-Salem State University to this day. When he dropped Hunt off at Griggs' house, Little couldn't stop himself.

"So, what you gonna do?" Little asked.

"I thought we weren't going to talk," Hunt replied.

Little pressed on.

"Larry, if I take the deal, how you gonna explain to people that you raised all this money for me?"

"Blame me. Blame me, and I'll say, 'I made him take the deal.' Look, we got contacts all over this country. We can get you out of here. I can send you my contacts of my friends in California. You want to go in Chicago, we got contacts—and you can build a new life. And you can move on, Darryl."[21]

But Hunt was adamant.

"Larry, Allah would not forgive me for bearing false witness."

"Allah is not gonna do this motherfuckin' time. *You* gonna do this time."

"Larry, I can't do it."[22]

The trial resumed. Ferguson and Stein decided to put up only two witnesses for Hunt's defense. The first was a man named Ronald McGee, who had seen three men attack Wilson. McGee testified that he chased the three attackers off in his car, catching a good look at all three in his headlights. He was the one who was certain Hunt was not any of the men he'd seen. The second was a psychiatrist whose testimony discredited Williams, the man who had first fingered Hunt in the case. Beyond those two, their strategy was to let the state's case collapse on its own. The strategy paid off. After just three and a half hours of deliberations, the jury acquitted Hunt in Wilson's death.[23] The man who served as foreman would later say there was no way they would send a man away for life based on the testimony of that crew of drunkards.[24]

In an interview after the acquittal with the *Chronicle*, Hunt said he had relied on his faith to get through this trial and hoped to be acquitted at the Sykes retrial as well. "I just want to live. I want to be employed. I wanted to make the next quarter at Winston-Salem-State."[25] But Hunt knew the experience would be different when they returned to Catawba County in September for his retrial in the rape and murder of a white woman.

Chapter Eleven

Life's Blood Ran in the Grass

Ferguson and Stein were the lead attorneys in the Sykes retrial, but Rabil was on the case too, and most mornings in September 1990 through the duration of the trial he picked Hunt up in his red Ram Raider at about seven for the 90-minute drive to the Catawba County courthouse in Newton, a brutalist building of brick and steel. The air was just beginning to cool, and if not for the dread that lay ahead, the drive west through rolling country would have felt good. But Hunt had a bad feeling about the retrial from the get-go. A Catawba County jury may have acquitted him of Wilson's murder back in the spring, but the justice system almost always went easy in cases in which a Black man was charged with killing another Black man, as dozens of other examples in Winston-Salem of such cases proved. Wilson's death made that clear; there was only a four-paragraph brief about the verdict in the *Winston-Salem Journal*[1] and no mention even in the Black-run *Chronicle*. Years later, a study in North Carolina found that in death penalty cases, jurors rarely sentenced defendants to death when the victim was Black. But they cared about white victims.[2] In Hunt's case, once the first jury sentenced him to life in prison for Sykes' murder, the death penalty was off the table—but the racial animus was just as real. The rape and death of a white woman, a young professional, demanded justice.

The state had all the same witnesses from the first trial. Johnny Gray. Marie Crawford. Thomas Murphy. Roger Weaver. And it had some new ones, turned up first by the state bureau in 1986 and then by city police in a third investigation conducted to prepare for this second trial. The city had assigned four detectives considered by the department to be their very best—Weavil and Hicks, both of whom had investigated the Wilson case, and two names new to Hunt and his team, Earl Biggers and Richard Nifong.[3] Stein and Ferguson would have loved to see their reports and the 3,000 pages produced by the state bureau in 1986, but it was still up to the district attorney to decide which ones to share and when. The defense attorneys did know about the new witnesses. The first, and the one they were most worried about, was a Black man named Kevey Coleman, who had been walking home along West End Boulevard the morning of the murder and could put Hunt at the scene. A man named Ed Reese, also Black, was saying he saw Sammy Mitchell nearby that morning. And two jailhouse informants claimed that Hunt had confessed to them in prison.

Ferguson and Stein had brought in a new investigator to help run down witnesses, an idealist named Richard McGough, who had studied anthropology in college and learned to investigate criminal cases in Central America, where he worked on cases related to crimes by the US-backed Contra forces. He came back to North Carolina fearless. Ferguson and Stein still believed, as Rabil had during the first trial, that Gray had something to do with the crime and had called 911 to cover his tracks. McGough spent hours that summer trying to track down people from Gray's circle, a cast of characters from the city's liquor houses and pool halls who may have heard Gray admit to some role in Sykes' death. McGough also wanted to nail down Hunt's alibi witnesses, the McKeys, whose testimony had fallen apart under cross-examination at the first trial.

McGough liked Hunt immediately.[4] They made an unlikely pair, a 25-year-old Black man from the streets and a 36-year-old white anthropologist from the college town of Chapel Hill, but McGough found himself seeking out Hunt's company. McGough's personal life was in turmoil that summer, troubles he kept to himself, but Hunt's easy manner and biting humor calmed him. With Hunt as the guide to the city's underbelly, they drove around town in McGough's beat-up Nissan, lingered over diner lunches, and laughed a lot, especially at McGough's ignorance of Black slang, like the time Hunt told him about "talking" to a girl back before he went to prison who was also "talking" to Sammy Mitchell.

"What's wrong with talking?"

Hunt looked at him and shook his head, then explained that "talking" meant something far more intimate than conversation. They both laughed hard, knowing they came from two different worlds but had been brought together by a common purpose.

Jury selection began as Sykes' mother, Sykes' husband, who by then had remarried, and detectives filled the benches behind the prosecution. Many days, as Hunt traveled between Winston-Salem and Newton with Rabil, his supporters followed in borrowed church vans, filling up the benches behind the defense. Ferguson and Stein had decided against putting Hunt on the witness stand. It was simply too risky, especially knowing how his alibi witnesses had fallen apart during the first trial.

Testimony lasted three weeks. Ferguson and Stein booked rooms at a motel off the interstate, hauling boxes of trial transcripts and notes with them to study at night. After more than 20 years in the courtroom, Ferguson knew how to shut off the outside world for the duration of a trial. In the evenings, he met with Stein, Rabil, and usually McGough to plan the next day's strategy.[5] Discovery was still limited to whatever reports the state decided they were compelled by the *Brady* Supreme Court decision to release, but the state's list of witnesses contained some names new to them, until McGough figured out that they were prisoners—snitches—who were prepared to lie against Hunt in exchange for a break in their own cases. All through the trial, McGough tracked down potential witnesses who would be used to discredit any of the snitches the state called.

After the Forsyth County district attorney recused himself from the retrial because one of his assistants had worked on Hunt's case as a law student, the state assigned Dean Bowman and James Yeatts from the rural judicial district just north of Winston-Salem. With their languid drawls and folksy references, the two prosecutors were right at home in Catawba County. By now, there were so many detectives involved in the case that they decided against putting police officers on the stand in favor of letting their case against Hunt unfold one eyewitness at a time, until the weight of so many ordinary people pointing at Hunt would erase any doubt.

A trial can be a disjointed presentation of facts, structured in a way that bears little resemblance to the way events unfold outside the courtroom. Sometimes these events overlap. Other times they occur independently from one another. But they are framed by time. In the courtroom, the rules of evidence interrupt the natural unfolding of events. Rather than using a chronological structure, a trial unfolds by witness, and because the prosecution gets to present its evidence first, it can dictate the manner in which jurors assemble what they believe to be the facts into a coherent timeline. Lawyers on both sides have the chance to help jurors shape that narrative with their closing arguments. As experienced trial lawyers know, the best story wins.[6]

Closing arguments began on Tuesday, October 9,[7] with Stein and Yeatts going first, leaving the final matchup to Ferguson and Bowman on Wednesday and Thursday. Like Rabil five years earlier, Ferguson and Stein were stuck with a story with no clear ending. They didn't know who had killed Deborah Sykes any more than Rabil did. They had a hunch that Gray had something to do with it, but they couldn't prove a thing. So Ferguson followed the conventional wisdom for defense attorneys and crafted an argument designed to create as much doubt as possible. It was a methodical approach that required him to pick apart every one of the state's witnesses, statement by statement, point by point.

His story centered on a police department that would do whatever it took to make an arrest in the Sykes murder. It would "hijack" buses to apprehend a runaway, pressure reluctant witnesses with "truth serum," and use anyone, even a prison snitch, who could help the state win a conviction. The jury's role was to finish the story by preventing any further abuse of power by the state.

As was his practice, Ferguson imagined his argument before the trial even began, laying out the pieces he would need through the way he questioned and cross-examined witnesses. He never spoke from notes, relying instead on a memory of the facts and on his gift of eloquence. He had tried cases in courtrooms across the state, and although he would have preferred a jury drawn from an urban community, he felt at home in Catawba County, which reminded him of the mountain town of Asheville, his childhood home. Ferguson moved the podium out of the way to bring him closer to the jury, and began by expressing sympathy for Sykes and her family, before reminding jurors of their sacred duty. It was the police who were really on trial here, and the DA, for they were the ones who had assembled a case based on a "trash heap" of evidence, a refrain he returned to over and over.

Ferguson reminded jurors of their duty to scrutinize the evidence carefully, then he tore into the state's evidence, witness by witness, pointing out the significance of conflicting statements, missing records, and any other exhibits jurors may have missed. Murphy, Ferguson reminded jurors, had no idea what he'd seen.

[Murphy's] riding with the police. He's become virtually an investigator with the police, and he's trying hard to help the police get someone. Perhaps he can be forgiven for that; but that doesn't mean that he knows what he saw or remembers what he saw or gave a description that fits Darryl Hunt. It means that he and Daulton were working together. Daulton has never explained and Mr. Murphy can't. That's what they're asking you to accept and believe beyond a reasonable doubt.[8]

And Gray was worse, he told the jury.

They say, Oh, don't worry about the inconsistencies. The inconsistencies make it true. But here is what Johnny Gray said the day they took him to this lineup. He said one. He said four. Let's see, eeny, meeny, miney, mo. One and four; either of them, just take your choice. Doesn't matter. And, of course, Johnny Gray having a creative mind that he has, later said, "Oh well, I put down one and four because the No. 1 suspect was No. 4." Does that make any sense to you at all?[9]

If there was one strength to the state's case, it was the sheer number of unrelated witnesses who could put Hunt at or near the crime scene that terrible Friday morning in August 1984. Without some guidance, it would be hard for jurors to see the holes. It wasn't that individually the witnesses were all lying, though some, like the prison snitches and Gray, certainly were. But memories can play tricks. And in spite of three investigations, police simply had not solved the crime. All afternoon, Ferguson threw witnesses to the "trash heap" until he wove his way to the story's ending. It was up to the jury to remember their Constitutional duty, a sacred one, to rely on their "common sense" and the "courage of their convictions" to see through the "trash heap" of evidence and acquit Hunt.[10]

Ferguson's skill impressed Hunt's supporters, but they wondered whether the jury had listened closely enough to see through the state's lies.[11]

Bowman took a different tack. Following conventional wisdom for a prosecutor, he centered his story on Deborah Sykes, an innocent victim, telling a far simpler story than the detailed one Ferguson had told. Bowman took his time establishing his rapport. First, the wooden podium Ferguson didn't need was returned. And as he began, he paused for a drink of water. It had been a long day.

Then he began his version of the story, all in the plainspoken style of a seasoned Southern prosecutor, with Hunt cast as the villain, his lawyers as his enablers, and the jury not as the defenders of the Constitution, but as the avengers in the rape and death of a woman who could easily have been their wife or daughter. There was nothing complicated about this argument. Bowman wasn't asking jurors to keep track of conflicting statements or question authority. This was a simple story about avenging a brutal crime. Why couldn't the defense account for Hunt's whereabouts on that awful morning? Where were the "Blues Brothers," the "Gold Dust Twins"? Bowman asked. And all those doubts Hunt's lawyers were raising, that was just a tactic to confuse, he told them. "They want you to get out here in Catawba County and chase rabbits around two or three days back there and throw your hands and forget it." Bowman stuck with the theme of chasing rabbits for a while, then turned to another folksy image, warning them against getting "lost in the fog" of doubt. From there, he defended each of the state's witnesses, starting with Johnny Gray. He was about to get to Thomas Murphy when court recessed until the following morning.[12]

The next morning, a Thursday, Hunt woke early, dreading what was coming. Bowman would finish his closing arguments. The judge would remind the jury of their sworn duty, then send them off to decide Hunt's fate. Ferguson and Stein had done their best. But Hunt knew what was to come in that rural courtroom. Without telling anyone, he packed up the belongings he would need back in prison: his books, the ones he'd read and loved and the ones he hoped to read; some new photos from these last months of freedom; and the pair of $70 red-and-white basketball shoes Little had bought for him, the most expensive shoes he had ever owned. He didn't need to listen to the rest of Bowman's closing argument or the judge's instructions. He knew how the day would go and what he would have to bear.[13]

Back in the courtroom, Hunt took his seat between Ferguson and Stein. At 9:30 a.m., the jury returned and Bowman went back to his story, turning away from the evidence to the final moments of the dead woman's life. In the event jurors had forgotten the lurid crime scene images of her bloody corpse, Bowman had them at the ready, to pass around. The testimony was over and done with. It was time to bring the case home, with raw terror at its core.

Bowman didn't rush.

It's raining this morning or it looks like it's going to. But you know, I know a story about another morning that wasn't raining that morning but some testified that it may have rained the night before. It doesn't matter. And I know a person, a young lady, this lady right here. She got up in the morning, just like I got up in the morning, just like you get up every morning. She got up; she did just what we all do. We knew—according to her husband, there's no doubt, you see her picture—she was tall. She was pretty. She put on that morning on August 10th, 1984—she put on a light-colored blouse. She put on this blouse right here when she got up to go to work. And she put on this sweater and she put on these blue Wrangler pants. Drive down to Winston-Salem. See, this is a real person. She put them on. She felt them. This sweater probably felt good on that morning at 5:00 or 5:30.[14]

Bowman held up the knit blouse, with its bloodstained holes, and wiped his face with a handkerchief, as if there were tears in his eyes. Jurors cried. A television reporter wept. Hardened detectives held back tears. Like all good storytellers, Bowman knew how to make his characters come alive, even the dead ones.

If she's like me, she probably thought about it was Friday. I admit that. Another week done. Weekend coming up. She might have been thinking about that trip to Georgia that her husband told y'all about. They were going to go down there that weekend; see some of their relatives and friends. And she might have just thought about getting to work, having a cup of coffee, reading the newspaper there where she worked. I don't know. I don't know what she thought about. Maybe like I've seen young women do—men too for that matter, maybe she was riding down the road; she didn't have any thought and glanced up in the mirror to see if her lipstick and her makeup was on straight and suited her just right.

He reminded the jurors that he had children and he knew they did, too, and just in case Sykes' story didn't make them think of their own daughters, he told another story.

This past weekend I saw a needlepoint in a frame and that needlepoint reminded me just like a sword going through me—it reminded me of Deborah Sykes. And on that needlepoint— you know what I'm talking about, how they're embroidered—I reckon that's what you call needlepoint—it said, quote, To have a daughter is to know a special kind of joy.

Then he turned to the crime scene photos, focusing on a close-up of Sykes' hand, her left hand, which made him think of her wedding ring, and of the pictures he imagined of her wedding day. A television reporter seated in the front row wept and through her tears could see jurors crying. Bowman imagined what had gone through her head when Thomas Murphy slowed his car, when Kevey Coleman walked by. "Was she afraid—was she afraid to cry out? Was she afraid at that time, well, maybe he'll help this man here?" He speculated, too, how she would have felt as her pants and then her underwear were torn from her body. "Was she still hoping for some kind of miracle?" He didn't worry about whether playing to his audience with the lurid details was right or just, and no one stopped him.

> And what was she thinking when this man right over here, this Darryl Eugene Hunt, what was she thinking when he pinned her down on the ground, held her arms up and he slashed and he slashed and he slashed and he slashed her some more, just like he was butchering some animal? What was she thinking then?

Though Hunt had never been charged with the rape itself, the rape was central to the story. Bowman continued.

> Finally, what was Deborah Sykes thinking when this man right over here, this real person Deborah Sykes. What was she thinking when he spread those legs right there apart and he crawled down inside her and raped her and ravaged her and deposited some thick yellow sickening fluid in her body? Did she feel—did she feel the blood trickling down her back? And her neck? Did she feel the blood running down dripping on her legs? Did she have—did she feel life itself just trickle right out of her body right there on the grass? What hope? What hope? What hope did Deborah Sykes cling to then? Where was the judge and where was the jury when life's blood ran on the grass?[15]

~

In his final hours of freedom, Hunt went to lunch with McGough at a Mexican place a short drive away from the courthouse, a place they'd been going to throughout the trial. McGough had noticed how Hunt had kept his cool throughout Bowman's argument, even when Bowman came up beside him and shook his fist in Hunt's face. Hunt's face fell into the familiar smile that police had always interpreted as a smirk, a smile that betrayed nothing. But now, with a verdict they knew was coming, McGough could feel a sadness in Hunt's bearing so profound that, years later, the memory would bring him to tears.[16]

To break the mood, McGough hatched a plan. They would stage a fight, right there in the restaurant. Hunt would knock him to the ground, grab the keys to the Nissan, and flee. With luck, he could make it to Mexico before they caught him. A stupid joke, really, but the absurdity of it made Hunt laugh.[17]

When jurors returned soon after lunch, Hunt noticed that not a single one looked his way, a sure sign of what was to come. Once again, he heard a voice in the otherwise silent courtroom proclaim his guilt in a crime he had not committed. He felt Stein rub his shoulder, a gesture he would long remember. He heard each of the jurors affirm their verdict. And once again he stared at the state seal on the judge's bench, determined that these lying fools would never see him cry.[18]

"Is there anything you'd like to say?" the judge asked.

There was so much, but the only words that came to Hunt as he stood there in the silence was the plain truth.

"I'd like to say in open court, I'm innocent of the charges, even though I've been found guilty."[19]

The judge gave him a few moments with his lawyers in an office outside the courtroom before the bailiffs locked him in the holding cell. McGough was allowed to visit him there, a glass partition separating the two unlikely friends. Hours earlier, they'd been telling jokes over lunch. It was hard now to know what to say in the face of such body-heavy sadness.

"I'm not going to let this go," McGough promised.[20]

Hunt had no time to return to Winston-Salem, no time to say goodbye to April or the rest of Griggs' family, no time for a final walk in the light rain that fell that cool autumn day. By evening, Hunt was back in prison, this time at the processing center for adults at Central Prison in Raleigh, a place that to Hunt smelled of death.[21] If Hunt regretted turning down the plea deal that would have set him free, he didn't say.

Chapter Twelve

We Will Not Give Up

Harnett Correctional Institution lies on the edge of town in Lillington, where the rolling hills of the state's Piedmont region give way to the coastal plain, not quite as remote as the prisons down east, but almost. The fall of 1994 marked a decade since Hunt's arrest, ten futile years fighting a system that so far was bent on keeping him locked up. Now science provided some hope in a new form of forensic analysis—DNA testing.

One September afternoon, Rabil and McGough met Hunt in the medical unit at the prison, a one-story building, smaller than but otherwise much the same as the rest of the brick buildings that house the cell blocks, kitchen, and vocational training shops for nearly 1,000 incarcerated men. They had driven down with a copy of a court order, just in case they needed proof, and the packaging a lab had sent for securing a blood sample. A prison nurse tied a thick rubber band around Hunt's arm and asked him to make a fist, while McGough took careful notes to establish the chain of custody, noting such details as the color of the orange tape they would use to seal the Styrofoam box, as well as the nurse's name, Doralene B. Knight, and the two minutes it took her to draw Hunt's blood, beginning at 1:35 p.m. and ending at 1:37.[1]

Hunt watched the two vials fill with blood, confident for the first time since the beginning of his ordeal that the end was in sight. "This is it," he thought. "This will prove, out of everything, this will be it."[2]

~

By the early 1990s, forensic scientists had perfected a technology that allowed a comparison between DNA from very small, even degraded, samples found at a crime scene and a suspect's DNA. In Hunt's case, that meant it was now possible to compare the DNA profile from the semen sample collected from Sykes' corpse, the sample that had not matched his blood type in 1984, to his DNA. The specious argument used at trial, that Sykes' blood type masked his, was now irrelevant. The new science could pick up DNA even in minute samples, giving police a reliable tool for convicting criminals and giving defendants the most powerful tool ever invented to prove innocence.

By 1994, 17 men had been exonerated by this new science,[3] setting off what we now know as the innocence movement. In April, Judge Melzer Morgan, who was hearing the rest of Hunt's post-conviction motions in Forsyth Superior Court, had agreed to the testing. Hunt's lawyers and the DA spent the entire summer negotiating over the laboratory that would do the testing, which was still new enough that the state crime lab hadn't yet set up a DNA unit. McGough left the prison at 2:05 p.m. that September afternoon and drove directly to Roche Biomedical Laboratories, in the Research Triangle, a high-tech center powered by the region's universities. He arrived at 3:26 p.m. and turned the package that held proof of Hunt's innocence over to the lab director and a technician, making sure that everyone signed the chain of custody forms to confirm that McGough delivered the box with the seal intact.[4]

With the samples safely delivered, all Hunt could do now was wait for the crime lab to prove him right. He had spent the four years since his conviction in Catawba County crisscrossing the state, moving whenever it suited the Department of Correction in the endless quest to balance out prison populations. The transfers seemed arbitrary, set by a vast bureaucracy where the rules for keeping order among caged men was determined by some combination of spreadsheets and the latest penal theory, with little regard to the stress to an individual such as Hunt. Each transfer required him to establish himself again in a new social order, each prison as predatory as the last, to form new alliances and shed old ones as he learned the whims of a new group of guards.

"You're shipping out," a guard would say, often waking him up before dawn so they could take care of the transfer before the breakfast rush. Hunt would empty his locker, pack his belongings in plastic trash bags for a ride that could easily last the day, by car, van, or the bus known in prison as the "gray goose," depending on how many others were shipping out that day. The first transfer took Hunt from Central Prison to Eastern Correctional Institution in a little place called Maury, where he found a strong community of Muslims. Numbering about 80, they protected one another, moving through the prison in groups of three and four, and, as Muslims did in other prisons, pooled their money so that they could borrow from each other and avoid the loan sharks who took advantage of others imprisoned with them.[5] From Eastern, Hunt was sent back to Southern, a little closer to home, then to Piedmont Correctional Institution in Salisbury, where he joined about 40 other Muslims. They were well organized, with jobs throughout the prison, in the kitchen, the canteen, the gym, and the library, which meant that they could watch out for each other. They organized classes in physical education and law and programs for Black History Month. Once again, his peers chose Hunt as their imam.[6] He later wrote with pride of the way Muslims were able to keep discipline among themselves, without interference from prison authorities.

We took care of our own problems. Brothers dealt with it always giving the brothers the benefit of the doubt, knowing that He and Allah will have the final judgement. Our job, is to keep the community in the best light, doing Allah's work. Sure we had short comings. There was brothers gambling, loaning money, selling weed. What we do, is work with brothers showing them the error they are committing, how it effect's them, and the community.[7]

Soon after his return to prison in 1990, Hunt drafted a letter to the editor of the *Winston-Salem Chronicle*, which from the very start had been willing to tell things from his point of view. Mendez "straightened up the grammar" of the original version, one that friends found even more moving[8] than what was published, and helped with references to such familiar civil rights icons as Rev. Martin Luther King Jr., Malcolm X, and Nelson Mandela. The *Chronicle* published it January 3, 1991, under the headline "Reader Has Faith He Will Prove His Innocence."[9] It was an eloquent promise that Hunt would keep up his fight against a rigged judicial system. It was also the first time Hunt spoke publicly about the plea deal he had rejected.

I know that the community has not heard from me since my recent incarceration following the miscarriage of justice during my second trial. I am presently serving a life term prison sentence because I refused to compromise my innocence by accepting a plea-bargain that would have eventually let me walk free. Yes, I wanted to be physically free but not at any price. If being free meant accepting anything less than the truth which is my innocence of the murder of Deborah Sykes, then I would rather be in jail. I am not prepared to sell my birthright. Too many people believe in me and have fought for my freedom and I cannot let them down by accepting a cheap plea bargain to make the police look good. You can enslave a person physically, but you cannot chain his spirit or mind unless you let them. My body may be incarcerated, but my mind is free because I have tried to stand for a cause I believe in and not bow to what is expedient or convenient to me personally.

Hunt ended by pleading with readers to remember his friend Sammy Mitchell, who was in prison for the Wilson murder. By then, Mitchell had also been charged in the Sykes murder, but no court date would ever be set. The two friends kept in touch with each other by mail, but the prison system made sure they were never incarcerated together. He also made a point that police and prosecutors fail to see when they convict an innocent man. His wrongful conviction meant that the real killer, whoever he was, had eluded justice.

In closing, thank you again, you the community, for all your support. I love you. Continue to support our Brothers and Sisters who are also being railroaded through the system and do not forget Sammy Mitchell. I want to say to the judicial system, "It Ain't Over Yet." We will not rest until the truth and justice prevail over the lies that have been told to hide the real killers of Deborah Sykes. Continue the fight to freedom. Again, thank you.
Your Brother in Struggle, Darryl Eugene Hunt.[10]

These were noble words, but they masked the grim reality of Hunt's daily life. In February 1992 he was moved to Odom, a more than three-hour drive for anyone who wanted to visit, deep in cotton country, across the Roanoke River from Caledonia, the state's largest prison farm. Before he arrived, he had heard rumors of death threats from white incarcerated men at both camps who knew about the rape and murder of the white woman in Winston-Salem. Just before his transfer, Stein wrote the secretary of prisons in an attempt to block the transfer:

Mr. Hunt informs me that he is about to be transferred from Salisbury, North Carolina to Caledonia over his protests to the Board that there are inmates at Caledonia who have threatened his life. As you may know, Mr. Hunt's cases have generated extensive publicity over the last eight years and strong animosity from violent white inmates who harbor racial prejudices against African Americans. He is resented by them both because the victim of the crime for which he has been convicted was white and because he has received vocal support from many in the African American community who believe he is innocent. Testimony at his last trial confirmed the intensity of feelings by one inmate regarding Mr. Hunt despite care on his part to remain peaceful and non-provocative.

When Mr. Hunt was incarcerated after the first trial, decisions were made not to send him to either Caledonia or Odom because of concerns for his safety. Those decisions were prudent then, and since the same problems remain, they should not be reversed now.[11]

The reply was swift, almost mocking in tone of Stein's fears:

Inmate Hunt has adjusted well to his incarceration and the "strong animosity from violent white inmates" to which you refer apparently has not hindered his adjustment based on his institutional records.[12]

The next 14 months were a lonely time for Hunt.[13] Few visitors made the 200-mile drive to visit. The winters were cold and damp, the summers stifling with heat, the dorms so cramped that the television hung above the toilet and there was no room even for a chair.[14] Imprisoned men figured that farmers in the region had been told to shoot any prisoner they saw fleeing through their land.[15] Hunt met men at Odom who had been there 20 years or longer, whose lives made him dread what lay ahead for him. No one ever wrote them or came to visit. Some had lost their minds. Others found comfort in sexual relationships with other men, but that held no appeal for Hunt, who thought of these men in disparaging terms as "punks."[16] Still others made a grim exit plan. They would contract HIV, which was then rampant in the state's prisons, with the idea that death by AIDS would be quicker than the slow, inexorable death that surrounded them. There was humor of the darkest kind in the way they talked about it, of going out with "a smile on your face."[17] For Hunt, Odom was the place the state sent you to die.[18]

In August 1992, Hunt was moved to Caledonia, a prison compound of 7,500 acres of soybeans and wheat, collards and sweet potatoes, chicken houses, and a cannery, with all the labor coming from men imprisoned there. Scholars today make the case that our system of mass incarceration is rooted in slavery, a history that helps explain how and why Black men are so disproportionately represented in the nation's prisons. With the abolition of slavery, Jim Crow laws created a new form of bondage by criminalizing unemployment, loitering, and other conditions of impoverished Black life. These laws led directly to the War on Crime, to the harsh sentences imposed for crack cocaine, to racial profiling by police, and to other forms of systemic racism, such that prisons became the new plantation.[19]

There's nothing abstract about that history at Caledonia. The vast floodplain was first cultivated in the eighteenth century by enslaved people. At the end of the Civil War, 271 men and women were freed from the Caledonia plantation, and those who stayed on the land became sharecroppers, exchanging their labor for a place to live and a small amount of wages.[20] In 1892, a generation after emancipation, the state bought the plantation for $61,000, substituting labor by the descendants of enslaved people with inmate labor, part of a national trend that included Parchman prison in Mississippi and Angola in

Louisiana.[21] By the 1990s, Caledonia imprisoned 590 men in closed and medium-custody units, with 208 more down the road at the minimum-security prison then called Tillery.[22] Today, with Tillery closed, Caledonia incarcerates more than 1,000 men.[23] A plaque near the entrance to the prison speaks in brief to its history, but even without the detail, the meaning of a prison born of slavery is clear.

By early November, the fields at Caledonia are mostly fallow, though prisoners still harvest wagonloads full of greens. The produce is preserved by imprisoned men working in the cannery, then shipped to prisons across the state as part of the state's Correction Enterprises, which runs industries throughout the prison system, billing itself as a job-training program. The land, with its rich, dark soil nourished by a river, reveals its brutal history. Berms built by enslaved men keep the river from flooding. At a break in the dike, you can see the black water of the Roanoke, deceptively calm. A man trying to escape the prison once drowned in the current.[24]

The fields lie outside the prison fence and today are patrolled by truck, a level of security feasible only because the prison now uses men in minimum custody to work the fields. In the 1990s, when Hunt was there, the scene more closely resembled the farm's plantation past: men from the closed-custody unit labored in the fields under watch by guards on horseback armed with rifles. Associate warden Ricky Duke said that at the time, guards would take 100 imprisoned men to the fields every day "and they would line them up all across the field with eight guards on horseback armed with rifles. We didn't have any problems. They'd do anything to get out of that cell block."[25] Duke said men in minimum custody also rode horseback during the same era. At the time, Caledonia raised 4,000 head of cattle and used the men in custody for the work of herding cattle and pulling calves. "We called 'em cowboys," Duke said.

Out in the fields, the resemblance between the armed guards on horseback and the overseers who once patrolled the plantation were obvious, but not surprising. Ronald Cotton, wrongly imprisoned like Hunt was for the rape of a white woman, was transferred to Caledonia shortly after Hunt's departure and assigned to the fields, picking field peas in the summer and collards in the winter. Cotton kept his humanity by defying the rules, making contraband wine in the evenings, turning a talent for drawing into a tattoo service for others imprisoned with him, and raising a stray kitten, one of many born on the farm, on sardines and milk from the commissary. But these distractions did little to change the fact that "when you go to prison you belong to the state."[26]

Hunt was assigned to work in the laundry, away from the armed guards, and did his best to resist and to lead others. In March 1993, he led a petition drive after a man who was complaining of heart trouble died in plain view. Hunt wrote with outrage and with compassion about the dead man, who, at 46, was serving a life sentence for kidnapping but nonetheless deserved to live.

> Life is precious to everyone, regardless of a person(s) present circumstances, and any chance to save a life should be allowed and not hinder by sickness, such as race, creed, color, not a childish mentality of being an inmate. God did not create inmates; He created human beings with hearts of love regardless of a person's statis in life.[27]

Twenty other men signed the petition, demanding that the administration look into the death and subsequent cover-up. The petition alleged that as part of the cover-up, guards had sent five men to solitary for inciting a riot when all they had done was try to offer CPR to the dying man.

Hunt was especially troubled by the presence of female guards at Caledonia, who were assigned, it seemed intentionally, to patrol dorms with a clear view of the open showers and toilets. Islam requires modesty, and Hunt wanted no part of the way others on the cell block turned showering into a lurid show. He later told friends that he also feared a set-up, that he could be accused of acting out in front of female guards to bolster the state's case that he was a rapist.[28] He filed grievances, but nothing changed. Finally, Hunt refused to work, landing in the hole.[29]

Caledonia's "restrictive housing" unit is desolate and may have been even more so for Hunt, an innocent man forced into such isolation. The cell doors are made of heavy steel, painted blue, with a barred window at eye level. The food slot is locked shut. The outside fenced area for exercise is divided into 12 covered sections, each cage measuring eight by eight feet.

Hunt stayed in the hole three months,[30] confined to an eight-by-ten-foot cell 23 hours at a time, with an hour of sunlight in a cage. The prison records confirm this, with no mention that he had refused to work not out of willful insubordination but to survive. In a letter to Rabil in December 1992, Hunt explained that he got himself sent into solitary to get away from a prisoner he was afraid might snitch to make a deal with the state. He didn't mention his unease over female guards. Either way, isolation seemed his best option.

> So I feel this is the best place for me. Everyone is trying to get out of prison, and they don't care how they do it. Out of 9 years, I've had more people lie on me than I even know in the world. I know I can't get around everyone, but at least this way here I don't see anyone no longer than 45 minutes a day. Plus I'm gaining more on lock-up. I'm able to read, study without the headache. I know I wouldn't like to be a monk, but now I'll deal with living like one.[31]

Rabil replied with an update on his appeals and a prayer:

> My Christmas prayer for you this year will be that this is your last Christmas in captivity. I do not want to see you enter a tenth

year in this system. I will do everything possible to help win a
new trial for you.[32]

There was more to the degradation witnessed at Caledonia Farm,
things Hunt confided only years after leaving the place, things that
no one would have believed if he'd complained at the time. One story
he told is still hard to believe, except that others who were incarcerated at Caledonia during the same era have told friends of the same
strange scene. On weekends, guards would set up tents in the fields
where incarcerated men, dressed in women's clothing, would turn
tricks with others, desperate for pleasure even if that meant finding
it in a makeshift brothel at the center of a former plantation.[33]

~

After the defeat in Catawba County in 1990, Stein and Ferguson
recruited a new team of lawyers because one of the potential issues
for appeal was their failure to object to the DA's lurid closing argument. Rabil was back on the case as attorney of record working with
Ben Dowling-Sendor, a Harvard-educated lawyer from the state's
appellate defender's office, which represented indigent clients free
of charge. They kept McGough on as their investigator, appealed
the conviction, and got to work on a different kind of appeal known
as post-conviction relief. Unlike other appeals, which are reviewed
by appellate courts and focus on issues that come up at trial that
violate a defendant's due process, post-conviction work is more
of a detective task. If a defendant can find new evidence that was
not presented at trial, the defense can file a motion for appropriate
relief. These motions are heard by trial judges in the county where
the case was first tried. The standard for a new trial requires that
the new evidence be strong enough that a new jury might come to
a different verdict at a retrial, a high and subjective hurdle.

Hunt's lawyers and McGough had been working for months
to discover new evidence that might persuade a trial judge to grant

Hunt a new trial. They'd been able to persuade Melzer Morgan, the judge appointed to their case and one known for fairness, to release thousands of pages of reports from the State Bureau of Investigation that until then had been sealed. The reports would have helped a great deal at trial to impeach many of the state's witnesses, especially Johnny Gray. It was clear, at least to Hunt's side, that the state had concealed evidence that should have been released from the beginning. Now they used the reports as a guide to evidence that pointed at Gray.

The legal battle weighed most heavily on Rabil, whose wife was battling breast cancer. She died in June 1993, just as the hearings before Morgan began. McGough spent hours that summer in pool halls and seedy parts of town talking to potential witnesses who could point their finger at Gray but had disappeared at trial and were saying that the police had intimidated them. The hearings also gave Hunt a reprieve from state prison. Rather than drive Hunt back and forth between Harnett and Forsyth Counties, the state kept him in the Forsyth County Jail for the hearings. Hunt shared a cell block there with an old friend from the neighborhood named Ayyub Rasheed, who was awaiting trial on a rape charge, and Thomas Michael Larry, charged with killing an off-duty police officer. The three of them established discipline among the other men on the cell block, with exercise and "quiet time" for reading and case work. Word traveled quickly around the jail that Hunt was back, and soon men lined up to see him for help with their cases.[34]

The hearings lasted through the summer, but none of the testimony about hidden evidence or Gray's potential role in the murder was enough. The following summer, Morgan ruled that the case against Hunt was so solid that the new evidence would not change a jury's verdict. Hunt had prepared for the defeat, doing one thousand push-ups with Rasheed to ease the tension. He would write about the moment later: "That old song by the temptations I wish it would rain, well it did rain, it rained in the shower with me crying, and it rained that morning before court."[35] When he heard Morgan's words, he was so angry he was ready to storm out of the courtroom.

The defeat hurt, but there was one more avenue his defense could take. Most mornings during the hearing, Rabil and Dowling-Sendor met for breakfast at Sherwood Barbecue, near Rabil's home. One morning, Dowling-Sendor was waiting at the register when a headline in the morning newspaper caught his eye. A man on death row in Maryland named Kirk Bloodsworth had just been cleared of murder and rape by DNA, which eliminated him as the source of the semen found in the nine-year-old victim's underwear. He was the first person on death row exonerated by DNA. Hunt's lawyers had heard about the new science and in fact had found evidence that the state knew about this testing in 1990, but it hadn't been tried yet in North Carolina.[36] Hunt agreed without hesitation to the new testing, just as he had in 1984 when Rabil lied to him about the possibility of testing for DNA. The district attorney opposed the motion, arguing that the science wasn't reliable. Not until April 1994 did Morgan order the testing. It took all summer for the state and Hunt's team to agree on a lab.

By then, Hunt was back at Harnett. The results came back on a Wednesday in October, three weeks after the nurse drew his blood. Hunt was done with his work in the meat-processing plant for the day when a guard came to the dorm with a message to call his lawyer. By the time the sergeant gave the go-ahead for the call, it was after 5 p.m. and Rabil's office was closed. He'd have to find the strength to wait another day. *Alhamdulillah*, he said to himself, *Praise be to Allah*.

The following day, the static on the phone line was so bad he could hardly understand a word Rabil had to say, but the sound of Rabil's joyful voice was enough. There was no trace of Hunt's DNA in the semen sample. Witnesses could lie or disappear. Prosecutors could say whatever they wanted. But DNA didn't lie. Hunt had been telling the truth all along. He hadn't raped Sykes and he hadn't killed her.

Hunt wept until his face was wet with tears.[37]

Rabil and the rest of the legal team also allowed themselves to believe in victory. With science now on their side, how could they possibly fail to get Hunt released? A court date was set for November 7, which meant three more weeks of waiting, three more weeks to figure out who had raped Deborah Sykes. The state agreed to test for Mitchell's DNA, but like Hunt's, his didn't match. And all the work the defense had put into finding witnesses who said Gray had something to do with the crime was for naught, as his DNA, too, was no match, so he clearly hadn't raped Sykes, either. The DNA also didn't match Sykes' husband.

Someone had raped Deborah Sykes, that much was true, but no one yet had figured out who had done it, meaning that the rapist, the real killer, was out there, somewhere.

With the facts on his side, Rabil could feel the burden of the last decade lifting. He had lived a full ten years since he began working with Hunt, lost his wife to cancer, raised two daughters, and endured the mockery of colleagues who called him "Don Quixote" for giving his life over to a lost cause. Even his girls were bullied at school for their father's work on Hunt's behalf. Now, all that—all those failures in court, dead ends, and grief—would be over. The night he learned that the DNA test that had cleared Hunt also cleared Mitchell and Gray, Rabil sat down at the dining room table and wrote in his journal.

New mystery today spawned from the DNA tests in the Hunt case: the State's testing shows the semen samples do not match Darryl, Sammy Mitchell or Johnny Gray. The assistant D.A., Eric Saunders, was very surprised: he thinks the testing must be wrong because everyone believes it had to be one of these three. I told him I was 90% sure it would be Gray, but not totally shocked. So the State, like a good defense attorney, will challenge the testing procedure. We now sound like them: well, Gray's still

involved even if he didn't leave semen—there's no other explanation for his conduct and lies. They say: well, Hunt still could
be involved—there's no other explanation for the eyewitnesses.
The results are the best case scenario for Darryl: they destroy the
State's backup theory (Darryl and Sammy did it together) and
the backup-backup theory (Darryl, Sammy and Johnny did it).
Darryl should go free, and me too.[38]

At Harnett, Hunt cleared his bunk and his locker for the trip back
to Winston-Salem. He'd done this so many times before, with little
reason for hope, but now he had proof. He packed up the few things
he really cherished—his Quran, two bags of letters from friends, and
his copies of the DNA motions. He gave his other things, books on
Islam, hair oils, and deodorant, away to other men in the unit. They
would need them more than he would. He was going home.[39]

～

Monday morning, November 7, 1994, Hunt was back at the familiar
defense table, in courtroom 5B, across the hall from where he had
first been convicted, seated between Rabil and Ferguson. Assistant
District Attorney Saunders represented the state. Evelyn Jefferson,
Sykes' mother, sat behind him, for yet another day of testimony
about her slain daughter. Doug Sykes came back to town from Tennessee to honor his former wife's memory. And once again, Hunt's
supporters filled the courtroom. The technician from the lab that
both sides had agreed on gave a long, technical explanation of DNA
testing. Saunders tried to discredit the science with questions about
the potential for contamination of the sample and the accuracy of
the reading. In the end he was left to make the far-fetched claim
that given Hunt's presumption of guilt, the science had to be flawed,
not the state's case.

When the court recessed for the night, Rabil allowed himself
to believe in miracles. Although Morgan had ruled against them

Darryl Hunt and Sammy Mitchell, August 1984, the night before the murder of Deborah Sykes.

Wake Forest Law Library Special Collections & Archives/ Wake Forest University School of Law

Darryl Hunt, identified as number 4, in the lineup in the Forsyth County Jail, September 1984.

Winston-Salem Journal

Mark Rabil and Darryl Hunt at Hunt's first trial, May 1985.
Winston-Salem Journal

Supporters of Darryl Hunt march through downtown Winston-Salem, just before his trial, May 1985.
Winston-Salem Journal

Detective Jim Daulton points to a map of the crime scene during Hunt's first trial.
Winston-Salem Journal

District Attorney
Don Tisdale prosecuted
Hunt and sought the
death penalty.
Winston-Salem Journal

Larry Little, the founder of Hunt's defense committee, while Hunt was out on bond awaiting retrial in February 1990.

Winston-Salem Journal

James Ferguson, renowned civil rights attorney, questions Detective Jim Daulton at Hunt's second trial.

Winston-Salem Journal

Darryl Hunt and Mark Rabil in the prison yard at Harnett Correctional Institution, 1995.

Winston-Salem Journal

Rev. Carlton Eversley,
pastor at Dellabrook
Presbyterian Church
and an early supporter
of Darryl Hunt.

Winston-Salem Journal

Rev. John Mendez, pastor at
Emmanuel Baptist Church,
and also an early supporter
of Darryl Hunt.

Winston-Salem Journal

Khalid Griggs, imam of the
Community Mosque, provided
Hunt with a home while he was
out on bond.

Winston-Salem Journal

April and Darryl Hunt posing for a photograph in front of a mural in the visitation room at Piedmont Correctional Institution, circa 2000.

Courtesy of April Hunt

Darryl Hunt praying in prison the summer before his exoneration.

Winston-Salem Journal

April and Darryl Hunt embrace at the moment of his release from the Forsyth County Jail in December 2003.

Winston-Salem Journal

Darryl Hunt reacts to the judge clearing his exoneration, February 2004.
Winston-Salem Journal

A film poster for the 2006 documentary *The Trials of Darryl Hunt* showing Hunt's mug shot from September 1984.

Winston-Salem Journal

Darryl Hunt
speaking at an event
for the NAACP, with
the Rev. William
Barber to his left,
Raleigh, 2010.
*Courtesy of
Tarrah Callhan*

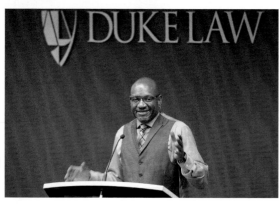

Darryl Hunt
speaking at the
Duke University
School of Law,
2014.
*Duke University School
of Law, Jared Lazarus.*

Rev. William Barber
delivering a eulogy for
Darryl Hunt March 2016.
Winston-Salem Journal

back in the summer on the evidence prosecutors had hidden, he was known to be thorough and fair. "I don't see how the judge can do anything other than grant Darryl a new trial on Thursday when he rules," Rabil wrote in his journal. "I will be shocked if he does not. It is time for his case to end, for the State to test other suspects."[40] By the following night, that optimism gave way to self-doubt and fear, and by Thursday morning, he was prepared for defeat. "I pray that the judge has ruled correctly," he wrote. "I pray for my mind to settle and the right course of action becomes apparent."[41]

That morning, in the holding cell outside the courtroom, the bailiff asked Hunt to remove his belt, on its face a simple request, but Hunt could think of only one explanation for relinquishing his belt. With its metal buckle, a belt could be used as a weapon. They must have been warned that the judge was ruling against him and didn't want trouble in the courtroom.[42] Science was no match for a system designed to keep men like Hunt imprisoned.

Hunt walked into the courtroom with a heavy heart. Taking his seat between his lawyers, Hunt whispered the news. From the bench, Morgan peered over his wire-rimmed glasses and began to read. He didn't get far before Hunt's supporters heard the gist of what Hunt already knew. In the judge's view, while the DNA evidence suggested that Hunt may not have raped Sykes, it had not weakened the murder case against him at all. In the judge's words,

The newly discovered evidence does not bear on kidnapping, robbery or homicide. While the state's theory on rape and sexual assault is somewhat weakened by the DNA evidence, its case overall is not fatally flawed. The state's case against the defendant at the second trial was strong. Even with the DNA evidence, it remains strong. On another trial, the newly discovered evidence is not of such a nature as to show that a different result, i.e. a finding of not guilty on all submitted bases of guilty, would probably be reached.[43]

It was hard to listen to the rest.

Hunt's motion to dismiss—denied.

His motion for a new trial—denied.

Hunt felt like a fool to have believed in the possibility of justice. They all had. Here was the twisted logic all over again: distorting plain facts, making a mockery of common sense. He was going back to prison.

His supporters shouted out in anger, with Dowling-Sendor calling the ruling a "judicial lynching." Rabil punched the metal door on his way out of the courthouse in a rage.

That night he wrote Hunt with words of encouragement.

I think I broke my hand when I slammed it on the courthouse door as I left following my brief statement to the media. So it will probably be a long time before I stop feeling this day. I went to the YMCA and ran one mile for each year of this case in the wind and rain. That calmed me down to a certain degree; at least it worked out some of the anger. We will not give up. We will be successful. You will be released. As long as you are shackled, so are we.[44]

If Hunt felt the rage of his supporters, he couldn't express it, not in prison. Such bursts of fury, a show of feelings of any kind, belong to the free.

The drive back to Lillington took about two hours. When the car pulled inside the prison gate, a man Hunt knew as "Shorty Red" was waiting for him in the yard.

"I'm glad to see you," Shorty Red said.

"What kind of sick joke is that?" Hunt asked.

"Ain't no joke," Red said. "I was getting ready to jump the fence, but now that you're back, I know I'll be OK."[45]

Hunt knew exactly what Red meant by "jump the fence." If Red had tried to climb the fence, the guards in the tower would have shot him dead, a quick end for a desperate man. Still in his early twenties, Red confided that he had just learned of his mother's death, a grief he could not bear alone. Now that Hunt was back, with all that he had endured, he would understand Red's loss. Hunt took the episode as a sign.[46] He was needed here at Harnett by men whose misery he understood.

Chapter Thirteen

In This Life or Another

Hunt's attorneys found a way to channel their fury by immediately appealing Morgan's ruling to the North Carolina Supreme Court. Surely the state's high court would see through the twisted logic Morgan used to send Hunt back to prison and, at the very least, grant him a new trial. Oral arguments were scheduled for early December 1994 and seemed to go well. A ruling was expected at the end of the month, on a Friday.

While Hunt waited for news in prison, his supporters, among them Rabil, Little, and Eversley, got together in a conference room in Rabil's office for a call with the court clerk. They were buoyed by the enthusiasm of two young filmmakers from New York: Ricki Stern, who had learned about Hunt's case in graduate school at UNC Chapel Hill from a classmate; the wife of Hunt's private investigator, Richard McGough; and Annie Sundberg, Stern's college friend and collaborator. They had started filming during the 1993 hearings on hidden evidence and had come to believe in Hunt's innocence. The ruling by the state's highest court held the promise of a dramatic moment, so they sent a cameraman to Rabil's office to catch it on film.

The film footage from the day is hard to watch.[1] The mood is somber, the men lost in thought. Rather than the hoped-for victory, the court ruled 4-3 against them. The three dissenters saw the DNA with the clarity it deserved. As the court's lone Black justice Henry Frye would later say, it was impossible for him to ignore that throughout the history of the South, Black men had lost their lives to false accusations over the rape of white women, real or imagined. Clearly that terrible history shaped Hunt's case. But Frye was unable to persuade a fourth justice to join him in granting Hunt a new trial.[2] The science that provided such irrefutable evidence of Hunt's innocence meant little to the majority, whose opinion focused on the hidden SBI reports and new witnesses McGough had found, without even a mention of the DNA.

The news fell hard. In the film footage, Rabil makes the call to Hunt by speaker phone.

"Well, we lost four to three. Justice Myers wrote the opinion and we have Exum, Webb and Frye on the dissent." Rabil pauses and his voice softens. "I'm really sorry, Darryl. I think Ben is going to call you at 10:30. OK?"

Hunt, his voice barely audible above the din of prison, replies. "OK, then."

The camera moves to Little, seated on the other side of the phone, pressing his fingers against his eyes, as if in pain.

"I was thinking we would have some good news, but we don't," Little said.

He shakes his head.

"Four to three, you know, that close."

Hunt's voice, again, is barely audible and then trails off.

"Thank everybody for me. And . . . hmm."

Then the sound of a woman's voice coming over the prison loudspeaker fills the room. Little calls out.

"Darryl, Darryl."

The line goes dead, the dial tone loud and angry in the silence. Rabil buries his head in his hands and weeps. It's hard to fathom how Hunt will bear another loss.

~

By the 1990s, the expansion of what is now called the "prison industrial complex" was well underway, fueled by the politics of fear and
the myth of Black criminality that the lone Black justice in North
Carolina understood all too well. Nationally, politicians in both
parties, including Black Democrats, were determined to fight back
against "super predators," code for Black youth. In North Carolina,
more than 23,000 men and women were imprisoned in 1994,[3] up
from 16,000 in 1985,[4] the year Hunt walked through the gates
at Polk. Few stopped to question whether it made sense to lock
away so many men and women in the name of law and order. For
example, in 1994, the year Judge Morgan rejected DNA evidence
as sufficient to grant Hunt a new trial, officials in North Carolina
dealt with overcrowding by sending 937 imprisoned men out of
state, to private prisons, and paying local jails to hold another 248.[5]
In many states, the unchecked growth was even steeper. One study
found that during the 1990s, a new prison opened once every 15
days.[6] The 1994 Crime Bill, authored by then-Senator Joe Biden
when he was chairman of the Senate Judiciary Committee, is often
blamed for what we now think of as the carceral state. But the truth
is that the bill's incentives for tough sentencing, its "three strikes
and you're out" provisions, and the billions of dollars it provided for
state prisons only exacerbated patterns that had begun years earlier.

Some scholars trace our current dependence on prisons as the
solution to entrenched social crises back to President Lyndon Johnson's administration, when the War on Crime replaced the War
on Poverty.[7] Others look to the federal Anti–Drug Abuse Act of
1986, which created the enormous discrepancy in sentencing for
crack cocaine such that possession of an ounce of crack was punished with the same amount of time as possession of 100 ounces
of powdered cocaine. This 100:1 ratio entrapped millions of Black
men and women drawn to the cheap form of cocaine while white

users who used the more expensive powdered form eluded harsh punishment. Only years later would the crisis of mass incarceration become visible to people outside the system, but inside, the insidious forces at work were clear.[8] As Hunt would later tell an interviewer: "Prison is just a warehouse, making money off of them, that's just sending them back on the street to go back again."[9]

Hunt relied on faith and discipline to ward off despair. After the state Supreme Court turned him down, Hunt wrote Rabil in January 1995 about the difficulty of accepting another defeat. In two months he would be 30, still a young man, but carrying the weight of a lifetime of loss.

> Dear Mark,
>
> I pray my letter will find you and your beloved family in the very best of health and spirits.
>
> As for myself, I'm doing much better. I apologize for taking so long to write. This latest injustice has taken me a long time accepting that the highest court in N.C. could make such a racist, political ruling. I had thought the worst was over after Judge Morgan's ruling. However I haven't given up. I believe strongly that God will bring about justice.[10]

Hunt's reading of criminal justice news made him well aware of how DNA had freed others trapped in similar circumstances. The innocence movement was just beginning, but these early exonerations revealed a pattern of systemic flaws all too familiar to Hunt. For anyone who paid attention, the cases exposed the dangers of relying on eyewitness testimony, as prosecutors had in Hunt's case. They showed how a host of forensic analysis, from the study of bite marks to the study of blood spatter, were so inaccurate they could no longer be regarded as science. They proved that defendants will confess to crimes they had nothing to do with. And they suggested that misconduct by investigators and prosecutors was more wide-spread than imagined.

The man who at 19 had assumed that if he simply told the truth he'd be released was wiser now. He had spent countless hours in prison studying his case files, reading the law, and learning how structural racism was ingrained in American history, his history. His letter to Rabil in 1995, written as he was trying to come to terms with what the state's high court had done, moves from his private anguish to a detailed discussion of his case, including the outrageous revelation that the state had known about the possibility of DNA testing as far back as 1990, before his second trial.

> It has taken me a long time to believe that the whole system was racist and could care less about justice, truth and fairness. It hurts like hell, Mark, but it also gives me the strength to continue fighting. Keeping my head high. My faith in God has gotten stronger when I feel bitter. I ask God to take that out of my heart because I will not commit a wrong in a blind attempt to correct a wrong. True, I don't know how I will deal with the next year or two. I'll just take it one day at a time, praying that God gives me the strength to make it.[11]

Hunt's letters and other writing during this period are filled with penetrating questions about legal precedent, history, and a growing frustration with a system more interested in a false narrative than in the plain truth. He was not writing regularly in his journals, but when he did, he no longer struggled with grammar and spelling as he had when he was first imprisoned. The raw prose of his youth had evolved into a more learned style, with entries that discussed the conditions he saw around him as a form of social control, even genocide, and his plight as that of a political prisoner. Inside prison, it was clear that the tough-on-crime polices enacted on the outside were causing unimaginable and permanent harm to the hundreds of men imprisoned with him. "It doesn't take a PhD to know that once you are in the system, you have used your last strike, you will always be an ex-convict."[12]

In spite of Hunt's growing eloquence, the agony of his false imprisonment was almost beyond words. He was not "some animal in the zoo, to be poked at,"[13] but a man whose only crime was "being born black."[14] In 1995, he wrote in his journal:

> I've found that, no matter how much you try to explain how it feels inside this jungle, the less people understand. At first look, we look fine, in side this crap eats you, you try to give people some understanding but there is no words that can express how you feel.[15]

His letters from this period hint at this misery. In 1996, three weeks before his 31st birthday, he wrote to Rabil of the slow passage of time behind bars:

> I trust my missive finds you and your beloved family in the very best of health and spirits. As for myself, I'm doing okay under these unjust circumstances. God has blessed me with strength to go on day after day, even though minutes feel like days, and days feel like months, and months feel like years. All praise due to the God Almighty. God willing this night-mare will end soon.[16]

~

Hunt had been hoping for a move from Harnett closer to home, but instead, in 1997, he was sent further away, to the new prison in Marion, a mountain town nearly two hours west of Winston-Salem. The prison was part of a $200 million expansion approved by voters in a bond referendum. With this new construction boom, North Carolina moved away from prison camps with open dorms, which had led to the lawsuit a decade earlier, in favor of prisons with

multiple floors and single cells. Marion was built for this higher level
of security as a three-story building that would eventually hold 900
single cells. As Hunt observed in a letter to Rabil in March 1997,
his move was driven by the state's need to fill the new prison and
justify the expense.

> It's no telling how long I'll be here. It's a new prison and the
> rules and policy is really stupid. It takes time to adjust to this
> place and staff. They treat us like trash. They have taken books
> and letters . . . I'm in medium custody but they treat us like we're
> on maximum or death row. Other than that . . . I'm doing okay.
> I'll deal with it. There is a saying in the Holy Quran, "the darkest
> hour is just before dawn."
>
> I don't think it could get any worse than this.[17]

Having failed in the state courts, Hunt's lawyers turned next to
the federal courts. The state was still arguing that the DNA proved
nothing, with new theories, each more preposterous than the next.
The most outlandish held that Hunt had raped Sykes but failed
to ejaculate and that the sample came from an "unindicted co-
conspirator," whom Hunt's team took to calling an "unindicted co-
ejaculator." Removed from the local fray, maybe the federal courts
would see through this nonsense.

Hunt still longed for the family he'd been seeking since childhood. Throughout these 12 long years, he would imagine a life with
children, maybe even a dog, wondering what it would feel like to
wake beside a "beautiful black queen."[18] At least in his thoughts,
he was free.

The first arguments were heard by a federal magistrate in June
1997. Two days later, a letter arrived at Marion that would forever
change the course of Hunt's life. He recognized the name on the
return address: April Clark Johnson, the imam's stepdaughter, the

woman he had fallen for in 1990 when he was out on bond for his second trial. And now she had written. She had married and went by Johnson, but was getting divorced, and had rifled through her stepfather's papers to find Hunt's address. Her letter filled two pages, but as Hunt later wrote, it "had meaning of three lifetimes."[19] He read it more than 50 times, and when he and April spoke the next day it was as if they had never been apart.

Hunt added her name to his list of approved visitors, and later that summer, Johnson headed west on the interstate to see him. She had never driven out of town on her own and was afraid. Coming off the exit ramp, she turned south on Old Glenwood Road for the last mile to the prison. She and Hunt had seen each other once since his second conviction, on a visit with Little and Johnson's daughter, Chanté, at Eastern Correctional.[20] After that, she did her best to forget him. Her second baby, born while Hunt was living with her family, died. She and the baby's father, Elston Johnson, married and had two more children, Jamal and Elston, now two and five. When the marriage broke up, her thoughts turned to Hunt.

She hadn't told a soul she was coming. They wouldn't approve. But the letters back and forth between her and Hunt were so full of love that she didn't care what others thought. Her heart racing, she checked in at the gatehouse to be searched, then followed a guard to the visitation room, where she picked a table and waited for the man she remembered with so much tenderness.[21]

The room was full of visitors—mothers, wives, girlfriends, and children who were growing up without their fathers. She barely noticed. The men imprisoned there were all dressed alike, in a clean white T-shirt and pants the color of a brown paper bag. Her hair in a short afro, she wore the cutest outfit she could put together. Finally, Hunt appeared and they held each other in a long embrace. Conversation came easily between them, the same rapport she remembered from the year he had lived with her family. He told her of the many losses in his life, his mother's death and his grandfather's, the girlfriends who had forgotten him as the months in prison turned to years, and friends he no longer heard from. Johnson promised she would never leave him.

From then on there was no turning back. Every other weekend, she was back on the road, sometimes with the three kids in the back seat. By their second visit, Hunt had cut the dreadlocks he had started to grow to a short afro, just like hers. Once she learned the way to Marion, the drive wasn't so frightening.

Their romance filled Hunt with hope, but the thought of losing her tormented him. Once, when he called her house and someone hung up the phone, the thought that she may have left him drove him to despair.

> I've been crying praying hoping I've misread what's happening, if it's true, I would rather be dead, I thought about hitting the fence, to make them kill me, I'm too big of a coward to do it myself. I know people will say this nigger has lost his mind, get over it, move on; however they are not in my shoes, they haven't been through what I've endured. I'm tired of losing people I love to this injustice.[22]

The year after their reunion, prison officials at Marion classified Hunt as a "Five Percenter," a member of an organization loosely affiliated with the Nation of Islam and later with hip-hop. It's not clear how or why Hunt was labeled as a Five Percenter, as his Islamic faith had nothing to do with the group. Its members were considered by North Carolina and a handful of other prison systems as security threats,[23] which made Hunt a threat too. His belongings were searched for material related to the Five Percenters, his mail was read, and he was required to submit urine samples for drug testing. There was no way to shake the label. When Hunt tried, the prison replied: "Policy does not provide an appeal for validation as a security threat group member."[24] Hunt took medication for depression that made urinating difficult.

When he was unable to produce a urine sample, even after drinking so much water that he vomited, they sent him to the hole.[25]

Hunt had endured solitary before, and had even sought it out. But now, the 60 days of solitary meant two months without seeing his beloved.

> She's my strength, my life. Not being able to see, hold or talk to her, is running me over the edge on the real. I've never had pain so intense. Fear of losing someone or something as deep as I feel now, hell I've never loved someone as much as I love her. Any way, I have no idea what Allah has in store for me, nor why He's sending me through this struggle, I've heard guys who been down a long time says that it get's easier as the time passes. That's bull, it's getting worse, because you can see all the dreams you have for life, go by, people you love disappear and their isn't a dam thing you can do about it, life go on without you.[26]

In the fall of 1999, Hunt was moved to Smithfield, near the state's largest slaughterhouse for hogs, and soon after to Franklin Correctional Center, another rural camp just south of the Virginia line, as unfamiliar to Johnson as the mountains had once seemed. They wrote each other weekly. Some of these letters, and the greeting cards Johnson sent him on anniversaries, birthdays, Valentine's Day, Halloween, and Muslim holy days, are preserved as part of an archive of Hunt's papers in the law library at Wake Forest University. Soon, Hunt began to think of Johnson as his wife, and her children as his.

> My dear April-Love,
> How is my Beautiful, Loving sweet, caring wife? I love and miss you dearly. Insha-Allah my letter will find you and our wonderful children in the very best of health and Islamic sprits and loving me as much as I love and miss you all.[27]

In March 2000, he was moved back to Piedmont Correctional Institution,[28] a nine-story prison in Salisbury, less than an hour from Winston-Salem. Johnson's mother tried to talk her out of a romance with a man who seemed doomed to spend the rest of his life locked up. But her heart was set. She converted to Islam and they called each other by Arabic names. She was Mu'mina. He, Muhammad. Once, in a snowstorm, her windshield wiper broke and she drove the entire way to Salisbury leaning out the open window to see her way.

By then their routine was set. Hunt knew of a window that looked out over the road. As she approached the prison, she would slow down so she could see him waving, then reach out the car window and wave back. Inside the visitation room, they'd buy popcorn, Doritos, and salt-and-vinegar chips from the vending machine, a Pepsi for him and a Mountain Dew for her. When she brought the kids, she'd bring extra quarters so they could amuse themselves buying snacks. Sometimes, she and Hunt would talk about his case, but he kept the misery of life behind bars to himself. "There's nothing to talk about here," he would say. "I'm just sitting here waiting."[29]

He always wanted to hear the details of her life—the kids, her family, her nursing job at a dermatology clinic. She asked his advice on everything. Simple home repairs. Child rearing. Office squabbles. The ordinary things she spoke of seemed to give him a sense of normalcy. He often told her that she provided him with solid ground, "a rock you can't move."[30] When their 90 minutes together were over and it was time for her to leave, she would walk to the door, her head turned back to catch the last glimpse of him as he was searched and led away, smiling and waving until he was back inside.

～

The federal courts were as obstinate as the state ones. In January 2000, the Fourth Circuit Court of Appeals in Richmond agreed to hear Hunt's case. Given the circuit's reputation for siding with the state, his lawyers were not optimistic. Rabil made the arguments, focusing on the *Brady* violations and the DNA. The justices were unmoved. The day after Hunt's 35th birthday, February 24, they turned him down. The following month, Hunt wrote Rabil of his despair.

> Mark, I want to apologize for not writing sooner. The court's ruling bothered me greatly. I didn't know how to deal with it, except to try not to think about it. As you know that's an impossible task. All in all though, I'm okay. God has given me the strength to continue on.[31]

It had been 16 years since Hunt's wrongful arrest, 15 since the first of two convictions, 14 years since he was wrongly charged with the death of Arthur Wilson, 10 since that all-white jury in Catawba County had called him guilty, 6 since the judge in Forsyth County had peered over his glasses to tell him the DNA did not matter and the high court of North Carolina agreed. Such a string of losses created layers of trauma for Hunt, a crushing burden he could not express and few would ever understand.

The weight of these disappointments is borne out by research into trauma. In his now-classic work, *The Body Keeps the Score,* Dr. Bessel A. van der Kolk writes of the way multiple traumas such as Hunt endured in prison, from the threats against his life to the repeated disappointments in court, become embedded in the body,[32] in the muscles of the back, in the neurons of the brain, in the pit of the stomach.

One misconception about trauma is that one can grow accustomed to pain, when the fact is that the reverse is true. Ultimately, there is only so much a person can handle. What's more, while the fight-or-flight response works well for survival, in warfare, in prison, and in the midst of a fight for justice, trauma lays the seeds for trouble afterward, when the crisis has ended but the body is still hardwired for distress. This is where the notion of "sustained catastrophe" helps explain the utter helplessness Hunt wrote about with each defeat.

He was nearly out of options. Technically, Hunt eventually would be eligible for parole, but because of the brutality of the crime and his refusal to admit guilt and show remorse there was no chance a parole board would ever free him. Rabil prepared an appeal to the US Supreme Court, always a long shot, with the court considering only about 1 percent of the 7,000 to 8,000 petitions it receives a year.[33] As a backup, Rabil also prepared a petition for clemency from the governor. A decision from the court on whether it would hear Hunt's case was expected in October.

October was also the month Hunt and Johnson had chosen to be married. They set a date for October 17, in the prison visitation room, in front of a mural painted with a tropical scene. Johnson's family opposed the marriage, but Nelson Malloy, a longtime member of the defense committee who had accompanied Johnson on other prison visits, agreed to serve as their witness. Like Hunt and Johnson, Malloy was a Muslim, diplomatic and soft-spoken. He and Little had a long history, having formed the local chapter of the Panthers together. Malloy was paralyzed, after a shooting in California that he rarely discussed publicly, except to confirm that the shooting was related to his ambulance work with the Panthers. In spite of those injuries, he served on the city's board of aldermen, representing the ward that had elected Little more than a decade earlier.

Johnson dressed in a simple green dress and head scarf for the wedding and settled into the driver's seat of the Camry that had taken her to so many prisons around the state to see her beloved. Seated beside her, Malloy carried heavy news. The day before, the Supreme Court had published the list of cases it agreed to hear. Hunt's case didn't make the list. There was no explanation for this final defeat. There never is.

Malloy kept the terrible news to himself until he could share it with the couple once they were together. Johnson turned into the familiar lot outside the prison, where she helped Malloy into his wheelchair, and together they made their way to the gatehouse, through security, to the visitation room. Hunt was waiting there for his bride only to learn the shattering news.[34] He had lost again, and in all likelihood he would spend the rest of his life in prison.

The news didn't change Johnson's mind, not in the least, but one final errand remained before they could be married. She had yet to pick up the marriage license from the local courthouse, a short drive away, so she left Hunt and Malloy to discuss the finality of the court's rejection. When she returned with the license, Hunt seemed distant.

"Do you still want to marry me?" he asked.

Johnson didn't hesitate to reply.

"If I can't have you in this life, I'll have you in another."

Chapter Fourteen

A Closer Look

In early August in North Carolina, the sun rises just after 6:30 a.m. as the long days of summer begin to shorten. In 2003, the 19th anniversary of the death of Deborah Sykes, August 10 fell on a Sunday. I am not an early riser, but I woke early that day, in time to meet up with photographer Ted Richardson and head downtown to West End Boulevard at dawn. Call me crazy, and Richardson certainly did, but I thought there was a chance that the killer would return to the scene of the crime. I hadn't thought through what we would do if he did, except that it would be a heckuva scoop. And if he didn't appear, we needed early-morning crime scene photos for the series of stories I was working on for the *Winston-Salem Journal*.

Richardson and I were exhausted, having driven seven hours late the previous day, heading back to North Carolina from Chattanooga, Tennessee, where we had gone to interview Sykes' mother and husband. The interviews had gone well, but Richardson was frustrated after shooting portraits in the unflattering light of a motel room.

We parked on the street where Sykes had 19 years earlier and picked our way through the wet grass, around the wooden fence, to the hillside where she had been raped and stabbed to death. The park was littered, as it had been back in 1984, with used hypodermic needles, random pieces of soggy clothing, and broken bottles. Her mother's anguished voice still present in my head, I tried to imagine the attack, the kind of attack I feared whenever I ventured out into a dark place alone. Her mother believed Deborah fought back and in the end knew she had died alone. I hoped Deborah's terror masked the agony of the attack. The streets were empty on that Sunday in 2003, with no one cutting across the park or driving down West End Boulevard on their way to work, but I could see that it would be hard for a witness to make out any features in the dim morning light. We picked our way around the trash, waiting for someone to appear. The sky lightened. Richardson shot the scene, looking west through the trees toward Crystal Towers, where a street light cast an eerie orange glow.[1]

I had been investigating Hunt's case since April and now, four months into the assignment, Sykes' death and the question of Hunt's innocence remained a mystery. I was 43 then and had followed Hunt's case from my first day on the job in July 1987, but always at a distance. By 2003, I was the newspaper's metro columnist, writing three columns a week on the news of the day and whatever human interest story I could come up with. Now it was up to me to sort through this 19-year-old case in the hopes of answering the question of Hunt's guilt with clear and convincing evidence in a way that had eluded so many others.

I'd like to be able to say that I was a crusading journalist, driven to risk it all to free an innocent man, but that wouldn't be the truth. In fact, several years earlier, I'd written about Hunt as part of a newspaper project on race, treating it as a local version of the O. J. Simpson case, which had divided the country along racial lines. At that time, Larry Little had begged me to get the paper to take a deeper look at Hunt's innocence claim, but I was in the middle of a divorce and didn't have the energy to take on a crusade. Five years passed, and with that came a new state law in 2001 that allowed defendants to ask for the DNA evidence in their case to be compared with what was then a new database of DNA from 40,000 people convicted of felonies in North Carolina, linked to a national system of 1.5 million DNA profiles.[2] Hunt's attorneys filed one of those motions, and in April 2003, a judge in Winston-Salem ordered a new round of DNA testing to compare the evidence in the Sykes case against the database. It was a chance, however slim, for Hunt to solve the murder and gain his freedom.

The newspaper's brief story about the court order caught the eye of the *Journal*'s metro editor, Les Gura, who'd arrived the previous year with a background in narrative writing and investigations. He'd won a national magazine writing award for a 2001 story about a Connecticut man falsely accused of murder. Coincidentally, Gura and I had been classmates at Columbia University 16 years earlier when we obtained our master's degrees in journalism.

With their open floor plans, newsrooms don't allow for much privacy. I watched Gura carry two file folders to his desk from the newspaper's library. They held 19 years of clippings, folded neatly into manila envelopes, which together told the history of Hunt's case. I watched him unfold every one of the clippings in the files and read them.

"We really need to look into this," he said to me when he was done.

"You should talk to Carl," I suggested, knowing that our executive editor, Carl Crothers, was interested in the case.

My desk had a clear view into Crothers' office, so I could watch them talk, first alone and then with the newspaper's managing editor and assistant managing editor. I remember the sense of dread I felt when the meeting ended and Gura headed straight to my desk.[3]

"We want to take you off your column for a few weeks and have you look into this case," he said.

Though not as large as newspapers in Charlotte and Raleigh, the *Journal* still took on big stories. Back in 1970, we'd won a Pulitzer Prize for a series of stories about a strip-mining project and other environmental threats throughout the state. In my time there, we went after political corruption, the region's high rate of infant mortality, and the legacy of the eugenics movement, and we had editors with the skill to oversee this kind of work. I should have been excited that my seniority made me the top choice for the assignment, but mostly I felt its weight. What could I uncover that all those lawyers, detectives, and judges had missed?

Crothers cleared out an office for me, a windowless room behind the mailroom. Many of my colleagues, especially those who had worked at the afternoon paper and known Sykes from her days on the copy desk, resented the time off I was getting from the daily grind to dig into a history that had already filled up so many column inches of print. Newsroom opinion about Hunt's conviction, much like the city's, was divided; many believed he was guilty. Others over the months would stop by to offer a word of support and inquire about the project.

Slowly, the windowless room filled with documents, first the news clippings Gura had pored over, then copies of all the police reports that had been released over the years and the appellate motions and the trial transcripts that Rabil let me borrow. He even let me borrow the Polaroid prints of the crime scene, graphic images that repulsed and fascinated me at the same time. I didn't want to forget the woman whose murder had set this all in motion.

Crothers wanted me to cover one wall with newsprint and outline the case, but I imagined the chart turning into the scribbles of a madwoman and resisted. I brought the transcripts home with me and read them either after my son and daughter, then seven and eleven, went to sleep or on the weekends they spent with their dad. Gura helped me with the police reports, which we organized in folders, one for each witness, with statements they made over the course of the many investigations, first in 1984, then in 1986, and finally in 1990. Gura summarized each one, highlighting the inconsistencies. When I got tired of reading case files, I talked to people connected to the case, beginning with lawyers and police officers, jurors and judges, and Hunt's defense committee. The most challenging interviews took me into the streets, where I tracked down as many witnesses as I could find, hoping to find someone who would provide a shred of new evidence to justify all the weeks I was spending on this story.

Most of the police officers involved with the case declined to talk with me, but Randy Weavil, who had investigated the Wilson case and reinvestigated the Sykes case before the second trial, saw the series I was writing as a chance to set the record straight. He felt that all the criticism against the police department had unfairly stained his reputation, and he still winced at the way Hunt's supporters had attacked his integrity, labeling him "Weasel" and part of the "goon squad." He was a lieutenant by then, with an office that still held the file cabinet they'd hauled to Newton in 1990, the same one Rabil had seen in 1994, securely locked with a padlock and a heavy chain to protect the evidence in the case. Weavil didn't disagree that there were problems with each of the witnesses, but he wanted to make sure I understood that witnesses are never perfect. He believed that taken together, the witnesses made a case against Hunt, imperfect pieces in a puzzle that nonetheless held together. And if Hunt hadn't killed Sykes, which Weavil was certain he had, he'd beaten up "old man Wilson" with such ferocity that his head had cracked open like a watermelon. I later learned that Weavil's memory of Wilson's death was contradicted by the autopsy, which found a single contusion, the medical term for a deep bruise, on the right side of Wilson's head,[4] just behind his ear. This finding suggested that Wilson may not even have been murdered, but rather stumbled drunk and hit his head.

After all this time, Larry Little was skeptical of the newspaper's intentions, but he talked with me, at length, and invited me to the first day of class at Winston-Salem State University, where he was teaching constitutional law, and told his students how his understanding of the law was rooted in Hunt's case. "I'm an activist," he explained. "So we'll teach what the law says and what the reality is." He also helped me find witnesses, especially Lisa McBride, the prostitute the defense had tried to find all through the second trial, the one who said that Gray had told her he'd killed Sykes and would kill her, too. Every week or so, my phone would ring. "I just seen her," Little would tell me. "She's over at Church's," the fried chicken place on a stretch of Patterson Avenue just north of downtown that prostitutes walked, day and night. I recognized her from photos I'd seen, a white woman about my height with stringy brown hair. The first time I met her, she was polite, but wouldn't agree to an interview. Every time Little called, I got in the car, hoping she would change her mind. Soon, we were on a first-name basis. "Here's that newspaper lady I been telling you about," she'd say, introducing me to whomever she was walking the street with, but she never agreed to talk. I was learning that she and many others were afraid to get involved in a case that had cost so many so much.

I found Marie "Little Bit" Crawford in Eden, a textile town about an hour east of Winston-Salem, where she was working as a maid in a motel. She didn't have a phone, but I found her through her grandmother, the one she'd lived with when she was a runaway back in 1984. Crawford didn't show for our first appointment. The next time we arranged to meet, she was late and then insisted she needed a ride to pay her utility bill. I bought her a sandwich and was finally seated with her in her living room. There were two dogs chained up outside. The coffee table was littered with empty cigarette packs and pill bottles she said were for her mental problems. Her husband wasn't home, and I was glad of it. She insisted that she'd told police about the grass stains and Hunt's confession only because she was afraid of being arrested and that after that, any statement she'd ever made against Hunt she made because of police intimidation. She believed Hunt was innocent and always had. I wanted to believe her, but it seemed she was making her story up as she went along, saying whatever she thought I wanted to hear. When I called again, to double-check my notes, she'd disappeared. Her grandmother had no idea where she'd gone.

I spent many hours parked outside a modest house on the south side of town, where Kevey Coleman, one of the new witnesses at Hunt's second trial, lived with his wife, waiting for someone to come home or answer the door. Gura and I had read through police reports of his seven interviews over the course of three years. Apart from Gray, Coleman was the only Black witness who had reported seeing Hunt at the scene and the only witness, apart from Gray, who had ever been treated as a suspect. His first interviews with the police were hesitant, the later ones more certain. I could understand why he would want to avoid yet another interview. I found his unlisted phone number and address through the newspaper's circulation department and tried calling mornings, afternoons, weekends, and weekdays. One afternoon, he came to the door and stepped outside. The police got it wrong, he told me. He never firmly identified Hunt and Mitchell. He said he told police that he was "not 100 percent sure, but I would honestly say that it looked like they are the two people I saw with her."[5] We spoke for five minutes at most. I heard his wife shouting at him in the background. He went inside and shut the door. After that, he never returned a phone call, and the next I heard they had canceled their newspaper subscription. This case had many injured parties.

I also spoke with people active in Hunt's defense committee, leaders whose voices my readers knew well, and less well-known supporters like Estella McFadden. McFadden and I met in her apartment, in the building where Sammy Mitchell's mother had lived, in the center of Hunt's former world. She helped me understand why so many Black people believed in the teenager they knew from the neighborhood. "I can tell you what I thought, that Darryl was telling the truth and just stuck to it. They told him if he told on Sammy, they'd set him free. But he didn't do that. He did what he was supposed to do and he told the truth," she said. "A lie can go around the world before the truth can get its boots laced up."[6]

A lot of the people I wanted to talk with had died. Johnny Gray died in prison in 2001, of throat cancer. Roger Weaver, the hotel clerk, was dead. I reached Thomas Murphy's home, but his daughter said he was dying of emphysema and couldn't see people. William Hooper, who had driven down West End Boulevard just before Murphy on the day of Sykes' murder, had died. His widow was trying to sell their house and had buried a statue of Saint Anthony in the yard for luck. She told me her husband had always believed the police had arrested the wrong man, but she knew nothing about the case that had not been revealed before.

I didn't see myself as Hunt's champion. That's not what journalists are. If anything, I saw myself as the champion of the truth, or to put it more simply, the champion of verified facts. My job was to investigate the case at every level, from the police work to the trials to the appellate work, in search of the facts. My notebooks filled with details, but the central questions remained. How could so many unrelated witnesses have put Hunt at the scene? And why, in spite of the DNA evidence, was he still imprisoned? I was learning a great deal about the way this case had consumed the lives of so many people, but I still couldn't put the pieces together into a coherent story.

The last week of June, still early in our investigation, Gura and I drove down to Piedmont Correctional Institution, about an hour south of town, to interview Hunt. I had written him to explain that we were looking into his case, and Rabil advised him to see us, provided he was there too. We had four hours with him, with a break in the middle, intending to save the toughest questions for last. I would handle most of the interview, with Gura jumping in as the "bad cop," as needed. We met Rabil in the reception area, where a guard searched my bag and inspected our IDs. Another guard led us through a metal door that closed with a crash behind us, through the yard, to an empty visitation room. We sat at a low table in hard chairs, the vending machines humming behind us, and waited for a guard to bring Hunt in to take the empty seat to my left.

Hunt wore a bright white T-shirt, prison-issued khakis, and a black knit skullcap. Gura took notes on the inside of a file folder, little details such as Hunt's long lashes, a brown spot on his left eye near his pupil, and a new pair of Converse All-Stars. I started off easy. "Tell us about your early life. During the trial, you talked about your grandparents and how you went to live with your aunt and uncle after his death."[7]

I liked Hunt right away. It was hard not to. But I reminded myself that my feelings didn't really matter. It was the facts that counted. Gura and I wanted to see how he talked about the morning of August 10 and whether there were any inconsistencies with what he had said before. I asked about his friendship with Mitchell, his life on the streets, and the events leading up to his arrest. He thought about each question, chose his words carefully, but never seemed to hesitate or hold back. His recall of details seemed uncanny. I noticed that he answered my questions without looking at Rabil for guidance or permission. Gura noted his gestures. "Thinks thru—at ease. Face betrays very different emotions. Seems to fight that."

With so much ground to cover, there was a lot I didn't ask or even think about. I didn't ask Hunt about his fears, or really much at all about his feelings. My notes from the interview reveal a great deal that at the time I ignored. The weight of the tremendous losses he'd suffered as a child, first the death of his grandmother, then his mother, then his aunt, didn't sink in. Neither did his sadness over losing touch with the baby girl he regarded as his own. Or the longing in the dreams he held to open a bed-and-breakfast with April, where they would serve halal meals for Muslim guests and build a nest egg for her children.[8] I didn't pay much attention to any of those details. My readers, especially those who believed in his guilt, wouldn't care much about the conditions of Hunt's life, or those of any of the other 950 men imprisoned with him. Mass incarceration and its disproportionate impact on Black families wasn't as big a part of the public dialogue back then as it is now.

I didn't inquire much about the racism he faced, either. Again, my readers had heard plenty over the years from Hunt's supporters about that. I needed more than righteous words. Instead, I listened for facts that would illuminate the case and for details that would make whatever story I wrote come alive. I asked about the plea deal he rejected in 1990, a key event that had never been reported by the mainstream media. "I know it sounds crazy," he told us. "For 19 years I'm going through pure hell in here. There isn't a day that goes by where I don't wish I were out. I just can't plead guilty to something I didn't do."[9] And I focused on DNA tests, the pending one and the one from 1994, which to me raised the central question in the case. Hunt hoped the new round of testing would solve the case. "It seems that the only way they're going to admit to their mistake is if they find the person who actually did it,"[10] he told me. He didn't seem angry as much as disillusioned by the years of defeat. For example, back in 1994, he had been so certain that the DNA evidence would set him free that he had given away his things to others imprisoned with him before the trip home for his hearing. These details moved me and would move a reader.

"What things?" I asked.

"My toiletries," he said.

"Which ones?"

I could tell I was annoying him. What did hair oil matter when he was talking about his freedom? But I had a story to write and pressed on.

Hunt was polite all morning, but it was clear he wasn't holding out a lot of hope in the newspaper or our work. We saved the tougher questions for the afternoon. I wanted to believe him, but my job demanded more. How could he explain that Cynthia McKey, his alibi witness, was now telling me that she was asleep when he left her house the morning of the murder? And how did the detective find out about his relationship with Little Bit? Why did he have newspaper clippings about the murder among his things at Mitchell's house? Why did he call Mitchell from the county jail on September 13? Why didn't he testify in 1990? How was he so sure Mitchell wasn't involved? He answered with the same calm I heard when he answered the morning's softball questions.

> If I'd a known Sammy had done this there's no way in hell I'd spend nineteen years in prison for him or no one else. Every day I go to sleep saying, "I'd rather be home." I can't see giving that up for nobody. If I'd a known he wasn't with me, I'd have said that. If I had any idea he or anyone I knew had anything to do with this, I'd have told them. I wouldn't want anyone to do my wife or my daughter the way Mrs. Sykes was done.[11]

We had come to the final question, the one we had planned for Gura to ask. Hunt had to turn in his chair to look at Gura and away from Rabil and myself.

> This case comes down to the DNA evidence on the one hand and eyewitness testimony on the other. Eyewitnesses put you at or near the scene of the crime that morning. You say you weren't there. Would you agree to an independent polygraph exam by an examiner hired by the *Journal* to test your truthfulness?[12]

Without even a glance back at Rabil (who had no idea we were planning to spring that idea), Hunt said one word: "Sure." Rabil quickly interjected, saying he wasn't positive he would be open to that, though he didn't close the door.

"I have no problem with it. If you want to hypnotize me. Whatever you want to do," Hunt said.[13]

We knew that polygraph tests are inadmissible in court because they are so unreliable, but they are still used as an investigative tool. And top editors at the newspaper were pressing for it as a way for the series to include some breaking news (if he took the test and passed) and also to lend credibility to my reporting. Hunt's willingness to be polygraphed told us a lot. If he were lying, it was unlikely he would have agreed. Rabil never did agree to the polygraph, but as the reporting continued, the top editors backed away from their insistence that the series hinged on having it.

I spent hours that summer talking on the phone with Sykes' mother, Evelyn Jefferson. I wasn't surprised that she was reluctant to talk about the case, but she always took my call, so I kept trying. Finally, we agreed on the weekend of August 8 for an interview. Photographer Ted Richardson and I stayed at a motel near her home, where we had agreed to meet Saturday. I always prefer to interview subjects at home or at their work because place reveals so much about a person. Apart from the details that came up at trial, and the closing argument at the second trial, Sykes' story had never been told in full. I wanted to correct that oversight. If I could make her mother come alive, it would help readers understand the full meaning of Sykes' death. Her husband, Doug Sykes, wouldn't invite us to his home, where he had started anew with a wife and children, but he did agree to meet us at the motel the night we arrived. Still shaken by her murder, he shared a bit about Sykes and the plans they had, but it was clear he didn't want to go too deep into such a painful time.

The following morning, Jefferson canceled the invitation to her home, but she agreed to see us at the motel. She arrived dressed in black, a statuesque figure, and had us carry stacks of scrapbooks and a framed photo of Sykes to my room. Richardson had set up a chair for her by the window, to catch the only light he could find in the dreary space. I sat across from her. She told me of the premonition she had the morning her daughter was killed as she got off work at a bottling plant just as her daughter was due at the newspaper.

"That morning a dark, dark depression came over me, like I was sinking," she said.[14]

I learned details that did, in fact, help make her daughter come alive. She'd won a beauty contest as a child, Little Miss Statesville, and spent afternoons with her grandmother while her mother worked. As a bride, she wore a garland of flowers in her hair. I learned just as much about the bitter loss felt by her mother, still wearing black for an interview 19 years after her daughter's death.

"You know, you remind me of her," she said.

The comment made me feel uncomfortable, so I didn't ask what she meant. I was roughly the same age Sykes would've been had she not been killed. Apart from brown hair and a big smile, I don't look like Sykes at all. Perhaps we shared a certain intensity.

~

Gura had learned by investigating other stories on miscarriages of justice that the most revealing documents would be the early police reports in the case. They would tell us more about what happened, especially about how the investigation unfolded, than the thousands of pages of trial transcripts ever would. Gura helped me build a simple timeline, a technique I've used many times since then, to map the month between the crime and Hunt's arrest. I hadn't found a smoking gun, but the timeline showed me how from the moment Johnny Gray used Sammy Mitchell's name, the rush to make an arrest led inexorably to Hunt. Random events that had nothing to do with the crime simply reinforced whatever suspicions Jim Daulton had, and no one on the state's side ever challenged those biases. It was clear that all Hunt had ever done was cooperate. It was Hunt who told Daulton about Little Bit, which set the stage for her to undermine his alibi. And it was Daulton's questioning of Hunt, observed throughout the neighborhood, that set off rumors about his role and led to calls to the tip line. Hunt's arrest over his relationship with a minor created the "Twin-City rapist" tag. The fact that someone overheard Hunt tell someone else that the police were trying to pin the crime on him, none of this was evidence, but it explained how, with the pressure to make an arrest, the case fell in place largely on the strength of a 911 call and a frightened 14-year-old prostitute.

People who study wrongful convictions look to the psychology of cognitive bias to explain how police investigations can go so tragically wrong. Rather than examine each piece of evidence for its merit, police seize on evidence that confirms suspicion and discard evidence that would lead them on another path. Such tunnel vision is a common thread in the hundreds of wrongful convictions around the country that have been confirmed since Hunt's. His defense attorneys developed tunnel vision themselves by fixating on Johnny Gray, spending years of effort on what turned out to be a futile attempt to find witnesses who might be able to confirm their theory of the crime—that Gray was involved and made the 911 call to cover his tracks.[15] Such tunnel vision is deeply embedded in the human psyche. People who are in love ignore obvious flaws in a future mate. Scientists ignore data that contradicts their hypotheses. The brain is programmed for confirmation bias. A compelling story is more powerful than fact.

The timeline helped me understand Hunt's arrest, but it didn't explain his two convictions for Sykes' murder or the court rulings that kept him in prison despite DNA evidence that should have set him free. Every court had made the same argument about the limits of the DNA evidence: Would it be relevant to jurors? Morgan and the judges who came after him concluded that a new jury would not see the DNA evidence as strong enough to override the eyewitness testimony. It seemed so speculative to me for a judge to imagine how a jury would weigh such a powerful piece of evidence. What would a real juror say? I tracked down two, the foreman from the first trial and a juror from the second. Neither had followed Hunt's case after the trials ended, so they both learned from me that DNA had ruled him out as the rapist, which meant that their response was unrehearsed. "Sounds like he may be innocent and, if he is, thank the Lord we didn't put him to death," the foreman from the first trial told me.[16] The juror from the second trial wasn't as decisive, but she, too, hoped another jury would have the chance to hear all the evidence. "I guess if it is taken to a jury again they'll have everything right in front of them and I just hope they'll be fair,"[17] she told me.

These interviews cut to the core of all the rulings that had kept Hunt in prison for the previous ten years. Even Donald Tisdale, the DA in the first trial, told me that if DNA evidence had been available back in 1985, he probably would have dropped the charges. "If DNA evidence had come back negative, I doubt very seriously I'd be trying that case,"[18] he told me. These interviews made it clear to me that the judges who'd considered the DNA evidence and kept Hunt imprisoned really had no idea how jurors think. They either took a guess or simply chose to downplay the DNA evidence for their own reasons.

The work I was doing also gave new meaning to the rhetoric about racism that had so defined Hunt's case. I could see now how racial bias played out in the way police treated Black witnesses as suspects yet treated white witnesses such as Thomas Murphy, who'd been a former Klansman, as coinvestigators. Jury selection also was defined by race, with the defense hoping for Black jurors and the state, ultimately, excusing all but one. And even at the appellate level, racial bias played a role. The December 1994 ruling against Hunt by the North Carolina Supreme Court had been split, 4-3, with Justice Henry Frye, the lone Black justice on the court, one of the three dissenters. Hunt's defense team had always assumed that Frye's race had something to do with his dissent. I wanted to know how he saw it. By 2003, he was retired from the court and in practice in Greensboro. He told me that, in general, he deferred to Judge Morgan, who had heard the testimony about the suppressed evidence in the case, but when it came to the DNA evidence, he saw things differently. For Frye, a Black man raised in the South, the rape was the central issue in the case. Any evidence that weakened the case against Hunt as rapist undermined the entire case. "There are so many of these that have been incarcerated and it turns out we had the wrong person. And so many of these are based on eyewitness testimony, on witnesses who say, 'I saw him. There's no doubt in my mind,' and it turns out this was not the one."[19]

~

When it was time to write, I was at a loss. The killer had not reappeared at dawn. There was no witness who had remained silent all these years who could identify another suspect. And all the obvious holes in the case—the inconsistent statements, the questions about Gray's credibility, the rush to judgment—had been reported all along. Gura was interested in another downtown rape that had occurred six months after Sykes was raped and killed, of a woman abducted outside the Integon building, but police told me that the suspect in that case had been in prison the day Sykes was murdered, so I dropped the lead without pressing for release of the records. There was so much else to make sense of. My first draft of part 1 in the series on Hunt was terrible. The piece began in 1994, with Hunt packing his things, certain that DNA would set him free, but the rest read like a lifeless research report. Gura advised me to think about the elements of narrative, with characters, scenes, and cliffhanger chapter endings. Maybe we had no earth-shattering evidence, but we had a story to tell that would help readers see old evidence in a new way. The news would be in the way we constructed that narrative, in a character-driven story that set aside balance in favor of truth, and unfolded in such a way that the public would come to understand what I had come to believe, and that was how deeply flawed the case against Hunt really was.

~

The series, titled "Murder, Race, Justice: The State vs. Darryl Hunt," ran in November 2003, with the first installment published on a Sunday, the 16th. When I got to work the next morning, I found an urgent message on my voicemail from a woman named Mary Lane, who told me about a crime that she always believed was related to Sykes' murder, the rape of her daughter-in-law, formerly Regina Kellar, in February 1985. It was the rape Gura had asked me to look into months earlier, the one police told me involved a suspect who was in prison when Sykes was attacked. The woman on the phone wouldn't let it go. Her daughter-in-law had identified someone, but the police had discouraged her from pressing charges. She was sure the man who raped her daughter-in-law was the same man who raped and killed Sykes.

The rest of the series had already been edited and laid out for publication, but I couldn't ignore such a compelling call. In the raspy voice of a heavy smoker, she gave me her daughter-in-law's name and phone number, then begged me not to tell her she had called. Regina Lane would resent her mother-in-law for interfering. She had for a long time. When I reached her by phone, Regina Lane was polite, but only spoke to me for a few moments. "I didn't see the similarities," she told me. "I really didn't."[20] I called the police again about Lane's rape and confirmed that the suspect had been in prison the day of Sykes' murder. I also called a forensic psychologist to learn more about serial rapists, who told me it was likely the two crimes were connected and that it would have made sense for the police to investigate them together. "Most sex offenders will continue to assault until they are stopped, especially those kind of violent rapists,"[21] she told me. It was a chilling thought, but I was out of time. I hastily wrote about the second rape as an unexplored lead, another flaw in the deeply flawed case against Hunt. I'd almost missed the crime entirely, but now, thanks to a reader's call, I had Regina Lane's name and the name of the man she had identified all those years ago, Willard Brown.

Chapter Fifteen

Without Bitterness

The last part of the "Murder, Race, Justice" series was published on a Sunday, and I went back to writing columns, depressed that in all likelihood Hunt would remain in prison for a crime I had come to firmly believe he had not committed. The state was taking its time to retest the evidence, and it was no oversight. Rabil learned that the technician at the state crime lab was ignoring the court order for DNA testing intentionally. As far as the technician was concerned, the case was closed and she had more pressing cases to work on. The series I wrote raised a public outcry and caught the attention of Anderson Cromer, the judge who had ordered the new round of DNA testing and now threatened to hold the technician and the entire crime lab in contempt.[1] In early December, seven months after Cromer's court order, the crime lab finally tested the DNA found in the semen sample, but a combination of the old sample and the lab's outdated equipment produced an incomplete profile. In spite of that, the technician ran that incomplete profile against the database anyway and found a partial match with a Winston-Salem man named Anthony Brown, whose criminal record included sex offenses.

Partial matches generally exclude a suspect, but in this case enough markers between the two DNA samples matched that instead of closing up the case, the technician sent the samples to a lab in Alabama that had more precise equipment.[2] In the meantime, the North Carolina lab got in touch with the city police department to let them know of the partial match with Anthony Brown.[3] Prompted by the renewed interest in the case, the police and the State Bureau of Investigation began a new investigation, this time looking at cases that might be related to the Sykes murder. They pulled the file on the Integon rape and two other rapes downtown, one in the summer of 1984 and the other in the winter of 1985. The file on the Integon rape led them to Willard Brown's name and to the discovery that, contrary to what police had told me, Brown had in fact been released from prison in June 1984, weeks before Sykes' murder. He was a viable suspect after all. What's more, Anthony Brown was his brother. Coincidentally, in December 2003, Willard Brown was in the county jail, this time for probation violation. He was 43, his hair in short braids, and so far had escaped punishment for anything more serious than a robbery.

The crime lab in Alabama was able to produce a clearer forensic profile of the DNA from the semen recovered from Sykes' body, but there was still no match with a suspect's DNA, only the partial one with Anthony Brown. Instead of dropping the matter, the technicians in Alabama called the police department in Winston-Salem and suggested that because the number of matching DNA markers was so high, the real rapist may have been a relative of Anthony Brown.[4] Winston-Salem police could no longer overlook Willard Brown. By another fluke, he would be getting out of the county jail the following Monday. Police would need to move quickly. Detective Mike Rowe had no grounds for a search warrant for a sample of Brown's DNA, but he had another plan. He arranged an interview with Brown about the Sykes case. During a break in the interview, Rowe left the room, leaving a pack of cigarettes on the table. Brown smoked two of them, tossing the butts on the floor. As expected, Brown denied raping or killing Sykes. But that wasn't the point of the interview. Once he sent Brown back to his cell, Rowe carefully collected the two butts. Test results came back two days later, a perfect match. Willard Brown had raped Sykes,[5] and when confronted with the DNA evidence that held his secret, he confessed to killing her too.

Brown's birthday fell on August 9. In 1984, he had stayed up all night celebrating his 24th birthday.[6] There's no telling how much he drank, what drugs he took, or how he ended up on West End Boulevard, behind the Crystal Towers high-rise at dawn the following morning. He couldn't remember.

At first, he thought about robbing the tall woman walking alone. He grabbed her by the neck and waited for a car to pass. "Do you have any money?" he asked. She said she didn't. By now, he had her on the ground, hidden behind some shrubs. Taller than he was, she fought back, and so did he, slashing her hands and arms with his knife. Her strength made him mad. He saw a man peering through the bushes. "Quiet," Brown warned. Forgetting about the robbery, he ripped off her slacks, then her panties, and raped her. She was still fighting and yelling. To keep her quiet, he stabbed her. Once. Twice. Three times. He lost count. He heard her take a deep breath and then he ran, across the field, past the corner grocery, across a four-lane street, past the fire station, to his mother's house about two miles away. She and his brothers were awake, but no one seemed to notice the cut on his hand or ask where he'd been. It was easy to slip into the bathroom and wash up. A week passed. "I think I may have killed somebody," Brown told his mother.[7] It would be their secret, locked up tight all those years in a strand of DNA.

~

April Hunt arrived at the Forsyth County Jail at 9:30 the morning of Christmas Eve 2003. She had waited for this moment for as long as she could remember, all through her courtship with Hunt and marriage; in truth, ever since she first laid eyes on him when they were both in their twenties. When the call came, there'd been no time even to clean the house or shop for dinner. She grabbed the black leather jacket she hoped would fit Hunt and a borrowed sport coat in case it didn't. After all the setbacks they'd endured together, it was hard to believe he was coming home. Soon, the crush of people would begin, the hordes of camera crews and newspaper reporters ready to capture her husband's moment of triumph, but for now, she was alone in the lobby of the county jail, her head covered in a white scarf, her husband's clothes folded neatly in her lap.

"Would you mind if I waited with you?" I asked.

"You're the only familiar face I know," she said, inviting me to sit beside her in one of the hard plastic chairs so many other mothers and wives had sat in before her. "I was just told to come and wait in the lobby."[8]

Back in the holding area, Hunt imagined the worst. A week earlier, the crime lab had found a DNA match with a man Hunt had never heard of, someone named Willard Brown. He always believed they would have to solve the crime if he was ever going to be free, and now they had. Brown had even confessed to raping Sykes and stabbing her to death and to having acted alone. But the police were still messing with Hunt, coming up with yet another scenario for the crime, that somehow he was still involved.

Hunt and I spoke by phone the morning after he learned of Brown's DNA match. He called me collect from the prison pay phone, optimistic, yet cautious after so many years of disappointments that he didn't dare tell any of the other men in his cell block. "I'm keeping it to myself."[9] We spoke again after his transfer from the prison in Asheboro, about an hour east of Winston-Salem, to the county jail. Other incarcerated men, even guards, had wished him luck and told him they would pray for him. But he'd been fooled once before and wouldn't be fooled again. "Basically, I was trying not to get over-excited because we had been close before and let down,"[10] he told me. They'd been promising to let him out since Monday and now it was Wednesday. It was hard to know what to believe.

At 11 a.m., a deputy arrived with the release order for Hunt to sign. It said Brown had confessed to having acted alone and that "Darryl Hunt was not involved."[11] The state was releasing him on a $250,000 unsecured bond with a court date set for February 6. He signed his name, Darryl E. Hunt, still imagining the deputy snatching away the signed piece of paper.[12] He changed from prison garb into the clothes April had brought, the first street clothes he'd worn in nearly ten years. Then he emerged, walking slowly down the corridor that led from the release area to the front desk, no cuffs or shackles, just a man of 39, his beard neatly trimmed, his head covered in a knit skullcap.

He heard the chants coming from the other side of the lobby.

"Darryl Hunt is free. Darryl Hunt is free."

Maybe he was. He wasn't sure. He met his wife first, lifting her off the ground in a long, quiet embrace, their foreheads touching.

"Darryl Hunt is free," came the voices of the men who had stood with him for nearly 20 years. "Darryl Hunt is free."

And then all at once he was surrounded. Little collapsed in his arms, weeping.

"Yes. Yes. Yes."

Ferguson reached him next.

"It's a long time coming, man."

The rest—Rabil, Griggs, Eversley, Mendez—all middle-aged or older now, grown from the young men they'd been at the start of their crusade, wiped away their tears.[13]

Outside, reporters shouted questions.

"Any thoughts on the man you are today compared to the man you were when you were first arrested?"

"Well, I'm older."

"What happens next?"

"I think justice will take its course, God willing. I always had faith that one day I would be free."[14]

A friend waited to take him to the Community Mosque. Inside the van, his wife stroked his hand and rubbed his back. Hunt said he felt calmer.

Little handed him the judge's order for his release and pointed to paragraph 11.[15] That was the one that said Willard E. Brown had confessed to murdering Sykes, that he had acted alone, and that Hunt was not involved, even that he was sorry for what he had done to Hunt.

"This pretty much seals it," Little said.

It was 12:15 p.m. Hunt had been a free man for 20 minutes and was at a loss for words.

"Does the jacket fit?" April Hunt asked.

The couple spoke so quietly to each other that no one else in the van could hear. They arrived at the mosque in time for the second prayer of the day. Hunt spoke to the other men gathered for prayer.

"I never gave up faith that one day I would be here. It's just been a tough road."

Nearby, people had been gathering since 9:30 a.m. at Emmanuel Baptist Church on Shalimar Drive, where Mendez was pastor. Hunt arrived at 12:45 p.m. Again, the cheers went up. "Darryl Hunt is free. Darryl Hunt is free." Inside the sanctuary, with its vaulted ceiling and walls lined in stone, people sang the gospel hymn "Victory Is Mine."

In 1994, Hunt had prepared a statement to read upon his release. Burned once before, he hadn't dared put words to paper again. Instead, he spoke from his heart, finding a story for each person seated with him.

"I want to start out with Larry," he said, struggling to compose himself.

"Take your time Darryl, it's all right," someone called from the audience.

"I remember not knowing what was going to happen to me and he asked me was I innocent? Did I do the crime? And I told him, 'No,'" Hunt said, recalling his meeting with Little the day after his arrest in September 1984.

He said, "If you didn't, I will fight for you, but if you did, I will fight against you."

It was that that helped me feel at peace and he has been with me through these 19 years. He is a blessing from God because at that point when I was arrested they probably could have shot me and gotten it over with and there wouldn't have been nothing said. The hell that I experienced the first couple of days, but after Larry became interested I was a little more at peace. I felt a little bit better, safer is the word I'm looking for.

At that time it was like, if you kill me now knowing I did not commit the crime at least someone will know about it.

Then he turned to Rabil.

I remember talking to Mark and not knowing if he would believe me or not . . . I didn't know if he believed me or thought I was some kind of freak, but he has always been there and always gave his heart. I remember when we was in court in '93 and his wife was sick and he was in court with us and the total sacrifice he gave.

At the mention of his late wife, Rabil collapsed in his chair in tears.

That gave me the strength to make it because there were times I felt like I was going crazy being locked up, and Mark, he always made a point to make me smile or laugh.

"I'll save my wife for last," he said, turning next to Griggs.

> In my saddest time, he has been there for me, inspired me and
> helped keep me focused.

Next came Mendez and the fire of his words.

> I remember the day they offered the plea bargain and everybody
> was in the room . . . everybody who was looking out for my good
> but I wouldn't take it. I think Reverend Mendez was the only
> one that really understood me on that point. I will never forget
> that because it was heart wrenching. He told me to go with my
> heart and that's what I had to do.

Eversley had that fire, too.

> I remember when I was out on bond, and we were playing
> basketball. It was the days I was in your church and listening
> to you preach, the message and the fire. The word of God is
> everywhere and his truth shines. If you can't feel it in your
> heart, you're missing something. I love the way, the fire, that
> Reverend Eversley has.

Nelson Malloy certainly understood survival.

> Next is brother Nelson. I ran his phone bill up since I been in
> prison, and he's always been there for me. He's always shown
> me love. His struggle and determination inspired me to keep
> going. He's been at some of my saddest moments too. I could
> always call him.

Finally, Hunt turned to his wife.

She came into my life when I was in a time of despair and picked me up and loved me when I thought nobody else in the world could and stood there with all the ups and downs . . . and she told me she would never leave, that if I can't have you in this life, Inshallah, we'll be together in the next. That put all questions, all doubts, out of my mind, and I love her with all my heart.

When we got married that Monday, the U.S. Supreme Court had just turned us down. I remember when she came in and I said, "We shouldn't do this." . . . We talked about the decision and she said, "I know about that but what does that have to do with what we're doing now?" So we got married and that was one of the happiest days of my life. Last night, that was one of the hardest nights because I was wondering, is she going through hell, like I was?

They stood and embraced, but Hunt had more to say, especially about Sammy Mitchell, who was in prison for the Arthur Wilson case, and Sammy's mother, Mattie Mitchell.

I want to talk about the people that's not here. One is Ms. Mitchell. Ms. Mitchell was like a mother to me. She would get on me if I didn't call on time or write like I was supposed to. When she passed, that was one of my saddest days. It was sort of like I lost my mother.

A lot of people talked about Sam. A lot of people don't like Sam, but I think with the news of what's going on, you don't have to like him, but he's just as innocent as I am and he should be here, too. Don't nobody forget him, because he's locked up unjustly. They refuse to give him any help because of the charges hanging over his head. I pray, don't nobody forget him.

Then it was time for questions.

"What's the one thing you want to do?"

"This might be crazy," Hunt said. "I just want to watch the sun go down."[16]

It was just after 2 p.m. when the rally was over, leaving Hunt free to go. But already, he felt the demands from people wanting his attention. Home, down the street from the mosque, where April had been living with her three children, would have to wait. With his friend Bilal Muhammad at the wheel, he and April headed east toward Burlington, a town of about 50,000 where no one would know them and they could get dinner undisturbed. Within minutes of leaving town, Hunt fell asleep. He was so very tired.

~

Hunt and April settled into her house, small for all five of them—Hunt, April, and her three children, ages 8 to 15. April worked during the day in a doctor's office, leaving Hunt time to figure out his life on the outside.

Everything had changed since he last walked the streets a free man. It had been 13 years since he drove a car. He'd never owned a cell phone, much less used one. Remote controls, the microwave, the ATM, were all new to Hunt. He'd even lost the habit of opening a door for himself, so accustomed to waiting for a guard to open the door and for it to slam shut automatically behind him. Institutionalization strips people of their agency, replacing it with an alertness to danger. Sociologists have a word for that: hypervigilance. In prison, Hunt rarely slept a deep sleep. At home, he remained alert, rarely sleeping through the night. When the rest of the household was asleep, he'd sit on the stoop, look at the sky, and fret. For Hunt, the layers of trauma from his childhood losses and the 19 years of defeat and imprisonment had made hypervigilance his normal state.

He told a newspaper reporter that he wasn't looking for an apology from district attorney Tom Keith, who had replaced Sparrow in 1990 and had numerous opportunities in his 13 years in office to see that justice was done in Hunt's case, or from any of the former DAs involved in the case. "What they need to do is apologize to Mrs. Sykes' family," Hunt said. "They lied to them for 20 years. Just leave me alone. Just let me live my life, what's left of it."[17] Even with the DNA and Brown's confession, he didn't believe he would be allowed to do that. The district attorney had been slow to let him out of prison after the DNA match was found. At first, it was the same old story, the crap they'd been saying for ten years. Rabil and everyone else was working toward the hearing in February, when the charges would all be dropped for good. Until then, ever alert to danger, Hunt could not, would not, relax.

~

Hunt rose early the morning of February 6, 2004, for court. Rabil had been working with the DA all month on the details. This time, the case for innocence was airtight. Together, they would ask Judge Cromer to drop the charges against him. Rowe would testify about the DNA match, Brown's confession, and the detective work to make sure that Hunt was not involved. With that, the charges would be dismissed "with prejudice," the legal way of saying that no one would ever again be able to pin Sykes' rape and murder on him. Still, without telling April, or anyone else, Hunt prepared himself to be sent back to prison, even packing up his Quran and prayer rug, just in case.

He knew the courtroom in Forsyth County well, with its wood-paneled walls, rows of benches, and harsh lighting. He'd been denied justice across the hall in 1994, convicted in the same place a decade before that. Things were different now. Before, he'd come in from the far-right corner, beside the jury box, from the door that led to the holding cell. This time he walked in the front door and took his seat beside Rabil, but still he felt that familiar sense of dread.

The room was packed, expectations high. Television and newspaper reporters filled the first two rows of benches. The filmmakers who had started their documentary in the 1990s flew down from New York and set up behind the bench, where they had a clear shot of the witness stand and of Hunt. There was one unexpected witness, Sykes' mother, who took a seat behind Hunt.

As the proceedings began, I noticed her steely gaze. As planned, Rowe took the witness stand and reviewed the evidence for Hunt's innocence. He explained the DNA testing, Brown's confession, and all the police work he had done to rule out any possible connection between Hunt and Brown.

"Is there anyone else?" Cromer asked.

Evelyn Jefferson rose. All she knew about Brown came from me. No one in the DA's office had bothered to make the trip to Chattanooga or even call her by phone to explain how they'd been wrong all along, that the story she'd believed about Hunt was a lie.

Nineteen years earlier, she'd taken the stand as part of the case against Hunt. She had told jurors about her beautiful daughter, her hopes for a family, and how she had died alone. Now she was the one alone. Her voice hard with bitterness, she spoke.

"I would like for the court to know that I do not believe in Mr. Hunt's innocence. What you're about to do today is set free a guilty man, who's guilty of my daughter's death."[18]

These were hard words to hear on a day so filled with expectation. Then it was Hunt's turn to speak. Someone else might have ignored Sykes' mother, or used the moment to deliver an angry tirade. Rising from his spot at the defense table, he turned to speak to her, his voice breaking with emotion.

Mrs. Jefferson, I had nothing to do with your daughter's death. I wasn't involved. I know it's hard. But I've lived with this every day trying to prove my innocence. I can't explain why people say what they say. Or why they lie. Or why all this happened. Only God can. That's how I tried to live my days in prison, knowing that only God can bring about justice. I just ask that you and your family know that in my heart you are in my prayers.[19]

His humility and his grace stunned us all.

Chapter Sixteen

Time for Me to Speak

Sgt. Chuck Byrom stared hard at the search warrant, the one police officers had drawn in 1984 for the apartment on Patterson Avenue where Hunt kept his things. Something about it didn't add up. Jim Daulton, the very first detective on the Sykes case, swore in the warrant that a witness told him he'd seen Sykes at the crime scene with a man wearing a black T-shirt printed with a spiderweb design. It was a very specific detail, the kind a witness would remember, but the thing was, not a single one of the eyewitnesses had ever mentioned a spiderweb design. Not Thomas Murphy. Not William Hooper. Not Johnny Gray. So where did the description of such a distinctive T-shirt come from?

Byrom and his partner, Joe Ferrelli, had been holed away in the conference room outside the police chief's office for weeks in 2005, assigned by the chief to work with the Sykes Administrative Review Committee, a group of seven citizens convened by the city council after Hunt's exoneration to figure out exactly how the police had arrested the wrong man all those years ago. Willard Brown was finally in prison for life, having pled guilty to Sykes' rape and murder in December 2004. But the question of how he had eluded justice all this time remained. Of the two detectives, Byrom was more skeptical of his fellow officers, and with good reason. He'd come up through the ranks, a Black officer in a largely white department, and had been on his way to making lieutenant six years earlier when some rap artists at a concert in the city's coliseum simulated sex acts on stage and the cops on duty didn't stop them. Byrom and two other Black officers on duty took the fall, and his career stalled. While he carried some bitterness about his department and some of its officers, it was not enough to keep him from seeing the facts, which right now filled up dozens of boxes stacked around the room. The facts would tell exactly where the missteps were in the Sykes investigation and whether any of these missteps had been intentional. Had Hunt spent all those years in prison because of sloppy police work? Or had investigators—men and women Byrom and Ferrelli had worked with for years—intentionally destroyed or hidden evidence that could have freed Hunt long ago?

They started with the police reports, the ones from the first investigation, the ones from the probe in 1986, and finally the ones from 1990, when the police were supposed to take a fresh look at the case in preparation for Hunt's second trial. The conference table was covered with these reports, each one dated and signed by an investigating officer. Byrom knew the drill well. The lead officer files the primary reports. Anyone else working on the case files a supplemental report. It's up to the lead officer to review them all, then send them up the chain of command, a system of checks and balances that could easily be subverted along the way. Byrom had his suspicions about the 1984 warrant, but he had to be certain about these suspicions, which meant rereading the dozens of reports on each of the eyewitnesses, looking for some mention of a black T-shirt with a spiderweb motif.

He and Ferrelli had fallen into an easy rhythm, each a check against the other. "Scab pickers," the chief called them, in admiration of their attention to detail and integrity, qualities that had landed them in internal affairs in the first place. They showed up every day in a suit and tie and headed up to the conference room on the third floor, their presence silencing the elevator banter. Neither one cared much that their old partners now called them "Darryl's detectives," or that some officers had stopped talking with them altogether. That was the culture of the department. Anyone who broke with the brotherhood would be ostracized. As the review dragged on, some in the department threatened to sue them. Undaunted, they were going to figure Hunt's wrongful conviction out, one report at a time. There was one important difference in their perspectives. Where Ferrelli saw incompetence, Byrom saw something far more sinister.[1]

The T-shirt with a spiderweb design had been the first hint of doctored evidence from the get-go, ever since Hunt told his lawyer that there was no way anyone had seen him with that T-shirt the morning Sykes was killed because he didn't buy it until the following week. Rabil had confirmed the sales date with the store clerk, which then became a rallying cry for Little. And now Byrom had finally figured out what happened. It was all there, in the reports, if you looked carefully. There was a report that mentioned a spiderweb pattern. It was a report not about an interview with a witness but about an interview with Hunt's girlfriend, Marie Crawford, the 14-year-old prostitute whom Daulton had arrested on a runaway warrant and who had told him, among many things, that Hunt owned a T-shirt with a spiderweb design. Byrom reached across the table, handing it to his partner. Contrary to what the warrant said, the description had not come from a witness to the crime.

"Is this what I think it is?" Byrom said.

"What's the big deal?" Ferrelli asked.

"The big deal is someone fabricated this to put it into a search warrant and that's basically a crime," Byrom replied.[2]

The only plausible explanation for the detail of the spiderweb T-shirt was that Daulton used what Crawford told him about the shirt to write a search warrant indicating that a witness who saw Hunt near the crime scene had seen him in the shirt. Writing the warrant that way guaranteed that when police searched the apartment where Hunt kept his things they would find something that could be used to confirm what eyewitnesses told them about the way the attacker was dressed. If investigators could fabricate evidence listed on a search warrant, Byrom wondered what else they had done to frame Hunt.

Byrom had seen cops play loose with the facts before. Raised in New Brunswick, New Jersey, he had moved to town at 19 to go to school at Winston-Salem State University, one of ten historically Black colleges in the state. A well-paying job at a metal fabrication plant lured him away from college. When he joined the department in 1981, he figured that police work would give him a chance to help others and provide him with the structure he knew he needed. He was 26 and confident, with training in martial arts as backup. He soon learned that the force was full of knuckleheads who were more interested in the hunt than in protecting the people they were called to serve. Often, it was easier to make a case, even if that meant fudging the facts, than to build one wherever the facts led. There was a saying around the department: use your tact and discipline. But old-timers told him that when those failed, trickery and deceit would do. Either way, it was still T & D. When Byrom and Ferrelli interviewed Daulton at the end of December 2005, he confirmed that he'd been the puppet of the higher-ups. He insisted that the chief or the police attorney had typed up the warrant and all he'd done was take it to the clerk's office and, without reading it, swear to its truth. It was clear to Byrom that someone high up had decided it was easier to frame Hunt than conduct an honest investigation.

Once he and Ferrelli were done with the police reports and trial transcripts from the Sykes and Wilson trials, they checked the files in the courthouse to see if there was anything in those files they hadn't seen.

Not surprisingly, there was.

In the file for the first trial in the Wilson case they found a legal pad with notes on witness testimony, something detectives routinely

produced as a trial unfolded. The pad included notes on each witness, whether they testified for the state or the defense, and their
key points. On one page, in the upper right corner, someone had
drawn a cartoonish face, with deep-set eyes and big lips. Beneath
the monkey-like face, the author had drawn a scorecard, labeling
one column "p" and the other column "n." The same scorecard was
drawn on another page, and the cartoon appeared beneath the name
of one of the Black witnesses from the liquor house.[3] It was clear to
Byrom what "p" and "n" stood for and what the crude cartoon meant.
It was "police" vs. "niggers."[4] It always had been.

When Byrom joined the department, the practice was to break
in rookie cops in East Winston. The neighborhood reminded him of
where he'd been raised in New Brunswick—Robeson Village, named
for the singer and political activist Paul Robeson. There were a lot of
calls in East Winston, but usually he saw tense situations that could
be de-escalated with calm authority. And he knew that beneath the
chaos of these calls was a community of men and women trying to
get by. A lot of the cops he worked with had a different attitude.
They enjoyed the adrenaline rush of conflict, the thrill of the hunt.
His training officer, who was white, treated Byrom and the people
they encountered with contempt. The training officer never actually
called Byrom "boy" or "nigger." He didn't need to. The first night out,
Byrom and his training officer took a call in East Winston about
a stolen bicycle. They found it nearby, tossed in the street. When
Byrom opened the trunk of the squad car so they could bring the
bicycle back to the property room, the training officer told him
to ride it there instead. It was pouring rain, but Byrom did as he
was told. When he rode up to the department, his training officer
was outside with half a dozen other officers, all white, all of them
laughing at the drenched Black rookie on the bike. At the end of
the month-long training period, the training officer asked Byrom,
"You think I'm a son of a bitch?"

"Yeah."

"You think I'm a redneck?"

"Yeah."

"You should meet my brother."

"I don't want to meet your fucking brother."[5]

Byrom soon heard about Sammy Mitchell, by his reputation, and about Hunt's case. Other Black officers, especially those in command, warned him away from a case that could be career-ending, especially for a young Black officer just starting out. Considering the lyrics, it didn't surprise him when a few years later the Guns N' Roses hit song "Welcome to the Jungle" became a kind of anthem for cops to sing as they headed out on patrol.[6]

~

A deep review of the police reports in the Sykes case shows how witness statements changed from one investigation to the next. The most glaring example was Kevey Coleman. He hadn't come forward for the first trial, but by the time the State Bureau of Investigation came in to reinvestigate in 1986, a coworker had called the police to let them know that Coleman was a witness.[7] Hunt's lawyers suspected all along that Coleman had been badgered into testifying. It wasn't surprising. He'd been treated as a suspect himself from the moment he came forward. He was fingerprinted and asked if he had killed Sykes for the simple reason that he was a Black man walking at the scene. At first, he said he couldn't identify anyone because he wasn't wearing his contact lenses. By the time of the second trial, he grudgingly said that the two men he saw with the white woman that morning might have been Hunt and Mitchell. The police weren't pleased with his waffling. Worse than that were threats he received from Hunt's supporters for turning on another Black man. By the time he spoke with Byrom and Ferrelli in November 2005, he was still uneasy about his role as a witness. Then he told them something not noted in any of the previous reports.

Back in 1986, when Coleman was first looking at mugshots
to identify the men he had seen the morning of the crime, he had
identified Willard Brown. Coleman told Byrom and Ferrelli that
he had even written down Brown's name, keeping the scrap of
paper for years, because he wanted to remember the name. But the
detectives told Coleman the same thing they'd told Regina Lane,
the woman who had identified Brown as her rapist—that Brown
couldn't have attacked Sykes because he'd been in prison in August
1984. Brown would have been an important lead, but not a single
report from 1986 or 1990 mentioned Coleman's identification of
Brown. Around the same time, Coleman had also identified Hunt,
and now, when he compared the pictures, he noticed that the two
men resembled each other. It was their eyes, he told Byrom and
Ferrelli, "real, real red eyes."[8] It would be hard to corroborate what
Coleman was telling them and easy for the police who questioned
him to deny his account. But Byrom believed him. The implication
of what he told them was damning. There was no way investigators had left his identification of Brown out of their reports by
accident.[9]

Once they were done with the reports and court transcripts
in the Sykes case, Byrom and Ferrelli started looking into other
rapes from the early 1980s. They knew about Lane's case, but there
were more. In June 1984, two months before Sykes was murdered,
a 40-year-old woman was attacked around the corner from the
Integon building and then again in the bushes where Sykes would
later be killed. To protect her identity, they called her Linda E.[10]
Then, in January 1985, five months after Sykes' murder and a month
before Lane was raped, a woman they called Kathleen D.[11] was raped
at an elementary school in the West End neighborhood just west
of downtown, by coincidence around the corner from where Rabil
had lived with his pregnant wife.

There were other rapes in that time period, attacks in public,
similar to these rapes downtown. Byrom and Ferrelli plotted them

on a city map and saw two clusters: the rapes downtown of white women and a handful of rapes on the east side of town of Black women. Byrom suspected that Brown may have committed all of them, but his work was supposed to be focused on the mistakes in the Sykes case, not on opening cold cases from the past, so he moved on.[12] If the unsolved rapes of the white women—Lane and Linda E. and Kathleen D.—could be swept away, the Black victims never had a chance.

It helped that Byrom knew not only what the reports he was reading meant but what the absence of a document meant as well. The reports revealed that about a year into the investigation of Lane's rape, police were able to get a sample of Brown's blood and have it tested by the state crime lab. If anyone had tried to make the connection between the Lane and Sykes cases, the results would have made Brown a viable suspect in the Sykes murder, more viable than Hunt ever was because Brown's blood type matched the semen sample in the Sykes case—type O. All the way back in 1986, police should have been able to make the connection between Brown and Sykes. Lane had made the connection. So had her mother-in-law. And the blood typing would have confirmed it. Byrom wondered whether this was an oversight or a cover-up. The one document that would have helped answer that question was missing. The reports mentioned a search warrant for Brown's blood, but the warrant itself was not in the files, and the reports didn't say how police had established probable cause. Byrom knew from the Sykes file that detective Carter Crump and other officers had interviewed Brown during the spring 1986 investigation as a suspect in the Sykes case. And he knew that during the same period, Lane had picked Brown out of a live lineup. But where was the probable cause for the search warrant? With no semen recovered in Lane's case, there'd be no reason to test Brown's blood type, and therefore no probable cause. Byrom and Ferrelli tore the files apart once again, looking for the search warrant. When it wasn't in the files, they searched the courthouse

and eventually found an order from 1999 to destroy hundreds of old
search warrants, including the one Crump had drawn up to obtain
Brown's blood in April 1986. Crump declined to speak with Byrom,
but the explanation that made the most sense to Byrom was that
Crump must have used the Sykes case to establish probable cause,
and when the results came back implicating Brown in her murder,
someone quashed it. Another piece of the cover-up.[13]

~

For 21 years, Regina Lane had been known only as the "Integon
victim."[14] All this time, someone else had controlled her story: first
the police, who did everything they could to conceal what had happened to her and to suppress her voice; then the media, including
me, who had made the story told about her sound as though she'd
had a choice in how her case unfolded. Now she had the chance to
set the record straight. Byrom and Ferrelli suggested she provide a
written statement. She'd tried that once before, when her case was
first investigated, and it hadn't worked. It was time, now, for the
public to hear her voice.

The Sykes Administrative Review Committee met February 2,
2006, in a conference room, with members seated at narrow tables
arranged in a square. City staff and visitors sat in chairs lined up
against the wall or in rows that faced the committee. There was
a podium off to the left for speakers. The night before she was
scheduled to testify, Lane had gone to choir practice as she did
every Wednesday, and choir members had sung one of her favorite
hymns, a piece that gave her courage for the words she was about
to speak. Her husband, mother, and a close friend came with her
for moral support. She also invited David Wagner, the man who
had opened his door to her and wrapped her in a bedspread. She
wanted him to hear her give thanks in public for what he had
done for her.[15]

Ten years would pass before the #MeToo movement gave so many women the courage to speak up, but Lane had decided that if she was going to speak, she would do it her way. She ignored the podium and instead found an open spot at a table so that she could stand among the committee members, the very people who would set things right. She had prepared her words carefully. She didn't want their pity. In spite of what they were about to hear, she wanted them to know that she had been blessed with a good life. But she intended to make it clear that she'd been victimized, too, first by the man who raped her and then by police who deceived her to protect their case against Hunt.[16]

Over the years, she had rarely talked about the rape. Her family, of course, knew, and a few people at work. But mostly, she kept the trauma buried and put her faith in God. She had married just three months after the attack, at a simple ceremony at her church. The cuts had mostly healed by then, with only a hint of a scar showing in her wedding pictures. She and her husband raised a son, Stephen, and they both worked, she at the insurance company and he as an electrician. On weekends, they set up booths at flea markets in the area, selling the antiques her husband collected.

Before the review committee began its work, she'd been mad at her mother-in-law for interfering, for calling me so that once again she had to read about what had happened to her in the newspaper. But with all she had learned in the past two years, she now understood that Mary Lane had been right. She never should have trusted the police. The man she had identified all those years ago had killed Sykes and gotten away with it. Who knows how many other women he'd raped?

All these years, she'd tried to put that horrible morning behind her and focus instead on her family, her job, and God. Any time she heard about Hunt's case on the news, she thought again about how close she'd come to death out there in those woods.

Now the city was taking an honest look at how Brown had eluded justice all this time. Unlike the detectives who had first looked into her case, Ferrelli and Byrom treated her with respect. When they took her to the crime scene, she felt heard for the first time. They shared the entire case file with her, reports that had been concealed back when she'd first been attacked, reports that made no mention of the connection she had seen with the Sykes case. And now she understood why.[17]

The first time she identified Brown from a photo lineup was just five days before the opening day of Hunt's 1985 trial.[18] No wonder they hadn't been eager to find him. She had badgered detective Bill Miller, and then Carter Crump when he took over her case, all the following year. It took a year for them to find Brown to put him in an in-person lineup. She could still remember riding that elevator in the old jail up to the third floor to view the lineup. Brown's attorney was there with her, a young woman who by coincidence was the daughter of the man who rescued her. Her knees nearly buckled. And there he was, number 3, the same man who'd attacked her. Afterward, she thought she would be sick.[19] But with no physical evidence linking the rape to Brown, the police always made it seem as though it would be her word against his. That's why she'd asked to hear a recording of his voice, to see if she recognized the gravelly voice that still haunted her. They'd turned her down. That made sense now, too. They were in the middle of reinvestigating Hunt's case. And Crump was part of that. Surely he'd made the connection.

She now saw how she'd been asking all the right questions all along, the same ones the investigators were asking now. She didn't know a thing about police work, but just eight days after she was raped, she'd asked about other rapes downtown. Now she knew that police had hidden them from her, hidden the fact that a woman named Kathleen had been raped a month earlier, within a block of where Brown had kidnapped her, and that another woman, named

Linda, had been raped two months before the Sykes murder, also within a block of her own kidnapping. They'd all been denied justice.

For 20 years, Brown had gotten away with rape and with murder while Hunt was stuck in prison, and the police had used her to protect their case against an innocent man. The new officers had also shared reports in Sykes' case with her. She now knew that Brown had briefly been a suspect in the Sykes murder at the same time police were trying to find him for an in-person lineup in her case. In fact, they'd interviewed him in the Sykes case in March 1986, when the State Bureau of Investigation was conducting a new investigation.[20] The following month, she picked him out of a lineup. No wonder they told her it would be her word against his. And then, in 1989,[21] they closed her case and destroyed the evidence—the swabs they'd collected in the hospital right after the rape, which may have contained Brown's skin cells, the glove Brown had worn, and her bloody clothes. There was nothing left from her attack to test for DNA. With the physical evidence gone, she had agreed with prosecutors not to charge Brown and that the life sentence in the Sykes case was enough punishment for both crimes. Still, knowing that the evidence had been hidden from her, she was more certain than ever that Brown was her attacker.

All along, she knew it was important that Brown had held her close so that she had to bend over to keep from tripping. He must have done the same to Sykes. That's why witnesses thought the attacker was taller than he was. She'd been right, too, to ask to see the pictures of Sykes. Now she'd seen them. She had studied the pictures police had taken of her in the emergency room, the slashes across her neck and cheeks, and the puncture wound below her ear. She saw the same pattern on Sykes' face.[22]

She'd been right all along. In fact, when the police had closed her case in 1989, she had said to Officer Crump: "Wouldn't it be wild if one day we found out that Deborah's attacker and my attacker was the same person?"[23] And now she knew that police had, in fact, made the connection between Sykes' murder and her rape. They had—and they had covered it up.

She wrote all that out in her statement and began to speak. She wasn't nervous. She had prayed about this moment and felt the strength of the Lord.

"My name is Regina and 21 years ago tomorrow, I was labeled by the *Winston-Salem Journal* as The Integon Victim."[24]

For far too long, she'd allowed the police to speak for her.

"It is time for me to speak."[25]

At 18, Lane had trusted the authorities. Now she knew better. For many people listening, the key moment in her testimony came when she described the very first inquiry she made two days after the attack about the possible connection between her case and the Sykes murder.

> Detective Miller walked away again and when he returned, he said in a very firm voice his answer. They already had the men or man that raped and killed Deborah Sykes in jail. Detective Miller told me that "they didn't want to do anything that would make people ask questions or put doubts in people's minds because it could hurt the case against the people in jail."[26]

It was the first admission anyone listening had heard of a police officer's intent to protect the case against Hunt. When "tact and diplomacy" fails, there's always "trickery and deceit."[27]

When she was done speaking, the room fell silent.

～

There were plenty of people in town who wanted to think that the police had simply fumbled a high-profile case. Lane's testimony now provided evidence of intent. Rabil and McGough had been trying to speak with her for more than a year, knowing she would be the key to proving that Hunt's 19 years in prison were no accident. All the misery he suffered, all those death threats and lost years, and their own pain, too—they were now convinced it had all been part of an intentional cover-up. For a while, McGough had called her every week, but she always told him that she wanted to let the review committee do its work first.[28] Now that she'd spoken, Lane proved, more so even than all the police reports that had finally been released, that police had gone to great lengths to cover up the trail that led from Deborah Sykes' murder to Willard Brown. They had railroaded Hunt and used whomever they needed, including an 18-year-old rape victim, to protect their case.

North Carolina law provided compensation for men and women exonerated of crimes. The pardon from the governor came in April 2004, and Hunt was awarded $358,545, which was eventually increased to $750,000. It was a lot of money, considering that 15 states still provide no compensation at all.[29] With a murder conviction still showing up on his record and no job experience, it was hard for Hunt to find a job, even the simple job he'd always dreamed of with the city streets department. With no work and a family to support, the money from the state would not last his lifetime.

As evidence of a cover-up emerged from the committee's work, Rabil and Little got to work on a civil lawsuit. The committee's work showed that police had fabricated and destroyed evidence, evidence that would have led to Brown, perhaps before Hunt's first conviction and certainly before he was retried in 1990. It all added up to compelling allegations of civil rights violations, fraud, and obstruction of justice. Rabil took a leave of absence from his job with the state capital defender's office and began negotiating with the city. In January 2007, he drafted a blistering letter to the city attorney that laid out, in detail, the evidence that would form the basis of a federal lawsuit.

I want to follow up on our phone conversation yesterday in which we rejected the City's latest offer of $800,000 (in response to our last offer of $2.3 million). Given the approaching statute of limitations deadline (2/6/07), we believe that the City needs to stop making incremental moves and accept Darryl's reasonable offer to settle.

I have closely examined the relevant cases and strongly believe that Darryl Hunt's case will survive any summary judgment motions in either state or federal court and that a jury will decide the amount of damages to be awarded to Darryl. I know that you have been briefed on the law, but I am not confident that you are familiar with the facts of Darryl's case that are to be applied to the law. The claims to be brought by Darryl include federal civil rights violations as well as state claims for malicious prosecution, fraud, intentional infliction of emotional distress and conspiracy to obstruct justice.

When one is aware of the institutional racism at play from the outset of this case, and of the fact that evidence that someone else—Willard Brown—was actually guilty of the Sykes murder and that this evidence was destroyed or covered up, and of the fact that the "eyewitness" evidence against Darryl was fabricated by the police, then one must conclude that a substantial yet reasonable settlement is in order. I will address some of these issues so that you may share them with the City Council as it considers a settlement in this case. I request that you share this letter with the members of the Council so that our position is clear.[30]

Three weeks later, the council agreed to settle, awarding Hunt $1.65 million.[31] After paying Rabil and Little the standard 25 percent commission,[32] Hunt had $1.24 million from the city and $750,000 from the state, which if invested wisely would be enough to

support him and April for the rest of their lives. Even as he negoti-
ated the settlement, Rabil knew that money would never be enough
to compensate Hunt for the trauma he had endured. Rabil wrote:

> How do we put a dollar amount on the loss of nearly 19 years?
> How do we compensate Darryl for being incarcerated in some of
> the worst prisons in the State for no good or justifiable reason?
> How do we make restitution for surviving the attempts on his
> life, the loss of sleep, the ulcers, the psychological distress? How
> do you go back in time and give somebody the chance to have
> a regular life, with a job, a retirement plan, children, grandchil-
> dren, a home?[33]

Chapter Seventeen

A Public Face

The documentary *The Trials of Darryl Hunt* opened at Sundance in February 2006. By then, Hunt and April were accustomed to his celebrity at home, where he couldn't even run out to the grocery store for a carton of milk without someone recognizing him. Now he was a film star, rubbing shoulders in the cold mountain air with money men and intellectuals. It was thrilling to be part of. Publicity photos taken that week in Utah show Hunt in a black leather jacket and turtleneck, another in a black cowboy hat, dressed for the celebrity role.

The film tells the triumphant story of Hunt's long road to justice, with him in the lead and with supporting roles played by Rabil, the lawyer driven by an overwhelming sense of duty, and Little, the activist fueled by a burning anger. It opens in court the day of Hunt's exoneration, with the bitter words from Sykes' mother and his graceful response. Then it traces the case, using gruesome crime scene photos, news accounts of the trials, and footage of his courtroom defeats and of his release—all set against a haunting score. The filmmakers, Ricki Stern and Annie Sundberg, wove the scenes they shot in the early 1990s, when they drove down from New York to look into the case, with contemporary and archival footage to make the strong statement that from the moment of his arrest, Hunt's race made it impossible for him to get justice in the rape and murder of a white woman.

I've seen the film at least a dozen times and I am always moved most by hearing portions of the interview Rabil recorded when he was preparing Hunt to testify in 1985, Hunt's voice layered over photographs of him at the time: a skinny kid with cornrows, a broad forehead, and an impish smile. The soundtrack is scratchy, recorded in the pre-digital age, but the voice is familiar, that of the same steady, humble man I came to know 20 years later.

"Do you pray, Mr. Hunt?"

"Yes. I pray every night."

"What do you pray for?"

"Justice."

"Do you pray for any particular result in this case?"

"Yes, I do."

"What is that?"

"That the police department would find the right person who did this crime."

"Do you pray for anything for yourself?"

"Yes."

"What do you pray for?"

"That I could live a decent life."[1]

The film brought Hunt's story to audiences around the world, and it gave him a platform to speak out against the systemic problems that led to his wrongful incarceration. But the work that meant the most to him was not the public advocacy but a more private role found in helping men and women coming home from prison. Hunt didn't care about their guilt. They had all suffered as he had in prison, and they would need help with the transition.

The year after his exoneration, Hunt founded the Darryl Hunt Project for Freedom and Justice[2] and opened shop downtown in an elegant turn-of-the-century bank building where the public defender and the capital defender also had their offices. Over the years, the organization employed a small clerical staff and social workers, with Hunt juggling many roles. Within a block of the jail and the courthouse, the office was convenient to potential clients. Soon, the reception area was filled with men and women waiting all day to see "Mr. Darryl."[3]

The idea for his reentry organization came from his own experience trying to find a job. Shortly after his release from prison, he heard that a local, established reentry project was looking for a caseworker. With his experience in prison and strong references, he thought he had a good shot at the job. He filled out the application, but with a 19-year gap on his resume, he never even got as far as an interview. The agency hired someone with a college degree.[4] The rejection hurt, but as he told my former editor, Les Gura, in a 2008 interview with the *Winston-Salem Journal*, it focused his attention on the larger problem of reentry. "So I know if they treated me like this, I could imagine what they treated others who were less fortunate than myself. And so that made me look into studying reentry problems."[5]

Hunt's interest in the carceral state put him at odds with some of the people advising him, who wanted him to focus on wrongful conviction. His advocacy for those incarcerated began in prison, when he had served as prayer leader for other Muslim men, organized petition drives, coached others on their legal rights, and taught men like himself, who had come to prison barely literate, to read. These experiences told him that reentry work was where he was most needed. Hunt never thought that his plight as an innocent man serving time for someone else's crime set him apart from the other men locked up with him. Prison was damaging all of them. As he had written at the beginning of his ordeal: "Each person here is a human being and deserves to be treated like one."[6]

More than 600,000 men and women are released each year from prisons around the country.[7] More than two-thirds are arrested and imprisoned again within three years.[8] What's more, in any given year a total of 4.5 million men and women sentenced for crimes are back in society, under supervision from a parole or probation officer,[9] at risk of returning to prison at any time. North Carolina releases 20,000 incarcerated individuals a year, with 77,000 under supervised probation or parole.[10] For each of the 2.3 million persons still imprisoned across the country, there is a child, a parent, a spouse, and in some cases entire communities also punished by the absence.

The burden of a record of imprisonment falls most heavily on Black communities. It's estimated that one in three Black men in America will spend time in jail or prison at some point in his life, compared to one in 17 white men.[11] Yet the approach to this often-hidden crisis is fragmented. The federal government pays for some programs, state governments for others. Local nonprofit groups, like the one Hunt founded, try to fill in the gaps. Most of the effort is aimed at necessities such as job training and finding housing, maybe some basic education or addiction treatment. But there is never enough money, or even a clear picture of exactly how much, or how little, is spent. For example, in 2020, the US Department of Justice spent $92 million[12] on grants to organizations working on reentry out of a total federal budget for spending on justice of $29 billion.[13] That comes to 0.3 percent of federal spending on criminal justice for reentry. Combining federal, state, and local spending on prisons and jails, we spend $80 billion a year on punishment[14] but next to nothing on recovery.

The odds against the men and women Hunt wanted to help are high, some would say insurmountable. In addition to a struggle for the basics required for survival—food, housing, and medical care—people coming home from prison face structural obstacles to their reentry. Critics of the carceral state, most notably Marie Gottschalk, author of the 2015 book *Caught: The Prison State and the Lockdown of American Politics*,[15] argue that a prison record amounts to a "civil death" for those with criminal records, what she calls a "purgatory" that "remains largely invisible." In many states, those with prison records are banned from public housing, food stamps, veterans' benefits, even pensions. The American Bar Association Criminal Justice Section counts 45,000 laws and regulations across 50 states that dictate the lives of people with criminal records, including where they may live, with whom they may associate, and the kinds of jobs they may hold.[16] They can't apply for student loans for college, licensure for any number of professions, or disability benefits. In spite of a 15-year-long effort to "ban the box," a reference to the box job applicants check to indicate whether they have a criminal record,[17] computerized databases make it easy for employers to check an applicant's record, and many still won't hire someone who has been convicted of a felony. People with criminal records are also stripped of their political voice, in most states losing the right to vote until the completion of their parole. In some states those with a felony record are disenfranchised forever.[18]

Still, Hunt dreamed big, imagining that his project would someday open a construction company to provide jobs for people coming home from prison and revenue to sustain itself.[19] It seemed to those working with him that what he really cared about was something far less tangible than food, shelter, and a job; it was restoring dignity to men and women whose spirits had been broken by a brutal system. Hunt well understood that the task he had set for himself was all but unachievable. As he told Gura in 2008:

> You got almost 100 people a month coming back to Winston
> from prison. So you try to do what you can, and a lot of it is just
> encouragement. You try to encourage people not to give up.[20]

Hunt's reentry project had a board and at times a staff of four, but the work revolved around Hunt, and in spite of grants, including a donation from the filmmakers of *The Trials of Darryl Hunt*,[21] much of the money used to run the project came from his settlement.[22] He was always well dressed in the office, in slacks, a matching shirt, and matching shoes. He told people there that after 19 years in prison-issued browns, he'd forgotten how to coordinate his clothing, so he bought outfits in different colors and stored them that way in his closet so that he would always look sharp.[23] The office, however, was a mess. The project's first director, a counselor named David Harold, would find sticky notes all over with phone messages and ideas Hunt had jotted down and forgotten about.[24]

Often it was Hunt who found jobs for clients, asking around in person at fast-food joints and a local cafeteria chain called K&W. Then he'd check on clients himself, knowing that there was so much more to their struggle than a job. As he told Gura:

> We have people at K&W, and I go eat, just to check on them. And they know I'm coming. Because it's easy to get a job and then everybody say, "OK, you OK," but that's not all of it. They have other issues. They gonna be behind from the beginning, so they trying to figure out how to catch up and we try to encourage them not to take it too fast. Just one step at a time.[25]

In the same interview, after Gura asked him what he was most proud of about the project's work, Hunt spoke of the satisfaction he took in the success of those he helped. His answer was personal, the story of a man he'd placed at a fried-chicken joint not far from Hunt's home.

> Lymon Sykes. Sixty-eight years old, first time he ever voted. The proudest moment was just seeing him, getting him a job, being able to check on him every day and know that he's doing great. He's at work every day, he's there early. Even when the doctor told him that he needed to quit because of his back. First job he ever held in his life. And he's proud of it.[26]

Many others coming home found stability with Hunt's help. Two sociologists at Wake Forest University, Angela Hattery and Earl Smith, spent the summer of 2008 interviewing clients at the project. They found that Hunt's mentoring, the individual attention he gave his clients, provided a form of "social capital" lacking in other reentry programs. Hattery and Smith published their findings in *Prisoner Reentry and Social Capital*.[27] The book tells stories of men returning from prison to battle drug addiction and homelessness and of one woman who gave birth while imprisoned, shackled to a hospital bed. The researchers found that in spite of the odds, Hunt's program helped many stay out of prison. They cite a remarkable statistic. Over three years, only 10 percent of Hunt's clients returned to prison, compared to a national recidivism rate of about 70 percent.

Early on, Hunt referred clients to a local body shop run by David Moore,[28] another man with a prison record who had made it his life's mission to teach auto-body work to people coming home from prison. Before his conviction on a drug charge, Moore had run a body shop that specialized in tricked-out cars and trucks. In prison, younger men recognized him from his TV ads and sought him out for advice on life after prison, knowing that prison would mark them for life. When Moore got out in 2004,[29] he opened his shop again, this time with the purpose of teaching formerly incarcerated men a trade so they could turn the entrepreneurial drive they brought to drug dealing into a legitimate business.[30]

Moore remembered Hunt from Piedmont Correctional Institution as an imposing figure who would come through the cafeteria with an entourage of Muslim men—one on either side, one behind him, one in front—each one looking as though they spent their free time lifting weights. "There's Darryl Hunt with his bodyguards," another man told Moore that day.

Hunt's approach to meeting the emotional needs of those formerly imprisoned made sense to Moore, but he worried that Hunt had too soft a touch. In prison, men pledge to help each other out when they get home. Moore will give $20 or $50 to men he runs into around town whom he knew on the inside. Hunt would give away $500. And he was equally generous with the clients he referred to Moore's shop. When it came time to paint their cars, Hunt took every one of them shopping, so that they could choose a color scheme for themselves.[31]

In 2007, Hunt made a pilgrimage to Mecca, with his wife and his in-laws. By then, *The Trials of Darryl Hunt* was in wide circulation on HBO and regularly winning awards at film festivals, securing Hunt's fame. After that, he traveled widely, almost always for his advocacy work, as far away as Los Angeles and Ireland. As his fame grew, so did demands on his time. In North Carolina, advocacy organizations used his case to lobby for reform. Hunt's story demonstrated clearly the risk of bias in eyewitness identification and led many police departments to change the way they conduct photo lineups. In Hunt's case, for example, department procedure permitted Jim Daulton, the lead investigator, to show witnesses the photo lineup. The reformed procedures require that an investigator with no knowledge of the suspects in a case administer the lineup to prevent any chance that police would influence, either intentionally or subconsciously, the selection witnesses make. Advocates also used Hunt's case to push for reforms in the way police interrogate suspects and to press for legislation for open discovery in all felony cases. Finally, Hunt's case and other innocence cases like his led to the creation in 2006 of the North Carolina Innocence Inquiry Commission, the only legal body in the country that hears and rules on claims of innocence.

Despite all of the acclaim, Hunt seemed most at home at the reentry project, hanging out with men and women who'd spent time in prison like he had. He didn't talk much about prison with his staff, but they could sense that all those long, lonely days had left their scars. Dale McCants, the client coordinator, came to the project after a career in nonprofit work. She and Hunt fell into an easy routine.

After lunch, he'd bring her a cookie from the coffee shop in the building's lobby. At the end of the day, he'd settle into the extra chair in her office, put his feet on her desk, and talk. He would joke that he was still trying to learn how to be a grown-up. Sometimes they'd simply review the day; other times he'd talk about the pressures he felt from all the different people in his life, from his wife at home to the advocates who wanted him as the face of injustice. McCants had come to see that some people coming home from prison struggled more than others with reentry. Hunt, she felt, was one of them. "He was so young and naïve when he went in," she said.[32]

In 2010, Hunt took a part-time job with the North Carolina chapter of the NAACP to lobby for the Racial Justice Act, which gave those on death row a chance to appeal a death sentence based on racial bias in their case. In that role, he traveled around the state, testifying before legislative committees and speaking to legal groups and civic organizations. One of the act's advocates was the Coalition for Alternatives to the Death Penalty. Its director, Tarrah Callahan, saw how the story Hunt told of his near miss with death row moved people in ways her own advocacy never could.[33] She also saw that he was in desperate need of health insurance.

By then, the reentry project had stopped paying him a salary or benefits for lack of money. His part-time work with the NAACP didn't come with benefits, either. Callahan made it a mission to find a way to get him the benefits she felt he deserved. In 2011, she secured a grant for him to work with the coalition full-time, with full health benefits. Some days, Hunt would make the hour drive from Winston-Salem to the coalition's office in Durham, showing up with coffee and a slice of cake. On days he worked from home, he and Callahan would spend hours on the phone, Callahan at her desk and Hunt driving around Winston-Salem, at the wheel of his Infiniti, or at home, talking through a Bluetooth head set.

"T, have you eaten lunch yet?" he would ask.

"No, I'm too busy."

"Go get you some lunch."

Theirs was an unexpected friendship, a fast-talking 28-year-old college grad and a soft-spoken man who had spent his adult life in prison. Some days they'd talk shop, reviewing Hunt's speaking schedule and strategizing over ways to keep the North Carolina legislature, now controlled by Republicans, from repealing the Racial Justice Act. At times, the conversation turned personal. Hunt confided in her about marital trouble at home and a host of girlfriends on the side. And she confided in Hunt, who matched her up with Rabil. When the stress of running a coalition made up of more than a dozen organizations overwhelmed Callahan, it was Hunt who comforted her with a nickname he had given her, the Arabic word for Moses.

"Breathe with me, Musa,"[34] he would say.

They didn't talk much about prison, but Callahan could sense his hidden trauma. If someone wanted to take Hunt to dinner after an event, Callahan made sure the restaurant could seat him at a table with his back to the wall, part of the hypervigilance left over from prison. He preferred it when Callahan came along, especially to fancy places, so she could interpret the menu for him. She could see that speaking gave him purpose. At the same time, repeating a story that had nearly claimed his life took a toll, as though Hunt owed the world his tale of anguish. They called it the "monkey-in-a-cage syndrome." She did her best to build in breaks between speaking engagements to give him a chance to recover. Still, there were weeks when Hunt would disappear for two or three days without calling. Then Callahan's phone would ring and "D" was back. They called these absences his "walkabouts."

Sometimes, their phone conversations lasted all day, with long silences while Callahan worked and Hunt sat in his backyard taking in the scene. There were two gray cats roaming the neighborhood, but one always stayed close by, pestering him for attention. Hunt liked to watch the deer that wandered through the patch of woods behind his house. One day, Callahan was lost in work when Hunt broke the silence.

"I need to get my chain saw."

"What the hell do you need a chain saw for?"

"For the deer. So I can cut down a tree and see them better."

Hunt let out a big belly laugh, imagining the headline.

"Yeah, exoneree goes cuckoo."[35]

~

After the documentary's release, Hunt decided he wanted to tell his own story, in his own words. He had his prison journals, but he hadn't written enough for a book. To fill in the holes, he started dictating his life story into an audio recorder.[36] Student interns at the reentry project transcribed the recordings and typed his handwritten journals.[37] Eventually, Hunt hired a local publishing company to finish the book. I was unable to locate the original journals or the audio files, but I did find a digital version of the transcriptions, now part of an archive of his papers at Wake Forest University School of Law. The manuscript fills more than 300 pages, with details drawn from his uncanny memory, which had impressed his lawyers way back in 1984. Whoever transcribed his words left his uneven grammar and added blanks where they were unable to decipher his handwriting. I was never able to discern with certainty which sections came from written journals and which were transcripts of audio recordings, or even whether the publisher he hired had edited his words.

Beginning with his birth in February 1965, the manuscript recounts stories of random relatives who came to his grandfather's house on Maryland Avenue, his mother's murder, the deaths of his grandparents, details about the various women he shacked up with during his teenage years, and his day-to-day rambles from one liquor house to another. He goes on to recount his arrest, each of his trials, and each of the defeats many times over, unable, it seems, to forget any of the painful details. What struck me most is that unlike the calm demeanor of his public statements, Hunt's anger over this genealogy of loss is raw.[38]

The unpublished manuscript ends abruptly with what appears to be a series of journal entries from the last day of May and the first of June 2002, more than a year before his release. April and her children had just left after one of their regular prison visits, and now that they were gone, the pain of his imprisonment and his helpless, lonely state enraged him.

> This is what truly pisses me off that I'm locked up away from those I love and need and who love and need me. All week I've been steaming about this when they ask me when am I coming home, I don't have an answer for it, other than, Insha-Allah soon E.J. and Jamal. I made paper footballs for them and we played until Mu'mina took them.

> So they went to playing spend the corn. When the visit was over, I felt truly weak inside after getting back to the block, I laid on my bunk replaying the whole visit I fell asleep thinking about the visit.

The last entry, dated June 1, trails off mid-sentence.

> 6-1-02, called this morning and spoke with Mu'mina. the first time I called she wasn't there, she had gone walking which was good, I admit, I was hot at first, I've been . . .[39]

Hunt showed the manuscript to friends, who told him it was disjointed and too revealing of the sexual exploits of his youth, so much so that rather than give voice to his life, it would damage his reputation. In short, they said it was unpublishable. At the end of 2011, Hunt broke off his agreement with the publisher, saying that the book did not turn out as expected. "I must end this project now," he wrote by email.[40] However, the idea of a book remained appealing to Hunt. He asked his wife to write their love story.[41] Later, he talked with Rabil and Little about writing a joint memoir, but that, too, never materialized,[42] which left his life story to others to tell.

~

In September 2011, Hunt drove with Callahan and other activists to Georgia to protest the scheduled execution of Troy Anthony Davis, a 42-year-old Black man who'd been convicted in the 1989 killing of a white off-duty police officer in Savannah. In spite of evidence of innocence and support from such public figures as former President Jimmy Carter, Davis had lost all his appeals, and the execution date was set for September 21.[43] The drive took them deep into rural Georgia. They sang old protest songs, reminding Callahan of a scene from the civil rights era—a lone white woman traveling with Black activists, in this case someone from Hunt's reentry project, another exoneree named Joseph Abbitt, a law student from Wake Forest University, and two students from Winston-Salem State University. They cracked dark jokes to make the six-hour van ride and the horror of what was to come more bearable. If they had to stop for directions, it was Callahan who got out of the car.[44]

Georgia executes people at the Georgia Diagnostic and Classification State Prison, a name that must have been chosen to conceal its true mission, in the town of Jackson, 50 miles south of Atlanta. They arrived well into a steamy afternoon. About 500 protesters lined one side of Prison Boulevard, with two rows of police in riot gear at the prison gate. Police helicopters flew overhead. Anyone who stepped onto the asphalt was arrested.[45] Callahan kept an eye on Hunt all afternoon as he wiped perspiration from his face. She worried about his health and the way he carried Davis' coming execution so close to his heart. They stood there all afternoon and into the night, with the officers taunting them for defending a "cop killer." Hunt kept

as far as he could from the asphalt. At about 7 p.m., the scheduled
time for the execution, news came that the Supreme Court was
leaning toward halting the execution. Hunt picked Callahan up
in his arms, all 117 pounds of her, and swung her in a circle. She'd
never seen him so happy.[46]

They piled into the van to get the students back to North Carolina in time for class the next day and drove off into the darkness.
They were gone from Prison Boulevard less than an hour when
Hunt's phone rang. The Supreme Court had only been stalling and
had now refused a stay, meaning the execution would happen. There
was no sense in turning the van around. Davis would be dead before
they got there. Soon, Hunt's phone lit up with calls from reporters
asking for comment. Hunt took every one of their calls, but otherwise was silent. Callahan wished the reporters had the decency to
leave him alone, to realize the weight he bore at the execution of a
Black man who Hunt believed had been wrongly convicted, as he'd
been, and whose death might have been his but for two holdout
jurors at his original trial.

Hearings on the first set of appeals under the Racial Justice
Act came the following year, in April 2012, from four defendants
in Fayetteville, home of the Fort Bragg military base. The presiding
judge was Gregory Weeks, one of a handful of Black judges in the
state, a distinction that only added to the pressure he came under.[47]
The legislature had already tried to repeal the Racial Justice Act, but
Republicans lacked the votes to overturn a veto by the governor, so
for now the act remained in effect. The defendants weren't claim-
ing innocence, but they were arguing that their death sentences
were tainted by racial bias. One of the cases in particular animated
the opposition. It involved the 2001 murder of a police officer. The
thought of driving to Fayetteville, where police were undoubtedly
on edge, frightened Hunt, but he wanted to be there in support of
the cause. With Callahan at the wheel, they drove to Fayetteville
almost every day for the duration of the trial. There was no formal

role for them. They simply sat and watched. Weeks ruled in favor of the four defendants, commuting their death sentences, and he would later say that Hunt's presence gave him courage.[48]

In May 2012, Duke University gave Hunt an honorary doctorate in recognition of his work for social justice. A picture from that day shows Hunt beaming with pride. It was extraordinary that he, a man who'd quit school and aspired, at most, to a job with the city streets department, now had a doctorate from one of the country's most prestigious universities.

In spite of his dedication to his work and his many accomplishments, Hunt was becoming less reliable. His erratic behavior worried Callahan. He begged off speaking engagements or simply failed to show up. His "walkabouts" grew longer. Callahan figured he simply needed some time to himself.

Chapter Eighteen

The Golden Egg

Ayyub Rasheed and Darryl Hunt understood each other in ways that people who have never been locked up could not. They first met in the late 1970s in the liquor houses that lined Patterson Avenue. Hunt would have been 13 or 14 but already knew his way around the city's rough sections. Rasheed, seven years older, could say the same for prison, having been convicted at 18 of breaking and entering.[1] Like Hunt, he spent his first months at Polk, the overcrowded processing center for men under the age of 21 that was known for violence and rape. In spite of that, Rasheed found camaraderie at Polk among hundreds of other young men looking for a card game or some pick-up ball. Hunt and Rasheed reconnected in 1993 in the Forsyth County Jail, where Hunt was waiting for hearings on the hidden evidence in his case and Rasheed was awaiting trial on a charge of rape.[2]

They had much in common. Rasheed had also been raised by grandparents, having lost his mother in infancy, and now he was fighting what he saw as a frame-up in a rape case, which, given his long criminal record, he had little chance of winning. By then, they had both converted to Islam and were preoccupied with the law and Black liberation. Hunt introduced Rasheed to popular fiction by authors such as John Grisham and James Patterson, lighter

than law books but still a good way to learn about the law. They
also read weightier stuff, such as books by the political activist and
Black Panther leader Eldridge Cleaver and the lawyer and activist
William Kunstler. With one other man on the cell block, Thomas
Michael Larry, who was awaiting trial in the murder of an off-duty
police officer, they established order, with morning calisthenics, filling trash bags with water for weights, and afternoon quiet time for
reading and study. Rasheed and Hunt would talk about Rasheed's
rape charge, one that Rasheed denied. Hunt urged him to go to trial
and fight for his innocence. Rasheed's lawyer advised him to plead
guilty because his long criminal record meant he had little chance at
trial. Rasheed took his lawyer's advice, which he now regrets. Once
they left the local jail, he and Hunt were never assigned to the same
prison camp, but they kept in touch. The week of Hunt's release in
2003, Rasheed wrote him from prison. With two years left on his
sentence, he was struggling to keep his faith and his heart free of
bitterness.

> I wrote to the imam a few times asking about you but I don't
> know if he got the letters or not. I know that I let you and the
> brotherhood down for accepting a plea deal. Praise be to Allah
> that it's about over.[3]

When Rasheed was released in 2005, he looked Hunt up at
the reentry project and they fell back into an easy friendship. Hunt
loaned him money to buy equipment to start a cleaning business.
Later, he gave Rasheed the keys to his truck and never took them
back. They saw each other at the mosque for prayer. Often, they'd
simply drive around town, with Hunt smoking Newports and drinking a Pepsi, old friends "chopping it up." During these easy days
together, Hunt always made a point of stopping at an ATM, even
if he didn't need cash. Without having to ask, Rasheed understood
the routine. The memory of prison still dictated Hunt's life, as it does

Rasheed's, to this day. At night, Rasheed sleeps with the lights on. He keeps a security camera monitoring his front door, partly against intruders but mostly for an alibi, should he need it. Likewise, Hunt wanted the receipt and the video record of where he'd been that day, just in case he ever needed proof.[4] He wasn't about to be sent away again for lack of an alibi.

Rasheed told me of their friendship during a series of interviews that began in 2016 and resumed in 2019. We first met at the mosque he attended, wary of each other. Later, he introduced me to some of Hunt's other friends and the easy camaraderie Hunt shared with them. We'd eat lunch and I would listen to the men tell stories about their teenage years, of neighborhoods like the 11th Street Bottoms and of the old county jail, where Miss Atwater ran the kitchen and made the best apple crisp, and the way Hunt, when he was back in jail in 1993 and 1994, would sit on his cell bunk in boxer shorts and a T-shirt, case files spread around him, drinking warm Pepsis, smoking, in those days Kools, and doling out legal advice.[5]

"You feel me?" Rasheed would ask, to make sure I was following the conversation. Most of it I did, especially their fierce love for Hunt.

One of the friends I met was Anthony Wright, born in 1965, like Hunt. He had been in and out of prison since he was 15 and now was working at a steakhouse as a cook. Like Rasheed, he reconnected with Hunt in the county jail in 1993, when Hunt was there for court hearings and Wright was coming down from a crack high. After Wright slept for two nights and three days, Hunt offered him a copy of a favorite book by Grisham, *A Time to Kill*.

"I don't know how to read," Wright told him.

Hunt gave him a legal pad and a pen and told him to write down every word he didn't recognize. The next day, they went over each of the words on Wright's list, beginning with "answer," the first word he had written down. Hunt gave Wright a second pad and instructed him to write the words over and over again until he could recognize and read each of them. This was the laborious method Hunt had used to teach himself to read the books that Little, Rabil, and Griggs gave him when he was first locked up.

By the mid-1990s, Wright was making enough money selling crack from his "trap house" in the Piedmont Circle public housing project that he could afford to spend thousands on a tricked-out Ford Bronco, whose paint changed from purple to gray to black. Every once in a while, he would take his customers in a rented van to a city park at dusk. Wright would stand at a distance as the lookout, watching their crack pipes light up the darkening sky "like fireflies."[6]

When Wright was released from federal prison in 2008, Hunt brought him to the house on Reynolds Forest Drive for dinner. April was cooking lamb stew and gave Wright a taste. She is a good cook and so is Wright. "It needs a little bit of salt," he said. She laughed and so did we, a laughter that helped me understand the spirit of this part of Hunt's life spent talking trash with friends.

One chilly Sunday afternoon in March 2020, just as the pandemic began and drove us outside, we met at a park in the area that had been the Black business district of their youth, now dubbed the Innovation Quarter for its research space, breweries, and high-end lofts. Wright brought some photos he had found of Hunt that he wanted me to see. In one, taken shortly after Hunt's release from prison, Hunt is seated on the bottom level of a bunk bed with Rasheed's two stepdaughters, a bright pink comforter hanging over their heads from the top bunk, all three of them grinning. The photo was sent to Wright, then serving time in federal prison, and he has kept it close since then.

"Look how handsome he is," Wright said. "I can't see this. I'm about to cry."[7]

Wright grew up just east of where we sat, in the 11th Street Bottoms, the Black neighborhood people living in the city in the 1970s and early 1980s knew to stay away from unless their shoes were tied tight and they were ready to run for it. Rasheed lived to the south, in the Happy Hill Gardens housing project, a two-mile walk from where we sat, less if he dared to take a shortcut through the graveyard. Just north of where we sat was Hunt's part of town, the stretch of Patterson Avenue where he had felt most at home.

All that was 35 years ago, a world away from where we now sat, yet present in the laughter and tenderness of the moment. Rasheed jumped up from the chair, pulled his shoulders back to demonstrate the pose Hunt struck as a teenager, his eyes squinted, a faint smile on his face, quiet as always, and, as Rasheed said, "high as a Georgia pine, with a cup of liquor in his hand."

Prison separated them for more than a decade, but once Rasheed and Hunt reconnected in 2005, their friendship resumed and with it a dark sense of humor. One afternoon, after Hunt received his settlement from the city, they were riding around town in Hunt's Infiniti, when he told Rasheed about one of the many women who were hitting on him. Rasheed had a theory about the attention his friend received from women. Hunt had gone to prison a bow-legged teenager and emerged a broad-chested man with the aura of a celebrity and a quiet dignity women found alluring. When word spread that he had settled with the city for more than $1.6 million, he became irresistible.

"You know what you are?" Rasheed said.

"Tell me."

"You're the goose that laid the golden egg."[8]

Wherever Hunt went, it seemed that someone wanted something from him. His work weighed on him—invitations to speak at screenings of the documentary, talks to give about his quest for justice, testimony to make about how he'd barely escaped death row. And privately, it seemed someone was always asking him for money or his time. Hunt didn't mind as much the requests from men he'd known in prison. But he hated it when he couldn't even run down the street for a quart of milk without someone from the old days asking him for a handout. In a 2008 interview, he put it this way:

You get the resentment that some people feel that, not that you didn't deserve it, but if you don't give it away, then you don't deserve it. It's a constant pull. It's hard because everybody assumes that you have this allotment of money that you got sitting in a bank account that you can just give away. And I'm pretty generous. I give a lot of money away, but at the same time I have a family, too, and so it sometimes makes it uncomfortable to make those kinds of decisions. When you say "no," it's like, "Well you got it, we know you got it," and I'm like, "No, I don't have it." That's the, if I can say one bad thing, that would be the one bad thing about having settled and having every dime of your money . . . everybody in town know exactly how much money you supposed to have.[9]

Once, he stopped at a gas station with a friend, who went inside to buy a snack. When Hunt went inside to pay for the gas, the clerk warned him that his friend had been bragging that he was getting as much of Hunt's money as he could.[10]

"You don't owe them nothing," Rasheed would tell Hunt.[11]

But the expectations and the betrayal ate at him.

~

Hunt gave hints of his private struggles soon after his exoneration. In 2006, he and Rabil were in Washington, DC, for a screening of the documentary, followed by a panel discussion. They were waiting in a hotel lounge, where the décor featured mid-century retro furniture, when Rabil noticed that Hunt had broken out into a sweat.

"Are you OK?" he asked.

Hunt's heart was racing, pounding in his chest. He hesitated before speaking.

"See that light over there?" Hunt asked.

In the distance, Rabil noticed a lime green light, one of many neon lights in the hotel décor, except that this one took Hunt back more than 20 years to the day he was first charged with murder. It was September 1984 all over again. He was in the basement of the courthouse outside the warrants office where police had locked him up in a holding pen, a cage, really, that had always reminded Rabil of what enslaved men might have been kept in at auction,[12] on full display for reporters who'd been invited over to witness the arrest.[13] Hunt had been a skinny kid then, wearing a black knit cap, rolled-up jeans, and white socks stretched over his calves,[14] with an impassive expression on his face that concealed his terror. He had focused his gaze on the vibrant green of one of the reporter's socks. He would use the same strategy of fixing his sight on some inanimate object each time a jury declared him guilty of murder, each time a judge refused to see the truth. Now the green light in the hotel lounge took him back to the moment his ordeal began. The flashback made his heart race. It was hard to breathe. He was not OK.

Hunt's panic attack is a classic symptom of post-traumatic stress disorder, for the body remembers what the mind tries to forget. If he was ever formally diagnosed, he never said. It shouldn't be surprising to anyone that years of wrongful imprisonment would leave those who suffer such injustice scarred, but the depth of these scars has only recently become a subject of research. That limited research suggests that post-traumatic stress disorder is widespread among men and women freed after a wrongful conviction. Virginia Lefever was exonerated in 2011 after 21 years in prison in Ohio for the murder of her estranged husband. After her release, she went back to school at South University for a master's degree in nursing. Wondering whether others suffered as she did from PTSD, she conducted a series of interviews for her capstone course. Her study has not been published, but she said that of her 249 subjects, all but one told her they believed that the wrongful conviction and the years in prison left them with PTSD. Their symptoms ranged from hypervigilance, nightmares, heart palpitations, and panic attacks to digestive disorders. Even the man in her study who denied having the illness told her that he triple-locked his doors and kept a golf club beside his bed, symptoms she chalks up to unrecognized PTSD. "Pretty much we've all sort of embraced it as part of being an exoneree," she observed.[15]

A published study by researchers Saundra Westervelt and Kim Cook of 17 men and one woman who had been wrongly sentenced to death reported a level of despair that surprised even the authors.[16] At first, their work focused on the trauma of wrongful imprisonment, what they had called the "sustained catastrophe," with the expectation shared by many who work on false conviction that exoneration opens a new and happier chapter. Instead, the trauma lived on, returning in their dreams, in their emotional distance from others, and in their broken relationships. The researchers coined a new phrase for what they were learning: continuing traumatic stress.[17] The traditional definition of PTSD, even of what's called "complex PTSD," does not account for the profound depression, paranoia, anxiety, and insomnia researchers were discovering, such exoneration, rather than marking the beginning of a new life, adds another layer of trauma.

Their interviews also revealed feelings of survivor's guilt, anger, and alienation. As Perry Cobb, who spent nearly ten years on death row in Illinois, told them:

> I can't say that my feelings were dead. I said that [they] had just fled . . . I didn't have no feelings. I didn't like. I didn't hate. I didn't dislike. I was just, I see you and that was it.[18]

Some of those they interviewed tried to face the trauma of their experiences head-on, through advocacy work, as Hunt had. Only half received compensation for their wrongful conviction. Many had trouble holding jobs and sharing intimacy, driving away the very people they loved and needed. Others found solace in drug and alcohol abuse. To the researchers, this seemed the least harmful of the options.[19]

Hunt rarely turned down an invitation to tell his story, which meant that his role as the face of injustice required him to relive the trauma of his ordeal as part of his job. To borrow language Westervelt and Cook came up with, his advocacy work added another layer to his continuing traumatic stress. His wife noticed the strain of these events. He never ate at receptions because he felt he had to speak to everyone.[20] If the audience members had been paying attention, they, too, would have noticed his anguish. Hunt rarely watched the entirety of *The Trials of Darryl Hunt*. Instead, he would creep into the theater toward the end, just in time to speak. He told friends that watching his case unfold on the screen, with the emotional tension the filmmakers so skillfully evoked, was simply too much for him to bear. As his friend Rasheed told me when we first met: "He was asking for help and none of you heard him."[21]

Perhaps it was prison that prepared Hunt for the double life he led after he was released. In prison, he learned to wear a mask to hide his fear, his frustration, and his despair. Now, he wore a public face as an eloquent champion for justice, while in private he waged a battle all too common among men and women wrongly imprisoned.

Within a year of his exoneration, April Hunt began to suspect a dark side to her husband's silence. Sometimes, he would simply stare off into space for hours at a time, or he would disappear without letting her know where he was going. At night, he had trouble sleeping, and even when he did sleep his dreams turned to nightmares. Islam as they understood it prohibits discussing nightmares; he never spoke of these terrors and she never asked. He spent hours holed up in his room. Some nights, he didn't come home. As April came to understand the pressure he was under, she was at a loss for what to do.

When Hunt was in prison, he would tell her that all he wanted was a simple life: a job, maybe with the city, like his grandfather had, a family, and a house where he could putter around. Sometimes, early after he won his freedom, he was able to live that life. He would throw on a pair of overalls and a straw hat, like his grandfather wore, and work in the yard, a dog at his heels.[22] But once he became a celebrity, that dream was gone. "I just felt like he had to put on this face and be this person that he was not," April recalled.[23]

One day, she found what she thought was powdered cocaine rolled up in plastic wrap among Hunt's tools in the basement. Rather than confront him, she moved it so that he would have to ask her where it was. When he did, he told her the cocaine was something to make him "numb." Then he left the house. That silence and reproach became their pattern. One day, a patient at the hospital clinic where she was working told her that people had seen Hunt coming out of drug houses. She began asking around to learn where he was buying drugs and followed him. Eventually, she told me, she'd catch him using powdered cocaine at home or popping pills, alone in his room. She didn't like it, but she couldn't stop it. Such deception is typical of addicts, and the betrayal she suffered was typical for their spouses. The tensions at home were terrible as the chasm between April and Hunt deepened. Finally, the stress created by Hunt's struggle was more than she could bear. Her life, too, was falling apart. "I was walking on eggshells and if I said something, he'd bust out the door again. I lost a part of myself and I still lost him."[24]

Rasheed knew of his friend's struggle with drugs, mostly opioids, but the code of the street requires loyalty, so he kept Hunt's secret. As he saw it, they'd been poor together, back in the day, two "cats roaming the streets." Now Hunt had money to do what he wished and needed a friend who would understand. Rasheed believes Hunt started abusing drugs in prison, maybe buying medicine from others incarcerated with him and probably relying on guards to bring in contraband. It was also easy to get Benadryl from prison infirmaries, even opioids for pain. Rasheed understood addiction, having beaten his own, and believed it would be futile to try to stop Hunt. Rather than talk about the pain Hunt was trying to numb, he made plans with Hunt built on dreams.

They would start a construction company together, an extension of Hunt's reentry project, hiring people coming home from prison to fix up run-down houses, then flipping them, and use the proceeds to invest in the company so that they could sustain the good work they wanted to do. They would also figure out a way to get Rasheed's criminal record cleared. At the very least, they would learn to play golf, something to keep them busy in old age.

Sometimes, they'd ride around town in silence. Rasheed would watch Hunt swallow pills, ten at a time, and chase them with a Pepsi. Hunt was terrified of being found out. They would trade cars so that Hunt wouldn't be recognized when he went out to buy drugs. Rasheed also booked motel rooms for his friend, because in addition to drugs, there were women. If Hunt asked, Rasheed would drive to drug houses for him and buy him opioids and whatever other pills he wanted. He still knew where to go from his days as a crack addict, and it was less risky for him to buy than for Hunt, whose celebrity status made him the subject of so much gossip. If Hunt wanted his help getting drugs, so be it. At least he could help keep Hunt safe. But it was clear to him that Hunt's addiction had consumed him. "It was like boom. A boiling pot. Like mixing ammonia and Clorox in the same bottle."[25]

In spite of Hunt's efforts to keep his drug use quiet, word did get out. Khalid Griggs first heard talk about Hunt's drug use from Muslim men incarcerated with Hunt when he was still in prison—rumors that still cannot be confirmed—but he never confronted Hunt directly. Instead, when Hunt was released, Griggs encouraged him to get counseling. Muslims with prison records who prayed at the mosque and others Griggs worked with in his prison outreach continued to warn him about Hunt's drug use, fearing if he were caught, the news could damage the reputation of the mosque. These men also understood how damaging it would be to Hunt's reputation and to his advocacy work if word got out that the poster child for wrongful conviction was strung out on pills.

When April confided in her stepfather that she had caught her husband with what she took to be cocaine, Griggs confronted Hunt. Hunt didn't deny it, but he also refused help.[26] Griggs confided in Rabil, hoping he and others would be able to intervene, but no one would believe him. When Rabil asked, Hunt denied any drug use. He also had a ready answer to explain why Griggs would spread false rumors. They had had a falling out, he told Rabil, because Hunt was not contributing as much money to the mosque as Griggs expected.[27] Addiction turns people of integrity into skilled liars. At the time, Rabil believed Hunt. It was easier for him to assume that Griggs was lying than to imagine that the man he so admired, in whom he had invested so much of himself, had succumbed to this all-too-human struggle.

Chapter Nineteen

Back in the Swamp

In September 2014, Hunt marked the 30th anniversary of his arrest with a walk through the Patterson Avenue neighborhood. He stopped at the very spot where he'd been picked up by police, where the red-brick apartments that Mattie Mitchell had lived in once stood. Much had changed about the neighborhood he had once thought of as home. The cigarette factories that had filled the air with the smell of sweet tobacco were now lofts and office space. Wake Forest University was renovating old factories for a downtown campus for its medical school. The liquor houses where Hunt had gone as a teenager searching for his mother's old crowd had been torn down years ago for urban renewal. The YMCA where he'd met Little on the basketball court, the cafés where his mother had taken him as a child, all gone. So was the convenience store where police had first questioned him about the 911 call by Johnny Gray, who gave his name as Sammy Mitchell and got this whole terrible thing started. Somehow, Lloyd Presbyterian Church, the rallying place for his supporters for so many years, had survived.

Hunt had accomplished a great deal since his release from prison. People often told him how much his voice mattered, that without him, North Carolina would never have created its Innocence Inquiry Commission. Executions would not have been put on hold by appeals under the Racial Justice Act. And police departments across the state wouldn't have changed the way they conduct inter-rogations or lineups. But there were still too many men in prison, Black men like him who'd been railroaded by a rigged system. It was time for another rally, this one in support of a Black man named Kalvin Smith, also from Winston-Salem, who was trying to prove his innocence in the near-fatal beating of a white woman.

Smith and Hunt had met in prison and, knowing what he knew about Winston-Salem detectives, Hunt found Smith's claim of innocence convincing. Like Hunt in the Sykes case, Smith had cooperated with police when they started questioning him in 1995 about the white woman who'd been badly beaten at a store in a busy shopping center. Under interrogation, he'd given a partial confession, as had a friend. But the holes in the case against him were obvious to anyone who looked closely. The Wrongful Conviction Clinic at Duke University had been working on Smith's appeal for 11 years.[1] I had written a series of stories that exposed the way police had ignored a viable white suspect to home in on Smith, using questionable tac-tics to secure his statement.[2] Detectives Byrom and Ferrelli, having documented the cover-up in Hunt's case, found similar problems in Smith's, and their findings were confirmed by a former assistant director of the FBI who was then working as a police consultant.[3] In spite of all that, Smith was still in prison.

Support for Smith was slow to build, but now the church was full of people calling for his release. Well practiced at projecting a public face, Hunt spoke with eloquence, exuding what seemed a quiet strength that hid the shambles of his private life. The Darryl Hunt Project for Freedom and Justice had all but shut down for lack of money. After years of breakups and reconciliations, he and April had split up for good this time, and he was living at Little's home until he found a place of his own. The grant supporting his job with the Coalition for Alternatives to the Death Penalty had run out, which meant that once again he was out of work and had no health insurance. Rabil, now teaching full-time at Wake Forest, was lobbying administrators in the law school and the college, where I was teaching, too, to bring Hunt on staff as a community liaison, formalizing the kind of work he did with law students and with my writing students.[4] That semester, for example, freshmen in my class were working with Hunt on a brochure about a legal clinic that helped people who'd been convicted of minor crimes clear their records. Their stories illustrated how even a misdemeanor criminal record lives forever, standing in the way of a job, an apartment, a regular life. By September, all that was needed for Hunt to be hired at Wake Forest was a final approval from the college dean.

The day after the rally, Hunt stopped by his old house on Reynolds Forest Drive. As their relationship was falling apart, April had struggled with the loss that went with her husband's drug abuse and now a broken marriage. She'd been hospitalized twice for psychiatric issues, and her grown children had moved home to help her. It's not clear what happened next. In April's version of the story, Hunt drove by, saw a strange car in the driveway, banged on the door in a jealous rage, and when she opened it, pushed her up against the wall in the entranceway. In Hunt's version, he came to the house to pick up a leaf blower so that he could clean up Little's yard. April was outside when he arrived and gave him permission to retrieve the key to the toolshed from the house, then followed him inside and attacked him in a fury. Hunt's glasses fell to the ground during the scuffle and his arm was scratched; there was no evidence that April was hurt. Whatever happened, the argument between them escalated until someone at the house called the police. Once again, Hunt was a wanted man facing the potential of jail.[5]

The moment would be difficult for anyone, but for Hunt to come so close to jail again was devastating. To borrow from the language of sociology, the sustained catastrophe that defined his life struck again. Back in fighting mode, Rabil met Hunt downtown. He hadn't worked 20 years to get Hunt freed for him to return to

jail on allegations Rabil could not believe. He and Hunt's divorce
attorney arranged for Hunt to speak with police officers outside
the department, where an officer took pictures of the scrapes on his
arm. The DA got involved and they agreed there were no grounds
for criminal charges, but by then April had gone ahead and filed
a civil action for a restraining order. A judge heard her complaint
that afternoon and continued the matter until the following week,
without even issuing a temporary order.

For most people, an allegation of domestic violence would remain
a private matter, but Hunt's life had long since ceased to be his own.
Three days later, the *Winston-Salem Journal* published a story with the
headline: "Darryl Hunt's Wife Files for Domestic Violence Restraining Order."[6] Newspapers and television stations all over the state
ran their own versions, focusing on the allegation without making it
clear that no one had yet confirmed it. The publicity shattered Hunt's
reputation. A restraining order was never granted against Hunt, but
the following month, as part of their divorce proceedings, Hunt and
April did agree to a mutual restraining order, meaning they could not
speak to each other or even contact one another.

There was more to the court record that the newspapers and
those who had Hunt's interest at heart missed. When April filed for
the restraining order, she asked the court to take away the handgun
he carried for protection. More than once, when they were still
together, she had seen him sitting in a chair, the gun beside him.
She didn't know whether he was paranoid or suicidal, but by then
she felt so alone that she had spoken to no one about these fears.
Now that she had the chance, she checked the box on the form that
said Hunt was suicidal, hoping that someone would pay attention
and help. "Darryl has talked about how worthless he is and should
die," she wrote. In other papers related to the divorce proceedings,
she also alleged that Hunt was using drugs.[7] If anyone noticed these
warnings, they didn't say, but it's clear that April understood her
husband in ways others did not. The allegations of domestic violence

were enough to contend with. Rabil put out a press release explaining Hunt's version of the facts, but the damage to his reputation could not be undone. I told Rabil I could no longer advocate with the dean's office on Hunt's behalf, and he put the idea of getting Hunt hired at Wake Forest on hold.

It was time for Hunt to get away from Winston-Salem. At the beginning of 2015, he moved to Atlanta, where he rented a split-level house on a wooded lot in a neighborhood where the suburbs give way to countryside, similar to the neighborhood around Reynolds Forest Drive. His friends at home hoped the change of scenery would help him recover from the disappointments at home.

Hunt's younger sister, Doris, lived in Atlanta. Hunt had started looking for her soon after his release from prison. He had always remembered her as a toddler who lived with him and his brother, Willie, at their grandparents' home on Maryland Avenue, until Doris' maternal grandmother claimed her and took her away. As a teenager, Hunt had tried to find her in Charlotte. Once he became famous, she had found him. Their reunion at Hunt's home in Winston-Salem, while he and April were still together, was a joyous one.[8] Now, Doris and her two children moved in with Hunt in Atlanta, an arrangement that his friends in Winston-Salem believed gave Hunt the family life he longed for.

It is difficult to piece together the details of his life in Atlanta. Doris declined to be interviewed, as did friends he made there. Hunt told friends in Winston-Salem that he liked the anonymity of life in a place where few people recognized him or knew his story. Pictures posted on Facebook from this period, taken at birthday parties and other celebrations, show a middle-aged man, always well dressed, surrounded by friends and relatives.

At some point during his year in Atlanta, Hunt began telling his friends in North Carolina that he had been diagnosed with cancer. He was vague on the details but said it was serious. He talked about treatments at Emory University Hospital. He mentioned surgery, maybe chemotherapy, and painkillers. Sometimes he sounded lethargic over the phone, but friends chalked it up to the treatments he was getting. In early spring, Rabil offered to go with him to the doctor, and drove the five hours to Atlanta for the appointment. They spent Sunday at Hunt's house and made plans to meet the following morning before the appointment. But when the time came, Hunt asked to meet instead at a Dunkin Donuts; he told Rabil he would see his doctor alone. On the drive back to Winston-Salem, Rabil's phone lit up with a text from Hunt, apologizing for being such a "punk." The word choice seemed strange to Rabil, but he was grateful for the apology. During that period, a woman Hunt was seeing from home, a childhood sweetheart, drove to Atlanta too, and got as far as the clinic waiting room with him, while he saw the doctor.[9] By the end of 2015, news of Hunt's illness had reached a wide circle of friends and supporters, who began plotting ways of getting him home so that they could better care for him.[10]

Hunt moved back to Winston-Salem at the end of 2015, thin and by all accounts gravely ill. He told people that things with his sister had not worked out as planned, another disappointment in his tangled family life. He kept his things at Little's house again but spent many nights with his childhood sweetheart. His old journals talk about that childhood romance fondly, how he and she rode bikes around the neighborhood, played basketball, and when no one was watching, messed around in the backyard. Now they talked of making a life together, somewhere out in the countryside, once his property distribution in his divorce from April was settled.

In spite of all that had come between them, Hunt and April were still seeing each other on the sly. That summer, they'd gone to Durham together for a conference. She worried the entire time they were together about his weight loss and the waves of pain that passed over his face. But he was determined, he told her, that he didn't want chemotherapy. One day that summer, during a visit he made back to North Carolina from Atlanta, they drove into the countryside, with the top down on Hunt's convertible, their favorite R&B singer, Kem, playing on the radio. A video April shot captures their easy camaraderie, Hunt in a red hat, April in oversized sunglasses that give her the glamorous air of a movie star.[11]

Even after the divorce was finalized at the end of 2015, he would stop by her house and she would wave from the door or the upstairs window. She showed me some of their email correspondence and text messages from that period, which reflect their ongoing connection. On January 5, less than a week after their divorce was final, her phone lit up with a text from Hunt:

I love you. I'm sorry things went wrong. You will always be my wife and soul mate. I'll call you tomorrow. Insha-allah. Infinity plus plus plus!!!!!

"Infinity plus plus plus" was a phrase they always used together. She replied the next day.

I love you too and I'm so sorry as well. I'll be here. Infinity plus plus plus!!!!

~

Back in 1990, when he was out on bond and awaiting trial, Hunt found a second home with the Burnette family. Gail Burnette, also Muslim, was active in his defense committee and worked at city hall for the Human Relations Commission. Her son, Anthony, was about Hunt's age and her daughters, then in elementary and middle school, adored him for his gentle manner and the noble cause he represented. He bought Jamika, one of her daughters, a pendant with the word "Allah" engraved in Arabic and taught her silly pranks that made her feel brave and grown-up.

"Does a fire burn twice?" Hunt would ask.

"No."[12]

Then he'd light a match, blow it out, and, when the tip had cooled down, touch it to her arm, where it burned that second time. It was a joke she taught her own children years later. Throughout Hunt's imprisonment, Gail Burnette had been a faithful letter writer and advocate. Over the course of his incarceration, she wrote to the state on his behalf, trying to get him moved to a prison closer to home and supporting his advocacy work with men incarcerated with him.[13] Now, early in 2016, the Burnettes needed Hunt. Anthony was battling lung cancer and Gail was home, taking care of her son and a house full of grandchildren. Hunt helped her with the children and stayed by Anthony's side during his rapid decline, up until his death on January 20.

Rasheed knew Hunt was back in town, but they only saw each other once during this period. He had heard that his friend had cancer, but when Hunt pulled up in front of his house, he was shocked to see him so thin. It seemed as though Hunt had simply crumbled. Hunt had never asked him for money, but now he did. He also pulled up his shirt to show Rasheed the scar from surgery, telling him it was related to his cancer, but wouldn't talk much about the illness. It was April he worried about. Hunt showed Rasheed where he kept the deed to the house on Reynolds Forest Drive, which he and April had once shared, hidden in the Infiniti. Rasheed promised that if Hunt died, he would make sure April found the deed.[14] After that, Hunt stopped returning his calls.

In spite of his poor health, Hunt resumed the advocacy work he'd let go when he was living in Atlanta. He spent his 51st birthday, February 24, 2016, in Washington, DC, for a conference sponsored by the US Department of Justice on the struggles that those wrongly convicted face after their release. Legal victories consumed so much time and effort that people in the innocence movement were just beginning to understand what Hunt knew so well, that release from prison didn't end the injustice of a wrongful conviction. Few in the justice system had taken the time to figure out how to help those wrongly convicted after exoneration—or to think about the impact of these miscarriages of justice on the victims of those crimes. The "listening session" was a start and a reunion, of sorts, for Hunt with other advocates he'd worked with from North Carolina. He knew the researchers from Greensboro and Wilmington who had studied life after exoneration for those released from death row. He also knew Jennifer Thompson. She was the woman who had mistakenly identified Ronald Cotton—whom Hunt met and spoke with after they were both released—as her rapist in 1984. She had served on the board of Hunt's reentry project and had just formed an organization called Healing Justice to figure out how to work with crime victims and those falsely imprisoned on their spiritual and psychological needs. The session in DC lasted two days, with men and women talking about struggles all too familiar to Hunt. Some were still fighting legal battles for compensation. In that way, Hunt had been fortunate. Others spoke of anxiety and despair and of relationships broken beyond repair. People who knew Hunt could tell he seemed sadder than usual, but they figured his cancer was troubling him. When it was his turn to speak, his words carried a plea. "When you're released, still nobody cares,"[15] he said.

~

Kalvin Smith's defense committee had also picked up steam. Smith was still incarcerated, after 19 years, at some of the same camps Hunt had endured, and some of Hunt's supporters had joined the campaign to free him. Smith's children, by now, were grown, and one son had had his own run-ins with the law. His father and mother still held out hope that he would be exonerated. But in Smith's case, there was no DNA evidence to test, only the flawed police work by some of the same detectives who had framed Hunt. Smith's supporters hoped that with Hunt back in town, he could provide some moral authority to move the state's attorney general to act on Smith's behalf. Just before his trip to DC, Hunt spoke at a rally for Smith at Winston-Salem State University. In a video posted on YouTube, the rally begins with Little firing up the crowd. Then Hunt takes the stage. The two men, Little in long dreadlocks and Hunt in a tweed jacket, embrace. For a moment, Hunt is overcome by emotion. When he finds his composure, he speaks of his incarceration—all 19 years, four months, and 19 days—and of Smith's quest for justice. "I know how it feels to go through getting turned down by the courts over and over again," he said, then repeated a favorite phrase: "The darkest hour is just before dawn."[16]

~

I last saw Hunt at the end of January 2016 on the Wake Forest campus, where I had invited him to speak with my students. His early-semester visit was the highlight of my composition course, a way for students to connect the issues of race and justice, which was the subject of the course, with a real person. Hunt played that role well. His warm smile and serene manner put them at ease. It was one thing for students to read about his nearly two-decades-long quest for justice, quite another to hear him speak about how he was arrested when he was their age, 19, a kid hoping only that someone would listen and believe him when he said he was innocent. We met outside the library and waited for Rabil to join us. I noticed that in spite of the cold, Hunt wasn't wearing a coat, and I could see he had lost weight since the last time I saw him. I had heard he had cancer but wasn't sure how or whether to bring it up.

"Welcome back," I said. "I'm sorry you've been sick, but you look good."

"Yeah. If I'm going to die, I might as well come home and be close to people I love."

Our exchange in the cold and the sun, awkward at the time, now seems prophetic.

Chapter Twenty

I Worried People

Hunt woke up the first day of March 2016, a Tuesday, at his girlfriend's house. She had already gone to work and left a plate of food for him and the remains of a sheet cake, decorated in red for his beloved San Francisco 49ers. He appreciated the gesture, but things weren't going well between them.[1] It was time for him to leave. The text he sent her, using his nickname for her, "Shorty," said as much.

"It seems as though I crowded you. I didn't mean to crowd you. I didn't finish the cake, but I liked looking at it. Thank you, Shorty."

Having lost his vehicles, the Infiniti and the truck, Hunt was driving Little's prized Ford F-150 with tinted windows. At 51, he was broke and homeless, just as he had been at 19. Later that day, he checked into the Baymont Inn, a transient but comfortable sort of place off the interstate on the northern edge of town. He had stayed there before, on trips home from Atlanta the previous year, and told friends that he liked the area precisely because it was so anonymous. The following day, he and Rabil confirmed travel plans for the annual meeting of the network of innocence projects, half legal conference and half coming-home ceremony for the newest group of exonerees. They wrote in the shorthand that friends use with one another, with Darryl signing off with the initial "D."

No hint of trouble there, just two friends making plans for a meeting they always attended together. These annual meetings serve two purposes, with sessions for lawyers on legal strategy and workshops for men and women like Hunt on the practical and emotional challenges of reentry. Hunt always made it a point to seek out those who had just come out of prison, knowing how hard reentry was going to be for them.

Hunt spent much of the next three days with the Burnettes, at their home in a cul-de-sac off University Parkway, the primary north-south route through town. Hunt told Gail Burnette several times over those first days of March that her home was a refuge. He sat on the couch in the front room and watched old Westerns, helped Burnette look after grandchildren, and talked. She was retired from the city by then, in declining health, and had the time. Hunt confided in her, private troubles Burnette would never betray, though she had no idea he was using drugs.[2] All he ever wanted was a family, an ordinary job, and some pets, but his life had become so much more complicated. It seemed to her that he suffered from the high expectations so many had of him, expectations that no one could meet.

When he left her house late Thursday, March 3, he hugged her in the doorway with such vigor she thought her back would break. Later, she would wonder if he knew that was the last time they would see each other.

~

The following day, March 4, Hunt checked out of the Baymont. It's hard to reconstruct what happened next because he stopped replying to texts and emails. He missed a court date, March 7, for a hearing on alimony. Still, he had disappeared before, for days at a time, and not until the middle of the week did his friends start looking for him in earnest.

Little stopped by Burnette's house several times, growing more and more frantic, telling her and her family stuff no one wanted to believe, that Hunt had gotten mixed up with drugs and prostitutes, and that Little was worried he was hurt somewhere. Hunt's girlfriend also was looking for him. She, too, had heard the rumors of his drug use and once even searched his arms for track marks, but Hunt had always chalked the rumors up to gossip. There was another reason she was now afraid. In February, when they had stopped at Little's for some of Hunt's clothes, she had found a pad covered with Hunt's writing that talked about him wanting to end his life.

"You want to commit suicide?" she had asked him then.

"That's just the way I felt at that time," he told her.

He insisted that he wrote on that notepad back in January, a day he remembered because it was the day his truck was repossessed. She asked for his word that he would not kill himself.

"Will you promise me?" she asked.

"I promise."

Thursday, with Hunt missing, his girlfriend remembered the pad they had left at Little's house and drove over to show Little. The pad with Hunt's note was still there. Little can recite its contents from memory.

> I hated to do it in your house, but I didn't have the money to
> get a hotel room. I don't want you to question yourself about
> anything you could have done to change this . . . Larry, don't hold
> this against April. She was there before any money.[3]

After reading the note, Little spent the night parked around the corner from Hunt's old house on Reynolds Forest Drive, hoping he would show up. He never did.

The next day, Friday the 11th, Little decided it was time to call the police, a move he hated to make because he feared that a police search would frighten Hunt. The missing person notice that went out to local media that night shows a photo of Hunt wearing a blue shirt and a light brown vest, his expression frozen in that same mysterious smile that so vexed investigators all those years ago. The notice read:

> Last known to be traveling in a white Ford F-150 pickup truck NC registration BDJ-9685.

That night, a police officer called Rabil to ask if he knew anything about Hunt using drugs. Rabil and Tarrah Callahan, who was in town for work, drove up to the north side of town together to the Baymont and the cluster of motels near the interstate, where they knew Hunt stayed sometimes to get away. Others checked out places where Hunt was rumored to buy drugs. On Saturday, Eversley, Mendez, and Little gathered in Eversley's office at Dellabrook Presbyterian Church and prayed. Late that night, Hunt's girlfriend pounded on the door to Rasheed's house, waking him. He and Hunt hadn't spoken in weeks. He told her he'd look for Hunt the next day, after morning prayers.[4]

April, who had last spoken with Hunt the previous week in a long, tearful conversation about the possibility of a reconciliation, sent the last of several desperate texts.

> I'm hoping that you are okay. I know Allah has something better for you baby. Just hold on a little longer. Let someone help you. I'm very worried about you and I love you so much. Always have and always will. Infinity plus plus.

There was no reply.

~

Little's nephew spotted his uncle's truck, lit up by street lights, from University Parkway just after midnight Sunday morning, the 13th of March. He turned into the parking lot at the College Plaza shopping center and, peering into the window, saw Hunt slumped in the driver's seat. Traffic had cleared by then from the coliseum across the street. Apart from Jimmy the Greek's, an all-night diner illuminated by a neon sign, the rest of the businesses—a rent-to-own furniture store, a pizza joint, a soul food restaurant—were closed up for the night. Little made it over from his house, five minutes away, before police arrived. Mendez and Eversley arrived soon after. Together, they watched with broken hearts as the police set up yellow tape to begin their investigation. There was nothing to be done for Hunt. Not now.

Hunt had dressed for cool weather, in long underwear, jeans, a long-sleeved shirt, a fleece jacket, brown boots, and a gray hat. He had $1.76 in his pocket and a notebook he used as a journal, with a final entry dated March 4, written from Pilot Mountain. The state park, with its rocky knob, would have been a refuge for him, drawn as he was to open spaces, city parks, and long drives. The drive back to Winston-Salem would have taken him about 45 minutes. Where he went next or whether he went directly to the College Plaza shopping center is unknown. He carried his .38-caliber revolver for protection. When he parked, in a space easily visible from the road, he left the ignition on but locked the doors and placed the journal on the seat beside him.

The medical examiner on call for the weekend, Dr. Anna McDonald, arrived at the scene about 5 a.m. on Sunday. She was never able to determine a time of death because the body already had begun to decompose, but it was clear that Hunt had been dead long before the police ever put out the missing person notice. The cause of death was clear too—a gunshot wound to the abdomen.

News of Hunt's death spread quickly. That evening, dozens gathered for an impromptu memorial in the sanctuary at Emmanuel Baptist Church, where many of the same people had celebrated his release in 2003, and where one of his early supporters, John Mendez, was pastor. I knew most of them, the lawyers who had worked his case, students whose lives he changed when they heard him speak, activists who worked with him to lobby for reforms. A neighbor spoke about how much Hunt had loved animals. A former client of the nonprofit Hunt set up to help with reentry told us that "Darryl Hunt saved my life." I told the stories he had shared with my class, stories that now seemed steeped with meaning. Some of us wept. "Once you're hooked by Darryl you can't be unhooked by Darryl," said Rabil. "It's this strength, it's this courage that you just can't let go."

Eversley struggled to compose himself. "I didn't know if I could do this, after last night," he said. He spoke about the trauma Hunt had suffered in prison and how he had kept it hidden. "That was Darryl's struggle," he said. "We saw Darryl on the outside, but a lot of us did not see Darryl on the inside."[5]

The formal memorial service the following Saturday, also at Emmanuel, lacked the intimacy of the earlier service. The sanctuary holds one thousand, and almost every seat was occupied. I recognized the people from Hunt's public life: Rabil and activists from around the state who worked with him after his release to lobby for criminal justice reforms; Khalid Griggs, the imam at the Community Mosque of Winston-Salem, where Hunt was a member; and the rest of the clergy who had led the rallies in his support. James Ferguson, the noted civil rights attorney who represented Hunt at his second trial, was there too. So were Judge Gregory Weeks, who presided over the first resentencing hearing under the Racial Justice Act; Superior Court Judge Andy Cromer, who exonerated Hunt in 2004; and Pam Peoples Joyner, a former director of the Darryl Hunt Project for Freedom and Justice and then a community liaison for the city police department.

The speakers cast Hunt as a martyr for social justice, with comparisons to Martin Luther King Jr., Gandhi, and Nelson Mandela. Eversley gave the prayer, Mendez a eulogy. Rev. William Barber, then the head of the state's NAACP and the Moral Monday Movement against North Carolina's Republican-led legislature, made a surprise appearance, delivering a second eulogy, later posted to YouTube, which hinted at Hunt's private life. "Too often our warriors can't even be human, even for a public second," Barber intoned. "The relief it might give to help, even this must die because very few, even those who look to them, can handle the truth that even our heroes get weak sometimes, so they have to smile when only crying makes sense."[6]

The oratory made the gathering feel more like a political rally than a memorial for Hunt the man. Little spoke about Hunt's legacy, in a rambling speech that brought people to their feet, with a speaking style cultivated from years spent stirring up the crowds at rallies. He showed a video, listed on the program as a "Message from Darryl Hunt." Most of it was scenes from Hunt's public life, combined with footage of the walk he made on the 30th anniversary of his arrest past landmarks from that period of his life.

But it was the opening scene that I found hard to forget. In it Hunt is seated in an ornate love seat, upholstered in white satin or brocade, looking directly at the camera. "If you see this," he says, in a voice that seemed flat and lifeless, "I am probably already dead."

The woman behind me gasped. "Jesus," she said.[7]

~

I hadn't intended to write about Hunt again. In fact, my friendship with Rabil and Hunt's work with my students meant that I had lost the distance expected of journalists. But it soon became clear to me that I had missed, even ignored, a story that demanded telling.

At first, I simply wanted to figure out what had happened. Where had Hunt been and when? Who had he talked with? And how had he died? I talked to clerks in the stores and restaurants in the College Plaza shopping center and tried to find surveillance tape that might tell how long Hunt had been slumped in the truck before anyone found him. I spent a lot of time tracking his final days, from his girlfriend's house to the motel by the interstate to the Burnettes' home and up to Pilot Mountain's rocky knob, a sacred place to Indigenous people and a beacon for early colonists.

Like many, I believed Hunt had cancer, and though taking his own life was a difficult decision, it would not be unfathomable given the physical deterioration I'd seen in Hunt myself. I knew of people with terminal cancer wanting to act on their own rather than waste completely away.

The rumors about drug use I heard as I began to investigate Hunt's death were new to me. I ordered the autopsy report and read it carefully, looking for clues about the cancer, as well as any evidence of drug abuse. What I found raised even more questions.

McDonald, the medical examiner, was new to town and didn't recognize Hunt's name, but a quick Google search provided her with the basic outline of his life story and why the police wanted to take such special care that they called her out of bed on a Sunday. Her preliminary report describes the scene:

> The decedent was found in a pickup truck with a .38 caliber revolver on his legs. The doors of the truck were locked and the ignition was still on, although the engine was not running. He'd been missing approximately 9 days prior to a missing person report had been put in place. He left a note with a friend and a journal entry (dated March 4, 2016 at 1:25 PM) was in the vehicle.

McDonald did not include Hunt's journal entry in her report, but investigators read the entry to Rabil and, according to notes he made of that conversation, Hunt wrote of the burden he feared he had become. He loved Little. His breakup with April was his fault. He feared going back to prison.

"I worried people," he had written. "Maybe they can rest easier."

The autopsy confirmed that the bullet had traveled from Hunt's abdomen through his heart and lungs to lodge in his left shoulder.[8]

He would have died in a matter of seconds, a comfort to those of us who had imagined a long, agonizing death. McDonald also found soot staining his undershirt, which suggested a contact wound and supported the ruling of suicide. There was no mention anywhere in the report of evidence of cancer, nor any firm evidence of drug use.

When I met McDonald that summer, I was struck by her combination of clinical detachment and warmth. Slides of tissue samples covered her office desk; enlarged photographs of her children hung haphazardly on the walls. She told me that she soon realized Hunt's death demanded more than a routine autopsy. A detective had told her that Hunt had been telling people he had cancer. If her autopsy was going to contradict what those who loved him understood about his final days, she would have to be certain.

She found no obvious signs of tumors in his prostate, stomach, or pancreas. She also took cross sections of tissue from the three areas, all types of cancer he had mentioned to others, as well as samples from other organs—lungs, kidneys, liver, heart, and brain—and sent them to a lab for analysis. Again, she found no evidence of cancer. She also ordered his medical records at Emory, in Atlanta, where Hunt told friends he'd been receiving cancer treatment. His record discussed surgery to repair a hernia, in May 2015, which explained the scar he had shown people, and follow-up care, but again, no mention of cancer. She found records from the medical center in Winston-Salem, where she works, which mentioned weight loss and fatigue. No cancer. Even the notes Hunt left said nothing about cancer.

She had heard the rumors about drug use and ordered a full toxicology screening. The state consented only to a blood alcohol test, which was negative, but declined to test for other drugs. With the cause of death clear, it was a waste of money to run more tests. She did find a bruise under the skin in the crook of his left elbow. This was consistent with intravenous drug use, but not conclusive. If Hunt had been abusing drugs, she could not confirm it.

At the end of March she ruled Hunt's death a suicide, a ruling that seemed unfathomable for a man who had faced so many adversities with so much grace and courage. What's more, the brutality of his death, a gunshot wound in the belly, seemed so at odds with the gentle strength he projected. The public knew Hunt as the triumphant hero who had conquered an implacable system of justice through determination and faith. But that story, one he told hundreds of times, concealed the dark, private struggle that he had lost.

Local news organizations reported on the ruling of his suicide but not on the findings about cancer. People who loved Hunt learned of those from me. The news that in all likelihood he was not suffering from cancer fell hard. Hunt, who had stood for truth and justice, had spent the previous year playing out an elaborate lie.

But why had he faked an illness? The facts surrounding Hunt's death didn't answer that question or the larger question of why, after all he had overcome, he could find no more reason for living. Suicide leaves these questions. It always does. But in Hunt's case, I came to see the explanation as larger than a single life. Rather, the answer lies in a confluence of forces Hunt could not escape: the legacy of slavery and Jim Crow, the false narrative of Black men as sexual predators, the violence and tenderness of his youth, the terror of a jail cell, the heartbreak of a false conviction, the long years lost to captivity, and the public pressures that came next, the full weight of which he bore until he could bear it no more.

There are many who simply do not believe that Hunt killed himself. They prefer a more conspiratorial explanation, that someone killed him, maybe over a drug deal gone bad or a robbery, and set the scene up as self-inflicted death, propping Hunt up in the truck, leaving the key in the ignition, and locking the door with the engine running. It's a more palatable ending for them than suicide, considered by some a coward's act. And Hunt was no coward. Suicide is especially hard for his Muslim brothers to fathom because it violates the word of God. Men in prison, past and present, also told me they refuse to believe that a man who had been a source of hope for so many, who had survived death threats, loneliness, and months in solitary, could not muster the strength to overcome whatever troubles he faced on the outside.

In the fall of 2019, I toured Caswell Correctional Institution, where Hunt had spent a miserable eight months early on in his incarceration. The place is better now than it had been in Hunt's day, the triple-decker bunks replaced by double bunks and more opportunities for job training. The cells for solitary, where Hunt had spent more than four months, were still there, all 16 of them, with their metal slots for meal trays, their locked showers, and a pen outside about the size of a dog run for a man's 45 minutes of daylight. At lunch time, guards lock the camp down to avoid a stampede to the chow hall. They close the commissary, too, which gave the prisoner who managed it when I visited an hour to himself, a refuge with the boxes of junk food and toiletries and a case full of sodas. This man was imprisoned for killing his wife's lover, with no chance of parole. He knew of Hunt, had even met him once, and like the others imprisoned there followed Hunt's exoneration and his rise as a champion for justice. Seen from inside prison, Hunt's was a success story, which made his suicide especially hard for the commissary manager to accept. As he said, "Coming from his experience, it seemed he had already been through the toughest of the tough. To go out and do that is unheard of. Why not do that while he's on the inside. He already had the toughest fight."

For Hunt, though, coming home was just as hard, maybe harder.

∽

The weekend Hunt's body was discovered, Hunt was expected at a retreat outside Chapel Hill, North Carolina, for men and women like him who had been damaged by wrongful conviction. Hunt had tried going to counseling, but not for long. This retreat would be different. The weekend of group therapy, art, and rituals had been organized by Jennifer Thompson to confront the spiritual and psychological pain caused by such injustice. She and Ronald Cotton, the man she'd wrongly identified as having raped her, had written a joint memoir, *Picking Cotton*, about the trauma each had suffered, he through ten years of his life lost in prison and she through the guilt over having made a mistake with such terrible consequences. The healing they both found in their friendship gave Thompson the idea of developing a program for exonerated men and women and crime victims to heal what she calls the "concentric circles of harm" and the broken places in the soul, none of which can be healed by a court order. Her work would be a form of restorative justice that the US criminal justice system has yet to take on.

Thompson recognized something else in Hunt, the added trauma of turning the telling of his story into his life work. With the success of her book, she, too, had fallen into the role of professional victim. Telling her story of rape was empowering and harmful all at once. She figured it must have been the same for Hunt. When she saw Hunt in February, at the listening session in Washington, he seemed exhausted. He had lost everything, he told her. His marriage was over. The allegations of domestic violence had destroyed his reputation. He was broke and broken. She thought the support of the retreat she was organizing might help him, and so she invited him to the one coming up in March. "I want to be there," he told her. "I need to be there."[9]

The retreat outside Chapel Hill began on a Friday. When Hunt didn't show, Thompson was hurt that he hadn't bothered to let her know he wasn't coming. There were other men like Hunt there, whose struggles would have been familiar to him. Thomas Haynesworth and Marvin Anderson came down from Virginia. They'd both been exonerated of rape by DNA evidence, after 27 and 20 years, respectively, in prison for the crimes of others. Thomas Webb flew in from Oklahoma. He had spent 13 years in prison for a sexual assault he hadn't committed.[10] After his exoneration, he battled depression and drug addiction until he was homeless and living in his car. The victims in those crimes came as well and shared their stories of trauma and of guilt over having identified the wrong man. The last day of the retreat, news came of Hunt's death. The participants managed an impromptu memorial, gathering in a circle to sing and pray. Someone spelled Hunt's initials out on the ground in wildflowers and broken branches,[11] a gesture toward something more hopeful than the terrible warning delivered by his death.

We are trained by news stories and our culture to see exonerations as stories of triumph. I saw Hunt's story that way for a long time. But it's clear to me now that this is a false narrative. Hunt knew this, but there were limits to what he could do to help himself or bring attention to his suffering. I imagine that knowledge added to his despair. When Henry McCollum and his half-brother, Leon Brown, were exonerated in 2014 after 30 years each in prison in North Carolina—among the longest wrongful incarcerations in the country—Hunt was there to celebrate. He soon made the hundred-mile trip to McCollum's home in Fayetteville to warn him, especially about the false friends who would come after his money once the state awarded him compensation.[12] Sure enough, unscrupulous investment advisors swindled McCollum and his half-brother out of much of their $750,000 payment from the state,[13] just as Hunt had predicted. Hunt once told Ronald Cotton that he "would never be right anymore."[14] He was speaking of himself, but the same is true for others. Cotton left prison in 1995, but the fear of returning remains a part of Cotton's daily life. He waves at security cameras in stores to establish an alibi should he need one, and 25 years after his release from prison, he still keeps receipts of most purchases stuffed in his vehicle's glove compartment, another record of his whereabouts. Anyone I have spoken with who has spent time in prison has a similar story about the fear of reincarceration and the despair and loss they feel even upon release.

On the second anniversary of Hunt's death, I drove up to Pilot Mountain, where I believe his final note was written. The parking lot covers a flat space near the top of the rocky knob. It was colder there than it was in town. And lonely. I looked over the edge to see if there would have been a place where Hunt might have considered suicide, but it looked to me as though trees and brush would break a fall.

In early April 2017, as I was finishing up a magazine piece, "The Last Days of Darryl Hunt," Little decided to show me the rest of a video he and Hunt had made, the one of Hunt speaking about his coming death that had so shocked mourners at his memorial service. "It was for public consumption," he told me. "I think I need to at least let you see that because Darryl wanted people to know how he felt about certain things."

We met at Little's house on Okalina, where Hunt had kept his things during his final weeks. I noticed the loveseat Hunt sat on in the video right away. Little had warned me that he still had no intention of talking about Hunt's last days, but I suspected we would talk, and we did, for nearly three hours. He talked about the beginnings of the Sykes case more than 30 years prior, his squabbles with others involved with Hunt's defense, and his disagreements with Hunt over Hunt's marriage and his personal life. It struck me, sitting in the house where Hunt had spent so much of his last year, how torn Hunt must have felt by these divided loyalties.

"That's a lot of pressure," I observed.

Little didn't disagree.

"He tried to please everybody. He's got to try to please me. He's got to please Mark. He tried to please April. He tried to be everything to everybody. I think it just tied him up in knots."

Little had heard from others I'd been interviewing that the autopsy showed no evidence of cancer, but he didn't believe it until I showed him the report and went over the medical examiner's explanation. We'd been speaking for more than an hour, and as the news that Hunt had not been suffering from cancer became clear, another plausible explanation for Hunt's weight loss emerged.

"If it's not that way, it's obvious he's using a lot of drugs," Little said.

Little told me that he and Hunt made the video in 2015, when Hunt told him he was dying of cancer. At the time, heart disease was making Little think about his own mortality and the legacy he would leave. The video opened the way I'd remembered from the memorial service. Hunt is seated, his back to the wood paneling in Little's living room. He is wearing a red tracksuit. A San Francisco 49ers cap, also red, lies beside him. But his tone is different from the way I had remembered, falsely cheerful, almost singsong.

"Good morning. Good afternoon. Good evening. If you're listening to this, I'm probably already dead."

Little told me a videographer had filmed more than an hour of footage about six months before Hunt's death and edited it down to 15 minutes to show at the memorial service. But after the edited version was done, Little decided against showing it because he was afraid mourners would be upset by seeing Hunt so thin and in so much pain. Hunt doesn't mention cancer in the video, at least in the segment I saw. He does talk about the people who meant most to him—his grandfather, who taught him to be truthful "even as he whupped my ass"; and three women who were active in his defense committee, women he called mother figures. He talks, too, of his desire to help people.

"I know what it feels like to be homeless. I know what it feels like to be hungry, not just for a day but for weeks."

That part seemed familiar from other public talks he'd given, but I was surprised to hear him speak about Little Bit, the prostitute he was involved with the summer of his arrest, who testified against him at his trial. He called that experience "the thing that hurt me the most," not because of what she did, but because of how he "disrespected her," a phrase I took to mean his role in her prostitution.

The forced cheer was gone, replaced by bitterness, especially about the way people treated him after he won his settlement from the city.

"The saddest part of my life is once I received money, I had people pretending to be my friends all over."

To hear Hunt's voice helped me understand the depth of his anguish during the final year of his life. Perhaps it was easier for him to create a false story about cancer than to tell the true one: that he was not superhuman, that he could not overcome the trauma he endured in prison or the injustice of spending all those years locked up for a crime he didn't commit; that the myth we built up around him as a man whose wounds had been healed by his own extraordinary grace and compassion, a story we needed because we all want to believe in the possibility of our own redemption, was founded on expectations for him that no one could have fulfilled. A lot of us kept those expectations alive.

At one point in the video segment Little showed me, Hunt stops, lost in thought, searching for words. If you believed he had a terminal disease, as Little did when he and Hunt made the video, you might think he was waiting for a wave of pain to pass.

"There's so much, God, I'm trying to express, something that's hard. It really is."

Little paused the video, to give space for Hunt's words.

"I never, ever wish this on anyone."

I'm not positive what he meant by "this." But if you believe, as I do now, that his death carries the weight of our failure to reckon with our nation's racist past and present, the damage inflicted by prison, the trauma of injustice, and the burden we all bear for letting Hunt down, then the reference becomes clearer. It is, indeed, time for that reckoning.

Epilogue

I pray for all of the people I left in prison and hope that they, too, one day will be free.[1]

Darryl Hunt, interview with Frank Stasio, host of
"The State of Things," WUNC radio, July 2007

Television reporters crowded around Kalvin Michael Smith on November 10, 2016, the moment he walked through the gates of the Forsyth Correctional Facility into his lawyers' arms. "If not for God Almighty, I wouldn't have been able to make it," Smith told them.[2] It was one of those warm November days in the South, with the air clear and the sun high in the sky, which made it possible to forget the perils that lay ahead.

Smith was out on a technicality. The day before, at a hearing in the Forsyth County Hall of Justice, lawyers had argued that an error at Smith's original sentencing hearing nearly 20 years earlier meant that he had served a full sentence for the crime of beating a woman with such brutality that she remains disabled by the brain injuries she sustained. Though Smith was not yet exonerated, it was still a moment of exultation. His supporters, among them some of the same ministers who had rallied to Hunt's cause, including Rev. William Barber, then the leader of the state's Moral Monday Movement and now the national leader of the Poor People's Campaign, filled the lobby outside the courtroom. The crowd was smaller than it had been for Hunt's release and perhaps wiser for Hunt's death eight months earlier.

Smith's father, Augustus Dark, waited at home for him, in a neighborhood not far from where Hunt had lived. Dark and Hunt had grown close during the final years of Hunt's life as they worked together on Smith's case. Sometimes, Hunt would drop by Dark's house, visits that gave Dark comfort because Hunt reminded him so much of his son. Hunt offered sobering advice for Dark to share. Smith's release, when it came, would be tougher than he imagined. He urged Dark not to put too much pressure on his son and to be sure to warn him of the disappointments that lay ahead, the betrayals, and the pain.[3]

His son's strength in prison always gave Dark hope, but even as early as that first day home, he saw signs of some of the trouble Hunt had warned him of. That first night, during the crush of well-wishers and reporters, Smith slipped off to another relative's home to escape the attention. The next day, Dark was surprised when Smith asked his father to watch his plate of food when he left the dining table to use the bathroom so that no one would take it in his absence. When he returned, he gulped what he'd left on the plate with a spoon in the ten minutes allotted in prison for a meal. "Dad, I haven't had a knife to eat with in 20 years,"[4] he told his father. Everything on the outside was new and hard to master, just as Hunt had predicted. At night, Smith barely slept in the unfamiliar quiet of his father's home. His lawyer bought him a cell phone and taught him to use it, but he kept misplacing it. That first week, on a trip to the mall for new clothes, Smith wanted to buy baggy pants and Timberland boots until a friend told him they'd gone out of style years ago. Harder still were the demands from people he barely knew who assumed that he'd received a settlement, as Hunt had. "When we going to get paid; when we going to get some of that money?" someone yelled at him that first trip to the mall.[5] Truth was, with no exoneration, he'd left prison with a check for $45, one that, without a bank account, he couldn't cash.

Smith went to prison in 1997, more than a decade after Hunt. While the details of what I believe was a wrongful conviction were different, the systemic racism, phony science, and police misconduct that infected Hunt's case played out in Smith's. The victim was a young woman named Jill Marker, who was beaten nearly to death one evening during the holiday shopping season at her job at an artificial plant store, the Silk Plant Forest. The crime had all the sensational elements of Sykes' murder. Marker was white and attractive. What's more, she was pregnant, conscious after the attack just long enough to tell paramedics of her condition. The news coverage was relentless, following the case through her five-month-long hospitalization and the delivery of her son, attention that created enormous pressure to solve such a brutal and apparently random crime.

Police had an early suspect, a white man with a history of domestic violence who knew Marker and had been stalking her, but they dropped him, without explanation, and settled instead on the notion of a random crime carried out by an unidentified Black suspect seen speeding away from the parking lot outside the store. A year later, a jealous girlfriend reported Smith to police. Like Hunt, he cooperated. Like Hunt, he faced a coercive interrogation, as did his girlfriend, by some of the same officers who had investigated Hunt's case. Unlike Hunt, Smith gave in to the pressure and signed a statement in which he admitted to being at the store with another man, whom he saw hit the store clerk. That was the extent of his admission. After that, Marker, still unable to speak, regained consciousness and partial sight, and identified him from a photo lineup.

Smith and Hunt met in prison, and Hunt encouraged him to reach out to the Wrongful Convictions Clinic at Duke University School of Law, which took on his case. With Hunt's encouragement, Smith also reached out to me, at the *Winston-Salem Journal*. Inspired by my work on Hunt's case, I investigated his case and wrote a series of stories that once again made a compelling case for innocence.[6] Since then, a host of others have found even more evidence of wrongful conviction. A city commission investigated the police work in the case, and while falling short of declaring

Smith innocent, found that in all likelihood Smith was not at the scene of the crime.[7] Later, a retired FBI agent, retained by Smith's defense committee, concluded that at the very least, Smith deserved a new trial.[8] Filmmakers also took up his cause, first a local filmmaker, Keith Barber, in *Ordinary Injustice*, followed by filmmakers for MTV, which included Smith's case in its series *Unlocking the Truth*. But as Hunt had learned before him, once convicted, the defendant carries the burden to prove innocence. Without DNA evidence, claims of innocence have little legal standing and are nearly impossible to prove.

Like Hunt, Smith faced the psychic toll of his wrongful imprisonment from the get-go. Soon after his release, he was diagnosed with anxiety and post-traumatic stress disorder.[9] Then one night in March 2017, just four months after his release, he was shot in the back by someone who sped away in a dark-colored vehicle. Police never made an arrest. His father told me that the bullet went clear through his abdomen, a wound that doctors told him few ever survived. They gave Smith OxyContin for the pain and soon he was addicted. People would call Dark with tips about the shooter, but Smith never wanted him to share those with police. "I'm not going to go to court and risk another innocent man going to jail," he'd tell his father.[10] Smith also began drinking heavily, and as his troubles grew, most of his supporters became disenchanted, and his chances of exoneration slipped even further away. In 2019, Smith was assaulted again, this time slashed in the face during an argument. He spent most of 2020 in jail, throughout a COVID-19 outbreak, on a series of petty charges, including larceny, trespassing, and illegal possession of prescription drugs.

In some ways, Smith had more support than most people coming out of prison. His father, retired from Reynolds Tobacco Company, provided him a stable home. Some of his supporters, including the lawyers from Duke, have remained loyal, even offering to put up money for drug treatment for Smith. But his father soon came to realize that reentry was harder for Smith and for his family than the nearly 20 years of his false imprisonment. "It's a sad story. I'm not saying it just because it's the story of my son or Darryl. It's the story of so many people."[11] Sometimes, Dark prays for Marker and her son, as he and his son did when Smith first came home from prison, in the knowledge that both families suffered from the crime.[12] He is haunted by Hunt's death and what it portends for his son. "He's so far gone. I don't know if we'll ever recover."[13]

~

Dark believes his son might have had an easier time had Darryl Hunt survived. It's hard to know, except to say that Hunt's death left so many bereft because his resilience had offered so much solace. Rabil felt suicidal for weeks following Hunt's death and now attributes his despair to his own version of PTSD.[14] He still wonders whether police fully investigated Hunt's death, or settled too quickly on suicide. He continues to represent others wrongly convicted in difficult cases like Smith's that lack DNA evidence. He teaches mindfulness to law students as a way for them to deal with the stress of the profession and is developing a course on race and the law. His research focuses on the secondary trauma faced by those who work on death penalty cases, including lawyers like him, investigators like those who devoted so much of their lives to Hunt's cause, jurors who must weigh the merits of a man's life against the cruelty of the crime, and prison staff who bear the burden of carrying out the punishment. The defendant is not the only one damaged by injustice.

Little has declined any further interviews. Publicly, he has said that Hunt's death left him brokenhearted beyond words. He is Hunt's executor, but closing his estate is on hold because Hunt and April had never distributed their property after their divorce. According to the records in his estate files, all the was left of the $1.9 million he received from his settlement with the city and from the state was the house he shared with April, four checks adding up to

$1,208, a 2002 Toyota valued at $2,000, and household belongings worth $1,500. In his will, written by hand in September 2015, Hunt left his house to his sister, Doris Hunt, and to his foundation. Everything else he left to the foundation, which was disbanded before his death. April still lives in the house with her grown children. She has gone back to school to become certified in medical billing and coding and now works in a nursing home. She remains a devout Muslim and early in the pandemic recovered from COVID-19.

Rev. Carlton Eversley died in September 2019 at 62 of a heart attack. He saw Hunt's addiction for what it was—the response of a good man to intolerable conditions. In an interview in 2016, he discussed his own struggles with depression and his effort to break the stigma of mental illness within the Black church.[15] Three months after Eversley's death, Rev. John Mendez retired at 69. He lives in Winston-Salem and works part-time in private practice as a psychotherapist. Khalid Griggs still leads the local mosque, which was closed for much of the pandemic, and works for social justice causes. Les Gura, who edited my work at the *Winston-Salem Journal*, left journalism and became a counselor, specializing in trauma-focused therapy. Hunt's story led him to this work. Tarrah Callahan, Hunt's friend and colleague in anti–death penalty work, now runs an advocacy group called Conservatives for Criminal Justice Reform. Most recently, this group persuaded the North Carolina legislature to pass the Second Chance Act, which allows for misdemeanor crimes to be removed from people's records.

Richard McGough, the private investigator who worked on Hunt's case all through the 1990s, is an investigator for the North Carolina Office of the Capital Defender, tracking down witnesses for the defense in death penalty cases. Chuck Byrom, the detective whose work detailed the cover-up in Hunt's case, is retired and spends much of his time caring for his ailing father. Regina Lane, who survived rape and was misled by the police to preserve their case against Hunt, still works at the insurance company. In 2012, she wrote a book about her case, titled *From Victim to Victory*, a story of survival and faith. Many of Hunt's closest relatives and friends are dead or scattered. Gail Burnette died in 2018 of cancer. Sammy Mitchell died in 2013 of liver failure. Doris Hunt, Darryl's sister and heir, lives in Atlanta.

The prosecutors who sent Hunt to prison and kept him there for nearly 20 years have either retired, moved into private practice, or died. Jim Daulton died in 2006, and most of the other police officers who investigated Hunt's case have retired. Willard Brown is in prison, and has been incarcerated in some of the same camps where Hunt was wrongly imprisoned. The Winston-Salem Police Department has a new chief, a Black woman named Catrina Thompson. She declined to release reports into Hunt's death, but she is seen by many as a beacon for a more humane approach to law enforcement. During the Black Lives Matter protests in the summer of 2020, she joined protesters in the streets and spoke of her fears for her teenage son.

I am reminded often of Hunt's achievements. No one has been executed in North Carolina since 2006, the death penalty having been effectively halted by the dozens of appeals pending under the Racial Justice Act. Among those saved by this reprieve is Hunt's friend Thomas Michael Larry,[16] known by Hunt as "Smoke," who shared a cell block with him and Rasheed back in 1993, establishing discipline and order in the county jail. Defense attorneys and prosecutors say that jurors in Winston-Salem are more skeptical now than they once were of shoddy evidence and police testimony. The Innocence Inquiry Commission, the judicial body inspired by Hunt's case, has reviewed 2,500 cases since its founding in 2007, looking for evidence of innocence. Its work has led to 12 exonerations. In 2020, the commission found enough evidence to refer two cases involving some of the same Winston-Salem police officers who framed Hunt for review by a panel of three judges. One is the innocence claim by four men who say they were coerced as teenagers in 2002 into confessing to killing the grandfather of NBA star Chris Paul. Rabil is representing one of the defendants.

Within the innocence movement, lawyers are beginning to pay attention to the recovery their clients need once the legal battle is won. A handful of innocence projects employ social workers, but most are too overwhelmed by requests for legal help to focus on what comes next. An organization called After Innocence, which offers reentry support for men and women like Hunt, has just started a pilot program in four states to find treatment for clients with such mental illnesses as depression and PTSD. It's a start, but not the comprehensive national plan such injustice demands. Nearly 30,000 years have been lost in prison by men and women proven to be wrongly convicted.[17] Many return home in states that offer no financial compensation for stealing those years. For some attorneys working to free the wrongly convicted, Hunt's death serves as a grim reminder of the mental scars of such injustice. "It's extraordinarily rare that anyone gets out of prison after being exonerated and is unscathed," says Ken Rose, senior attorney with the Center for Death Penalty Litigation in North Carolina. "It just doesn't happen."

Hunt's story has been framed as a story of wrongful conviction, but more than anything, he wanted to speak for the thousands of men and women he left behind in prison, regardless of their innocence or guilt. Incarceration in North Carolina is at its lowest since 1995, but as of April 2021, the state imprisoned 26,656 men and 2,015 women and monitored almost 80,000 formerly incarcerated men and women under supervised probation or parole.[18] Chances are, most will be back in prison within three years. One study of recidivism, for example, found that of 412,731 people released in 2005 from prisons in 30 states, 45 percent of the men were arrested within the year. By the end of nine years, more than 80 percent were charged again with a crime.[19] Long before politicians began campaigning against mass incarceration, Hunt saw the system he had left behind for what it is, a trap that condemns millions of men and women, and their children, to living on the fringe, barred from jobs, housing, bank loans, food assistance, and more—barred, in short, from a reasonable chance at a decent life.

The struggles Hunt's friends have faced in the time I've known them bear out these challenges. Anthony Wright was released from probation in February 2021 at the end of his federal sentence, but has dealt with hardships I cannot fathom. He survived a gunshot wound and multiple surgeries but cannot afford the medicine prescribed for the resulting blood clots. One of his daughters has lost custody of her children, grandchildren Wright adores. And an old girlfriend has accused him of assault, which means he is not allowed to see the child they had together. Rasheed has been home for more than 15 years. He still runs the construction business Hunt helped him form, but glaucoma has destroyed his eyesight, which makes it hard for him to work. And his criminal record prevents him from bidding on many jobs, even from borrowing money in his own name. He also suffers from PTSD, but as he would say, he is surviving. Hunt advocated for so much more.

As a country, we are just beginning to grapple with the most rudimentary elements of prison reform. The conversation Hunt pushed for when he got out of prison on how to bring people home with dignity has barely begun. Policy makers hold up model reentry programs as examples of what we should try on a national scale. Some offer men and women sales jobs while they are still incarcerated so that they are employed when their sentence is up. Others teach people coming home to start their own business. Another aims to sort out the bureaucratic hurdles that prevent former prisoners from obtaining a simple state ID card.[20] If Hunt were still alive, he'd be part of that work, a voice for men and women who, as he told an interviewer in 2007, cannot speak for themselves because the rest of us refuse to believe what those convicted of crimes, even those who are innocent, have to say. "Once you commit a crime, you cannot be forgiven for it," he said in 2007. "It's like a life sentence."[21]

Timeline

1984

AUGUST: Deborah Sykes is raped and murdered on her way to work at the *Sentinel* in Winston-Salem, NC.

SEPTEMBER: Darryl Hunt is charged with murder. Soon after, Larry Little organizes the Darryl Hunt Defense Committee.

1985

FEBRUARY: Regina Lane is kidnapped near the Integon Corp. building, across the street from the *Sentinel* offices, and forced at gunpoint to drive to a vacant drive-in movie theater, where she is raped.

MAY: Regina Lane identifies Willard Brown as her attacker from a photo lineup. The following week, Hunt's trial begins.

JUNE: Hunt is convicted of murder and sentenced to life in prison without parole.

1986

JANUARY: The State Bureau of Investigation begins a review of the Sykes case.

MARCH: Winston-Salem police detective Carter Crump, who is assisting the State Bureau of Investigation with its probe, interviews Willard Brown in the Sykes case. It's not clear why. Crump is also lead investigator on the Lane case, but his report for the Sykes case does not mention that Lane had identified Brown the previous year.

APRIL: Hunt and Sammy Mitchell are charged in the 1983 murder of Arthur Wilson in Winston-Salem. This same month, Lane identifies Willard Brown in a live lineup.

MAY: The state crime lab tests Brown's blood as type O, the same type found in the semen from the rape kits in the Sykes case. The report is filed with the reports in Lane's case.

OCTOBER: Mitchell is convicted in the death of Wilson and is sentenced to 50 years in prison. The State Bureau of Investigation completes its probe into the Sykes murder, without bringing any new charges.

NOVEMBER: A report by the city manager blasts the police department for its shoddy work in the Sykes case.

1987

OCTOBER: Hunt is convicted in the Wilson murder.

1989

MAY: Hunt wins a new trial in the Sykes murder.

SEPTEMBER: Lane's case is closed and the evidence is destroyed.

OCTOBER: Hunt wins a new trial in the Wilson case and is released on a $50,000 bond. He lives with Imam Khalid Griggs.

1990

MARCH: Hunt is acquitted at his second trial in the Wilson murder. During the trial, he rejects an offer to plead guilty to the Wilson murder and the Sykes murder in exchange for the time he has already served in prison.

OCTOBER: Hunt is convicted at his second trial in the Sykes murder and returns to prison.

1994

NOVEMBER: DNA testing excludes Hunt as the source of the semen in the rape of Deborah Sykes, but Judge Melzer Morgan rules that the evidence is insufficient for a third trial.

DECEMBER: The North Carolina Supreme Court agrees with Melzer.

2000

FEBRUARY: The US Court of Appeals turns down Hunt's appeal.

OCTOBER: The US Supreme Court refuses Hunt's petition. He marries April Clark in prison.

2003

APRIL: Judge Andrew Cromer orders a new round of DNA testing of the evidence in the Sykes case.

NOVEMBER: The *Winston-Salem Journal* publishes "Murder, Race, Justice: The State vs. Darryl Hunt," reviving interest in the 1985 rape of Regina Lane.

DECEMBER: Brown is identified by DNA testing as the source of the semen in the Sykes case. Hunt is released from prison and Brown is charged with murder.

2004

FEBRUARY: Hunt is exonerated.

APRIL: Hunt is pardoned by Gov. Mike Easley, which entitles him to compensation from North Carolina for $360,000, an amount that eventually is increased to $750,000.

DECEMBER: Brown is convicted and sentenced to life in prison but is not prosecuted for Lane's rape. The Sykes Administrative Review Committee begins work.

2005

Hunt opens the Darryl Hunt Project for Freedom and Justice to help men and women coming home from prison.

2006

FEBRUARY: *The Trials of Darryl Hunt* opens at Sundance, making Hunt a celebrity.

2007

FEBRUARY: The Sykes review committee report concludes that police should have been able to connect Brown to the Sykes case as far back as 1986 and provides evidence of a cover-up. Hunt wins a $1.6 million settlement from the city of Winston-Salem.

2011

APRIL: Hunt begins working for the North Carolina Coalition for Alternatives to the Death Penalty.

2012

MAY: Duke University awards Hunt an honorary doctorate.

2014

SEPTEMBER: April Hunt seeks a restraining order against Hunt, which is reported by news organizations across North Carolina. A month later, they agree to a mutual restraining order.

2015

EARLY 2015: Hunt moves to Atlanta, where he lives with his sister, Doris, and tells friends he has been diagnosed with cancer.

DECEMBER: Hunt's divorce from April is finalized.

2016

JANUARY: Hunt moves back to Winston-Salem, where he lives with Larry Little.

MARCH: Hunt is found dead from a gunshot wound to the abdomen, and his death is ruled a suicide.

Notes

This book relies heavily on excerpts from journals, letters, trial transcripts, and other primary sources. With the exception of a few errors of punctuation in trial transcripts, I have quoted verbatim from these sources, leaving errors of spelling, grammar, and syntax to preserve their authenticity.

Preface

1   National Registry of Exonerations, A Project of the University of California Irvine, the University of Michigan Law School, and Michigan State University College of Law, accessed Jan. 14, 2021, https://www.law.umich.edu/special/exoneration/Pages/about.aspx.

2   Sam Gross et al., "Rate of False Conviction of Criminal Defendants Who Are Sentenced to Death," *PNAS*, April 28, 2014, https://www.pnas.org/content/111/20/7230.

3   Jack Betts, "Behind Bars: North Carolina's Growing Prison Population," *North Carolina Insight*, published by the NC Center for Public Policy Research, https://nccppr.org/wp-content/uploads/2017/02/Behind_Bars-_NCs_Growing_Prison_Population.pdf.

4   NC Department of Correction 2003 annual report, http://www.doc.state.nc.us/NEWS/annrep/2003annrepWEB.pdf.

5   North Carolina Coalition for Alternatives to the Death Penalty, "N.C. Death Penalty Fast Facts," accessed, May 2021, https://nccadp.org/nc-death-penalty-facts/.

6   US Census Bureau, Quick Facts North Carolina, last modified July 1, 2019, https://www.census.gov/quickfacts/NC.

7   Eli Hager, "A Mass Incarceration Mystery," Dec. 15, 2017, The Marshall Project, https://www.themarshallproject.org/2017/12/15/a-mass-incarceration-mystery?ref=collections.

Chapter 1

This chapter relies heavily on a series of newspaper articles I wrote for the *Winston-Salem Journal* titled *Murder, Race, Justice: The State vs. Darryl Hunt*, which was published Nov. 16–23, 2003. My reporting in 2003 included a review of hundreds of pages of police reports, trial transcripts, and appellate briefs as well as interviews with witnesses, police officers, lawyers, community activists, and others involved with the case.

1   Call transcript, Phoebe Zerwick, "Murder, Race, Justice: The State vs. Darryl Hunt," part 1 of eight-part series, *Winston-Salem Journal*, Nov. 16–23, 2003.

2   Zerwick, "Murder, Race, Justice" (part 1).

3   Zerwick, "Murder, Race, Justice" (part 1).

4   Zerwick, "Murder, Race, Justice" (part 1).

5   Zerwick, "Murder, Race, Justice" (part 1).

6   *The Trials of Darryl Hunt*, documentary directed by Ricki Stern and Annie Sundberg (New York: Break Thru Films, 2006); and Zerwick, "Murder, Race, Justice" (part 1).

7   Zerwick, "Murder, Race, Justice" (part 1).

8   Zerwick, "Murder, Race, Justice" (part 1).

9   Zerwick, "Murder, Race, Justice" (parts 1 and 2).

10   Zerwick, "Murder, Race, Justice" (part 1).

11   David Snyder, "Woman's Murder Heightens Anxiety," *Winston-Salem Sentinel*, Aug. 13, 1984.

12   Tom Sieg and David Snyder, "Murder Case Has Boiled Down to Plain Old Footwork," *Winston-Salem Sentinel*, Aug. 23, 1984.

13   Tom Sieg, "Tragedy Hits Home, We Often Write of Death; This Time We Lived It," *Winston-Salem Sentinel*, Aug. 13, 1984.

14   Criminal Justice Information Services Division, Federal Bureau of Investigation, Offenses Known to Law Enforcement: Crimes Reported; State: North Carolina; County: Forsyth; Crime Type: Murder, 1984 (Data Planet Statistical Datasets: A SAGE Publishing Resource).

15   Alexia Cooper and Eric B. Smith, "Homicide Trends in the United States: 1980–2008," Nov. 2011, NCJ 236018, Bureau of Justice Statistics, Office of Justice Programs, US Department of Justice.

16   Clip files, *Winston-Salem Journal*, folder labeled "Murder: Statistics, Thru 1993."

17 Jesse Poindexter, "Man Sentenced to 6 Years," *Winston-Salem Journal*, Aug. 24, 1984.
18 Zerwick, "Murder, Race, Justice" (part 2).
19 Zerwick, "Murder, Race, Justice" (part 2).
20 Zerwick, "Murder, Race, Justice" (part 2).
21 Zerwick, "Murder, Race, Justice" (part 2).
22 Zerwick, "Murder, Race, Justice" (part 2).
23 Zerwick, "Murder, Race, Justice" (part 2).
24 Zerwick, "Murder, Race, Justice" (part 2).
25 Zerwick, "Murder, Race, Justice" (part 2).
26 Zerwick, "Murder, Race, Justice" (part 2).

Chapter 2

This chapter relies heavily on Darryl Hunt's unpublished journals and transcripts from audio recordings made for his memoirs that are part of the Darryl Hunt Collection, Wake Forest Law Library Special Collections and Archives, Wake Forest University School of Law, Winston-Salem, NC. These journals exist in paper format, stored in a three-ring binder, and were given by Mark Rabil to the Darryl Hunt Collection, with restricted access. I have left most of the grammar and spelling as they appear in the transcriptions, making corrections only when needed for clarity. Hunt's original handwritten notebooks and the original audio cassettes are not part of the archive.

1 Phoebe Zerwick, "Murder, Race, Justice: The State vs. Darryl Hunt," part 2 of eight-part series, *Winston-Salem Journal*, Nov. 16–23, 2003.
2 "Darryl Hunt Journals," n.d., section titled "Darryl Hunt Prison Journals—1983-," Darryl Hunt Collection, Wake Forest Law Library Special Collections and Archives, Wake Forest University School of Law, Winston-Salem, NC.
3 Hunt, Journals, section titled "Darryl Hunt Prison Journals—1983-."
4 Zerwick, "Murder, Race, Justice" (part 2).
5 Hunt, Journals, section titled "Darryl Hunt Journals, 1979–1989."
6 Hunt, Journals, section titled "Darryl Hunt Prison Journals—1983-."
7 Hunt, Journals, section titled "Darryl Hunt Prison Journals, Oct. 6, 1995 & 1984."
8 Weatherunderground, Weather History, Piedmont Triad International Airport weather station, Aug. 10, 1984, https://www.wunderground.com/history/daily/us/nc/winston-salem/KGSO/date/1984-8-10.
9 Hunt, Journals, section titled "Darryl Hunt Prison Journals—1983-," and Darryl Hunt, testimony at his first trial, pages 1770–1830.
10 Hunt, Journals, section titled "Darryl Hunt Prison Journals—1983-."

11 Hunt, Journals section titled "Darryl Hunt Journals, 1979–1989"; and Vernessa Wright, interview with the author, Oct. 10, 2019. All interviews took place in Winston-Salem, NC, unless otherwise noted. All interviews in the author's personal collection, unless otherwise noted.

12 Allen H. Johnson, "'Police Know I'm Innocent'—Darryl Hunt: Police Know I Didn't Murder Sykes," *Winston-Salem Chronicle*, Feb. 7, 1985.

13 Hunt, Journals, section titled "Darryl Hunt Journals, 1979–1989."

14 Johnson, "'Police Know I'm Innocent.'"

15 Hunt, Journals, section titled "Darryl Hunt Prison Journal."

16 Hunt, Journals, section titled "Family Tree."

17 Forsyth County Department of Social Services, Face Sheet, labeled Defendant's Exhibit 2, located in Box 1, File 1 in "Correspondence," Darryl Hunt Collection.

18 Death Certificate, Hattie Stroud, Nov. 16, 1973, uncertified copy in the author's collection.

19 Hunt, Journals, section titled "Family Tree."

20 Wright, interview with the author.

21 Hunt, Journals, section titled "Family Tree."

22 Jo Anne North Goetz, *Long Time Coming*, as told to Leigh Summerville McMillan (Bloomington, IN: AuthorHouse, 2007), chap. 1.

23 North Goetz, chap. 1.

24 North Goetz, chap. 1.

25 Hunt, Journals, section titled "Darryl Hunt Journals, 1979–1989."

26 Death Certificate, William Stroud, Oct. 5, 1977, uncertified copy in the author's collection.

27 Hunt, Journals, section titled "Darryl Hunt Prison Journals."

28 Hunt, Journals, section titled "Darryl Hunt Prison Journals, 1982."

29 Jon Healey, "Man Already in Jail Is Charged with Sykes Murder," *Winston-Salem Journal*, Sept. 15, 1984, and Hunt, Journals, section titled "Darryl Hunt Prison Journals, 1982."

30 North Goetz, 17.

31 Zerwick, "Murder, Race, Justice" (part 3).

32 Zerwick, "Murder, Race, Justice" (part 3).

33 Zerwick, "Murder, Race, Justice" (part 2).

34 Zerwick, "Murder, Race, Justice" (part 2).

35 Zerwick, "Murder, Race, Justice" (part 2).

36 Hunt, Journals, sections tiled "Darryl Hunt Prison Journals, Sept. 11, 1984," and "Darryl Hunt Prison Journals—1983-."

37 Jim Daulton, interview with State Bureau of Investigation officers, Feb. 12 and 18, 1986, SBI file 367-H-10, author's collection.

38 Zerwick, "Murder, Race, Justice" (part 2).

39 Zerwick, "Murder, Race, Justice" (part 2).

40 Zerwick, "Murder, Race, Justice" (part 2).

41 Hunt, Journals, sections titled "Darryl Hunt Prison Journals, Sept. 11, 1984" and "Transcripts," Darryl Hunt Collection.

42 Hunt, Journals, section titled "Darryl Hunt Prison Journals, Sept. 11, 1984."

43 Hunt, Journals, section titled "Darryl Hunt Prison Journals, Sept. 11, 1984."

44 Hunt, Transcripts and Journals, section titled "Darryl Hunt Prison Journals, Sept. 11, 1984."

45 Hunt, Transcripts and Journals, section titled "Darryl Hunt Prison Journals, Sept. 11, 1984."

Chapter 3

1 Larry Little, interview with the author, April 7, 2017.

2 Phoebe Zerwick, "Murder, Race, Justice: The State vs. Darryl Hunt," part 3 of eight-part series, *Winston-Salem Journal*, Nov. 16–23, 2003.

3 Larry Little, interview with the author, April 21, 2003.

4 Zerwick, "Murder, Race, Justice" (part 3).

5 Mark Rabil, unpublished manuscript on loan to the author, 2007, chap. 4, "Enter the Panther."

6 Zerwick, "Murder, Race, Justice" (part 3).

7 Estella McFadden and Vernessa Wright, interviews with the author, summer 2016 and Oct. 10, 2019.

8 Zerwick, "Murder, Race, Justice" (part 3).

9 Nikole Hannah-Jones et al., "The 1619 Project," *New York Times Magazine*, Aug. 18, 2019.

10 National Registry of Exonerations, accessed Dec. 2020, https://www.law.umich.edu/special/exoneration/Pages/about.aspx.

11 National Registry, accessed Dec. 2020, https://www.law.umich.edu/special/exoneration/Pages/about.aspx.

12 Tom Steadman, "First and Foremost an Activist," *Greensboro News & Record*, May 29, 1988.

13 Steadman, "First and Foremost an Activist."

14 Carlton Eversley, interview with the author, July 22, 2019.

15 Eversley, interview.

16 Eversley, interview.

17 Lee O. Sanderlin, "After 36 Years of Ministry and Fighting Injustice, John Mendez Is Leaving the Pulpit," *Winston-Salem Journal*, Dec. 14, 2019, https://

www.journalnow.com/news/local/after-36-years-of-ministry-and-fighting
-social-injustice-john-mendez-is-leaving-the-pulpit/article_5a7a7e6b-247f
-598b-a60d-71568e90dd7a.html.

18 John Mendez, interview with the author, July 10, 2019.

19 Karen Bethea-Shields, as told to David Cecelski, "In Joan Little's Cell," part
    of the "Listening to History" series, *Raleigh News & Observer*, Jan. 12, 2003,
    reprinted in https://www.ncpedia.org/listening-to-history/bethea-shields;
    and Christina Greene, "'She Ain't No Rosa Parks': The Joan Little Rape–
    Murder Case and Jim Crow Justice in the Post–Civil Rights South," *The
    Journal of African American History* 100, 3 (2015): 428–447, https://www.jstor
    .org/stable/10.5323/jafriamerhist.100.3.0428?seq=1.

20 Wayne King, "Joan Little's Lawyer Scorns Legal System and Says He Bought
    Her Acquittal," *The New York Times*, Oct. 20, 1975, https://www.nytimes
    .com/1975/10/20/archives/joan-littles-lawyer-scorns-legal-system-and-says
    -he-bought-her.html.

21 Jordan Green, "Joan Little: Dramatic New Footage Casts Light on Historic
    Black Panther Activists," *IndieWire*, Dec. 10, 2019, https://www.indiewire.
    com/2019/12/joan-little-footage-Black-panthers-1202190788/.

22 Jaye Sitton, "Old Wine in New Bottles: The Marital Rape Allowance," *North
    Carolina Law Review* 72 (1993) 261, http://scholarship.law.unc.edu/nclr/
    vol72/iss1/9.

23 John Mendez, interview with the author, July 10, 2019.

24 Eversley, interview.

25 Zerwick, "Murder, Race, Justice" (part 4).

26 Zerwick, "Murder, Race, Justice" (part 3).

27 Rabil, Manuscript, chaps. 4 and 5.

28 "Facing Controversy: Struggling with Capital Punishment in North Caro-
    lina," UNC Libraries Exhibits, Jan. 14–Mar. 15, 2008, at Davis Library,
    University of North Carolina at Chapel Hill, digital exhibit retrieved June
    29, 2020, https://exhibits.lib.unc.edu/exhibits/show/capital-punishment/
    controversies/legality.

29 Seth Kotch and Robert P. Mosteller, "The Racial Justice Act and the Long
    Struggle with Race and the Death Penalty in North Carolina," *North Carolina
    Law Review* 88 (2010): 2031, http://scholarship.law.unc.edu/nclr/vol88/
    iss6/4.

30 Papers in the personal collection of Robert Korstad, professor emeritus of
    public policy, Duke University, loaned to the author.

31 Korstad Collection.

32 Barron Mills, "Clyde Brown, Speller Pay with Their Lives for Crimes," *Win-
    ston-Salem Journal*, May 30, 1953.

33 Associated Press, "Clemency Is Denied Speller," *Greensboro Daily News,* May 26, 1953; and Associated Press, "Speller and Brown Pay for Rape with Lives," *Greensboro Daily News,* May 30, 1953, Korstad Collection.

34 Seth Kotch, *Lethal State: A History of the Death Penalty in North Carolina* (Chapel Hill: University of North Carolina Press, 2019), 113.

35 Mills, "Brown, Speller Pay with Their Lives."

36 Jonathan Michels, "Marker to Honor 1940s Labor Union," *Winston-Salem Journal,* April 15, 2013, https://journalnow.com/news/local/article_a7dcbaa2 -a56c-11e2-abbe-0019bb30f31a.html.

Chapter 4

This chapter relies heavily on the book Regina Lane wrote with Linda F. Felker, *From Victim to Victory,* which tells the story of her rape, her faith, and her experience with the Winston-Salem Police Department.

1   Regina Lane and Linda F. Felker, *From Victim to Victory* (Winston-Salem, NC: Clear Light Books, 2012), 2; and Regina Lane, interviews with the author, June 10, Sept. 12, 19, and 26, 2019.

2   Lane and Felker, *From Victim to Victory,* 2–4; and Lane, interviews with the author.

3   Lane and Felker, 3.

4   Lane and Felker, 3.

5   Lane and Felker, 4–6; and Lane, interviews with the author.

6   Lane and Felker, 7.

7   Lane and Felker, 8.

8   Lane and Felker, 9.

9   Lane and Felker, 10.

10 Lane and Felker, 17.

11 Lane and Felker, 18–20.

12 W. G. Miller, supplement report, Feb. 2, 1985, Winston-Salem Police Department, appendix 10–1, 20, Sykes Administrative Review Committee Report, City of Winston-Salem, 2007, https://www.cityofws.org/1957/ Sykes-Administrative-Review-Committee-Re.

13 Sykes Report, appendix 10–1, 51.

14 Sykes Report, 28.

15 Sykes Report, 51.

16 Mary Lane, interviews with the author, 2003 and 2004, dates unknown.

17 Sykes Report, 134; Lane interviews with the author; and Phoebe Zerwick, "Murder, Race, Justice: The State vs. Darryl Hunt," part 8 of eight-part series, *Winston-Salem Journal,* Nov. 16–23, 2003.

18 Lane and Felker, 134.

Chapter 5

This chapter relies heavily on Mark Rabil's unpublished memoir, written in 2007, which he generously loaned to me, and on dozens of conversations with him—some formal interviews, others informal—about his experience as Darryl Hunt's lawyer.

1   Mark Rabil, unpublished manuscript on loan to the author, 2007, chap. 2, "The Presumption of Guilt."

2   "Darryl Hunt Journals," n.d., section titled "Sept. 11, 1984," Darryl Hunt Collection, Wake Forest Law Library Special Collections and Archives, Wake Forest University School of Law, Winston-Salem, NC.

3   Tracie Cone, "Employee of Integon Corp. Is Kidnapped and Raped," *Winston-Salem Journal*, Feb. 5, 1985.

4   Cone, "Employee of Integon."

5   Rabil, Manuscript, chap. 8, "The Integon Rape."

6   Rabil, Manuscript, chap. 8.

7   Rabil, Manuscript, chap. 2.

8   Rabil, Manuscript, chap. 2.

9   Rabil, Manuscript, chap. 3, "Interview with the Accused."

10 Rabil, Manuscript, chap. 3.

11 Rabil, Manuscript, chap. 3.

12 Rabil, Manuscript, chap. 4, "Enter the Panther."

13 Rabil, Manuscript, chap. 2.

14 Rabil, Manuscript, chap. 4.

15 Rabil, interviews with the author, 2017–2019.

16 Hunt, Journals, section titled "Darryl Hunt Prison Journal."

17 Hunt, Journals, section titled "Trial Cont, 1986–1987."

18 Mark Rabil, interviews with the author, 2016–2020.

19 Hunt, Journals, section titled "Darryl Hunt Prison Journal."

20 University of North Carolina Library Exhibit, "Facing Controversy: Struggling with Capital Punishment in North Carolina," accessed June 29, 2020, https://exhibits.lib.unc.edu/exhibits/show/capital-punishment/controversies/legality, and Ken Rose, former director of the Center for Death Penalty Litigation, interview with the author, June 29, 2020.

21 Rabil, Manuscript, chap. 2.

22 Rabil, Manuscript, chap. 2.

23 Rabil, Manuscript, chap. 5, "Investigating in the Dark."

24 Rabil, Manuscript, chap. 2.

25 Rabil, Manuscript, chap. 5.

26 Rabil, Manuscript, chap. 15, "The Case against Gray."

27 Rabil, Manuscript, chap. 15.

28 Rabil, Manuscript, chap. 15.

29 *The Trials of Darryl Hunt*, documentary directed by Ricki Stern and Annie Sundberg (New York: Break Thru Films, 2006).

Chapter 6

Much of this chapter is told from Hunt's point of view, and relies on "Darryl Hunt Journals," n.d., Darryl Hunt Collection, Wake Forest Law Library Special Collections and Archives, Wake Forest University School of Law, Winston-Salem, NC, especially sections titled "Sept. 11, 1984" and "Darryl Hunt Prison Journals, 1973–May 1988."

1   Phoebe Zerwick, "Murder, Race, Justice: The State vs. Darryl Hunt," part 4 of eight-part series, *Winston-Salem Journal*, Nov. 16–23, 2003, http://www.journalnow.com/app/specialreports/hunt/about.html.

2   Hunt, Journals, section titled "Darryl Hunt Prison Journals, 1973–May 1988."

3   Hunt, Journals, section titled "Darryl Hunt Prison Journals, 1973–May 1988."

4   Hunt, Journals, section titled "Darryl Hunt Prison Journals, Sept. 11, 1984"; and Mark Rabil, interviews with the author, 2016–2020.

5   Hunt, Journals, section titled "Darryl Hunt Prison Journals, Sept. 11, 1984."

6   Hunt, Journals, section titled "Darryl Hunt Prison Journals, Sept. 11, 1984."

7   Zerwick, "Murder, Race, Justice" (part 4).

8   Allen H. Johnson, "'Police Know I'm Innocent'—Darryl Hunt: Police Know I Didn't Murder Sykes," *Winston-Salem Chronicle*, Feb. 7, 1985.

9   Don Tisdale, letter to acting police chief Joseph Masten, Oct. 19, 1984, Darryl Hunt Collection, Wake Forest Law Library Special Collections and Archives, Wake Forest University School of Law, Winston-Salem, NC.

10 Zerwick, "Murder, Race, Justice" (part 4).

11 NC State Bar, Rule 3.8, Special Responsibilities of a Prosecutor, https://www.ncbar.gov/for-lawyers/ethics/rules-of-professional-conduct/rule-38-special-responsibilities-of-a-prosecutor/.

12 Zerwick, "Murder, Race, Justice" (part 4).

13 Gordon Jenkins, letter to Don Tisdale, May 22, 1985, Box 1, File 15, Hunt Collection.

14 Don Tisdale, letter to Police Chief Joseph Masten, Feb. 6, 1985, Hunt Collection.

15 Hunt, Journals, section titled "Darryl Hunt Prison Journals, Sept. 11, 1984."

16 Hunt, Journals, section titled "Darryl Hunt Prison Journals, Sept. 11, 1984."

17 James Luginbul, letter to Mark Rabil, April 10, 1985, Box 1, File 13, Hunt Collection; and Zerwick, "Murder, Race, Justice" (part 4).

18 Luginbul, letter to Rabil, April 10, 1985, Hunt Collection.

19 General Population Characteristics, North Carolina 1980 Census, PC80–1-B35, Table 14, https://www2.census.gov/library/publications/decennial/1980/volume-1/north-carolina/1980a_ncabc-02.pdf.

20 "Transcripts," 105, Darryl Hunt Collection, Wake Forest Law Library Special Collections and Archives, Wake Forest University School of Law, Winston-Salem, NC.

21 Transcripts, 105–107, Hunt Collection.

22 Zerwick, "Murder, Race, Justice" (part 4); and Mark Rabil, letter to Adam Stein, March 1, 1987, Hunt Collection.

23 Zerwick, "Murder, Race, Justice" (part 4).

24 Transcripts, 303–343, Hunt Collection.

25 Ronald F. Wright, Kami Chavis, and Gregory Scott Parks, "The Jury Sunshine Project: Jury Selection Data as a Political Issue," *University of Illinois Law Review* 2018, no. 4, https://papers.ssrn.com/sol3/papers.cfm?abstract_id=2994288; and Ronald Wright, "Yes, Jury Selection Is as Racist as You Think. Now We Have Proof," *New York Times*, Dec. 5, 2018, https://www.nytimes.com/2018/12/04/opinion/juries-racism-discrimination-prosecutors.html.

26 Hunt, Journals, section titled "Darryl Hunt Journals, Sept. 11, 1984."

27 Zerwick, "Murder, Race, Justice" (part 4).

Chapter 7

1 Tracie Cone and Rebecca Olmstead, "Hunt's Trial to Begin Tuesday," *Winston-Salem Journal*, May 26, 1985.

2 Phoebe Zerwick, "Murder, Race, Justice: The State vs. Darryl Hunt," part 4 of eight-part series, *Winston-Salem Journal*, Nov. 16–23, 2003, http://www.journalnow.com/app/specialreports/hunt/about.html.

3 Jo Anne North Goetz, *Long Time Coming,* as told to Leigh Summerville McMillan (Bloomington, IN: AuthorHouse, 2007), chap. 2.

4 Rebecca Olmstead, "Bomb Threat Interrupts Darryl Hunt's Trial," *Winston-Salem Journal*, June 6, 1985.

5 Tracie Cone, "Hunt Says He Didn't Kill Mrs. Sykes," *Winston-Salem Journal*, June 11, 1985.

6 "Transcripts," 1770–1850, Darryl Hunt Collection, Wake Forest Law Library Special Collections and Archives, Wake Forest University School of Law, Winston-Salem, NC.

7 Transcripts, 1770–1850, Hunt Collection.

8 Transcripts, Brenda Dew testimony, 920–937, Hunt Collection.

9 Transcripts, Don Tisdale testimony, 967, Hunt Collection.

10 Transcripts, Thomas Murphy testimony, 1027, Hunt Collection.

11 Transcripts, Murphy testimony, 1028, Hunt Collection.

12 Zerwick, "Murder, Race, Justice" (part 4).

13 Transcripts, Roger Weaver testimony, 1193–1194, Hunt Collection.

14 Transcripts, Weaver testimony, 1225, Hunt Collection.

15 Transcripts, Weaver testimony, 1225–1226, Hunt Collection.

16 Carlton Eversley, interview with the author, July 22, 2019.

17 Transcripts, Don Tisdale and Brenda Morino (aka Marie Crawford) testimony, 1310, Hunt Collection.

18 Transcripts, Tisdale and Morino testimony, 1312, Hunt Collection.

19 Zerwick, "Murder, Race, Justice" (part 4).

20 Mark Rabil, interviews with the author, 2016–2020.

21 Transcripts, 1411, Hunt Collection.

22 Robin Adams, "Assistant DA to Daulton: 'You Blew It,'" *Winston-Salem Chronicle*, June 13, 1985.

23 Transcripts, 1819–1820, Hunt Collection.

24 Zerwick, "Murder, Race, Justice" (part 4).

25 Notebook, Box 3, File 33, Darryl Hunt Collection.

26 "Darryl Hunt Journals," n.d., section titled "Darryl Hunt Prison Journals, 1st trial cont. . . . 1985–1987," Darryl Hunt Collection, Wake Forest Law Library Special Collections and Archives, Wake Forest University School of Law, Winston-Salem, NC.

27 Mark Rabil, unpublished manuscript on loan to the author, 2007, chap. 16, "The Bullpen."

28 Hunt, Journals, section titled "Darryl Hunt Prison Journals, 1st trial cont. . . . 1985–1987."

29 Rabil, Manuscript, chap. 16.

30 Zerwick, "Murder, Race, Justice" (part 4).

31 Hunt, Journals, section titled "Darryl Hunt Prison Journals, 1st trial cont. . . . 1985–1987."

32 Hunt, Journals, section titled "Darryl Hunt Prison Journals, 1st trial cont. . . . 1985–1987."

33 Larry Little, "Hunt: Will He Die like Clyde Brown?" *Winston-Salem Chronicle*, May 30, 1985.

34 Jon Healey, "There's No Justice for a Black Man, Little Says," *Winston-Salem Journal*, June 15, 1985.

35 Douglas Linder, Famous Trials website, University of Missouri-Kansas City School of Law, based on the Archives at Tuskegee Institute, https://famous-trials.com/sheriffshipp/1083-lynchingsstate.

36   Seth Kotch and Robert P. Mosteller, "The Racial Justice Act and the Long Struggle with Race and the Death Penalty in North Carolina," *North Carolina Law Review* 88, no. 6 (2010).

37   Kotch and Mosteller.

38   NC Department of Public Safety, Executions 1984–present, https://www .ncdps.gov/adult-corrections/prisons/death-penalty/list-of-persons -executed/executions-1984–2006; and "Velma Barfield," Wikipedia, last modified Dec. 2, 2020, https://en.wikipedia.org/wiki/Velma_Barfield; "James W. Hutchins," Wikipedia, last modified Dec. 15, 2020, https://en.wikipedia .org/wiki/James_W._Hutchins.

39   Hunt, Journals, section titled "Darryl Hunt Journals, 1999."

40   Rabil, interview with the author, 2017–2019.

41   Zerwick, "Murder, Race, Justice" (part 4).

Chapter 8

1   *Greensboro News and Record*, "Polk Youth Institution Is North Carolina's Shame," May 10, 1993, https://www.greensboro.com/polk-youth-institution -is-north-carolinas-shame/article_07e9a9dc-42e2-5d37-be8e -11561de6e5f5.html.

2   Small v. Martin, 5:85-cv-00987 (E.D.N.C. 1985).

3   "Prisons in North Carolina," A Report of the NC Advisory Committee to the US Commission on Civil Rights, Feb. 1976, NC Room, Forsyth County Library.

4   *Greensboro News and Record*, "Polk Youth Institution."

5   "Darryl Hunt Journals," n.d., section titled "Hunt Prison Journals, Sept. 11, 1984," Darryl Hunt Collection, Wake Forest Law Library Special Collections and Archives, Wake Forest University School of Law, Winston-Salem, NC.

6   Hunt, Journals, section titled "Darryl Hunt Prison Journals."

7   Hunt, Journals, section titled "Darryl Hunt Prison Journals."

8   Saundra Westervelt, interview with the author, Feb. 21, 2020.

9   Saundra Westervelt and Kimberly Cook, "Continuing Trauma and Aftermath for Exonerated Death Row Survivor," In *Living on Death Row: The Psychology of Waiting to Die*, 301–329, ed. Hans Toch, James R. Acker, and Vincent Martin Bonventre (Washington, DC: American Psychological Association, 2018), https://doi.org/10.1037/0000084–013.

10   Zieva Konvisser, interview with the author, July 11, 2019.

11   Hunt, Journals, section titled "1st trial cont. . . . 1985–1987."

12   Mark Rabil, unpublished manuscript on loan to the author, 2007, chap. 3, "Interview with the Accused."

13   Hunt, Journals, section titled "1st trial cont. . . . 1985–1987."

14   Hunt, Journals, section titled "1st trial cont. . . . 1985–1987."

15   NC Department of Public Safety, Offender Public Information, "Darryl E. Hunt," https://webapps.doc.state.nc.us/opi/viewoffender.do?method=view &offenderID=0197495&searchLastName=hunt&searchFirstName=darryl &searchMiddleName=e&searchDOBRange=0&listurl=pagelistoffenderse archresults&listpage=1.

16   Hunt, Journals, section titled "Darryl Hunt Prison Journals."

17   Khalid Griggs, interviews with the author, July 15 and 31, 2019, and Feb. 25, 2020.

18   Allen Trelease, "Ku Klux Klan," NCpedia, 2006, https://www.ncpedia .org/ku-klux-klan; and Natalie Allison Janicello, "KKK Parade to be Held Saturday in Caswell County," *Burlington Times-News*, Dec. 2, 2016, https://www.thetimesnews.com/news/20161202/kkk-parade -to-be-held-saturday-in-caswell-county.

19   Griggs, interviews.

20   Hunt, Journals, section titled "Darryl Hunt Prison Journals."

21   Ayyub Rasheed, interview with the author, Oct. 31, 2019.

22   Hunt, Journals, section titled, "Darryl Hunt Prison Journals."

23   Hunt, Journals, section titled, "Darryl Hunt Prison Journals."

24   Josh Shaffer, "NC's 'Little Alcatraz,' Famous Jailbreak Prison is For Sale," *Raleigh News & Observer*, Jan. 13, 2017, https://www.newsobserver.com/ news/local/news-columns-blogs/josh-shaffer/article126361489.html.

25   Prison guards interviewed by the author during visit to Caswell Correctional Institution, Nov. 6, 2019.

26   Hunt, Journals, section titled "Darryl Hunt Prison Journals."

27   Griggs, interviews with the author.

28   Hunt, Journals, section titled "1st trial cont. . . . 1985–1987."

29   Hunt Journals, section titled "Darryl Hunt Prison Journal, March 25, 1998– Sept. 4, 1998."

30   "Snapshot," *Business Journal North Carolina*, October 1995, NC Room, Forsyth County Public Library.

31   Photos, NC Room, Forsyth County Public Library.

32   Patrick A. Langan, "Race of Prisoners Admitted to State and Federal Institutions, 1926–1986" May 1991, NCJ-125618, US Department of Justice, https://www.ncjrs.gov/pdffiles1/Digitization/125618NCJRS.pdf.

33   Langan, "Race of Prisoners."

34   Rasheed, interview.

35   "Prisons in North Carolina," report of the NC Advisory Committee.

36 Arthur Brisbane, "A Get-Tough Philosophy Starts a Building Boom," first of two in "Crime and Punishment, the Push for Prisons," *Washington Post*, March 3, 1985.

37 Marie Gottschalk, *Caught: The Prison State and the Lockdown of American Politics* (Princeton, NJ: Princeton University Press, 2015), 121.

38 Associated Press, "North Carolina Prison Population Reaches 18,000, Triggering So-Called 'Supercap' for Second Time," Jan. 18, 1990.

39 William Claiborne, "Making Sentences Fit the Prisons: North Carolina Tries to Balance Punishment, State Resources," *Washington Post*, July 16, 1994.

40 NC Department of Public Safety, "History of North Carolina's Corrections System," accessed Jan. 13, 2021, https://www.ncdps.gov/adult-corrections/history-of-corrections.

41 Small v. Hunt, 858 F. Supp. 510 (E.D.N.C. 1994).

42 Andre Weaver, speaking to NPR reporter Adam Hochberg, "North Carolina Wants More Prisoners in Same Space," *Morning Edition*, May 19, 1994.

43 Carlton Eversley, interview with the author, July 22, 2019.

44 John Downey, "Maybe Fund Should Pay Hunt's Legal Fees, Tisdale Says," *Winston-Salem Journal*, July 12, 1985.

45 "Blacks Need Unity, Angelou Says," news brief with no byline, *Winston-Salem Journal*, Aug. 25, 1985.

46 James Ferguson and Adam Stein, interview with the author, summer 2019.

47 Phoebe Zerwick, "Murder, Race, Justice: The State vs. Darryl Hunt," part 5 of eight-part series, *Winston-Salem Journal*, Nov. 16–23, 2003.

48 Zerwick, "Murder, Race, Justice" (part 5)

49 Carlton Eversley, interview with the author, July 22, 2019.

50 Eversley, interview.

Chapter 9

1 L. A. A. Williams, "Police Making Progress on Reopened Murder Cases," *Winston-Salem Chronicle*, April 3, 1985, http://newspapers.digitalnc.org/lccn/sn85042324/1986–04–03/ed-1/seq-1/#date1=04%2F03%2F1986&index=0&date2=04%2F03%2F1986&sequence=1&lccn=sn85042324&rows=20&words=&dateFilterType=range&page=1.

2 Phoebe Zerwick, "One Crime, Two Verdicts: The Death of Arthur Wilson," part 2 of eight-part series, *Winston-Salem Journal*, June 13–14, 2004.

3 Sharon Kelly, clinical psychologist, letter to Donna E. Tanner, associate director of the NC Innocence Inquiry Commission, May 29, 2019, in "Commission Hearing Handouts," 1459, https://innocencecommission-nc.gov/cases/state-v-williams/.

4 Zerwick, "One Crime, Two Verdicts" (part 1).

5   Police Report, Sept. 17, 1983, in "Commission Hearing Handouts," 919, https://innocencecommission-nc.gov/cases/state-v-williams/.

6   Zerwick, "One Crime, Two Verdicts" (part 2).

7   Phoebe Zerwick, "Murder, Race, Justice: The State vs. Darryl Hunt," *Winston-Salem Journal,* part 5 of eight-part series, Nov. 16–23, 2003, http://www.journalnow.com/app/specialreports/hunt/about.html.

8   Zerwick, "One Crime, Two Verdicts" (part 1).

9   Zerwick, "One Crime, Two Verdicts" (part 1).

10 "Darryl Hunt Journals," section titled "Darryl Hunt Prison Journals" (there are two sections with similar titles, in this one "Journals" is plural), Darryl Hunt Collection, Wake Forest Law Library Special Collections and Archives, Wake Forest University School of Law, Winston-Salem, NC.

11 Hunt, Journals, section titled "1st trial cont. . . . 1985–1987."

12 Hunt, Journals, section titled "Family Tree."

13 Hunt, Journals, section titled "Darryl Hunt Prison Journals."

Chapter 10

1   Adam Stein, letter to Darryl Hunt, March 28, 1988, in Darryl Hunt Collection, Wake Forest Law Library Special Collections and Archives, Wake Forest University School of Law, Winston-Salem, NC.

2   Hunt, letter to JoAnne North, Feb. 23, 1987, Hunt Collection.

3   "Darryl Hunt Journals," section titled "I Wasn't at Reidsville," n.d., Darryl Hunt Collection, Wake Forest Law Library Special Collections and Archives, Wake Forest University School of Law, Winston-Salem, NC.

4   Hunt, Journals, section titled "I Wasn't at Reidsville."

5   NC Department of Public Safety, prison record provided to the author via email, July 10, 2017.

6   NC Department of Public Safety, email to the author, July 10, 2017.

7   Hunt, Journals, section titled "Darryl Hunt Prison Journals May 4, 1989–1991"; and Richard McGough, interview with the author, Sept. 6, 2019.

8   Brian O. Hagan et al., "History of Solitary Confinement Is Associated with Post-Traumatic Stress Disorder Symptoms among Individuals Recently Released from Prison," *Journal of Urban Health: Bulletin of the New York Academy of Medicine* 95, no. 2 (2018): 141–148, doi:10.1007/s11524–017–0138–1.

9   Hagan et al., "History of Solitary Confinement."

10 Laura Brinkley-Rubenstein et al., "Association of Restrictive Housing During Incarceration with Mortality After Release," *JAMA Network Open,* Oct. 4, 2019, https://jamanetwork.com/journals/jamanetworkopen/fullarticle/275 2350?resultClick=3.

11 Hunt, letter to Mark Rabil, postmarked Dec. 7, 1988, Hunt Collection.

12 Robert Korstad, interview with the author, Jan. 8, 2020.

13 Phoebe Zerwick, "Murder, Race, Justice: The State vs. Darryl Hunt," part 5 of eight-part series, *Winston-Salem Journal*, Nov. 16–23, 2003.

14 Hunt, interview with the author, Piedmont Correctional Institution, June 25, 2003.

15 Hunt, interview; and Zerwick, "Murder, Race, Justice" (part 5).

16 Phoebe Zerwick, "The Last Days of Darryl Hunt," Atavist, May 2017, available on WordPress, https://thelastdaysofdarrylhunt.wordpress.com/.

17 Hunt, Journals, section titled "May 4 1989–1991."

18 Hunt, Journals, section titled "May 4 1989–1991."

19 US Census Bureau, https://www2.census.gov/library/publications/decennial/1990/cp-1/cp-1-35.pdf.

20 Zerwick, "Murder, Race, Justice" (part 5).

21 Larry Little, class lecture at Winston-Salem State University, Oct. 16, 2019, as transcribed by Jordan Green, senior editor at *Triad City Beat*, in the author's collection.

22 Little, class lecture.

23 Tonya V. Smith, "Hunt Not Guilty in Murder Trial, Defense Team Ready to Face Next Round," *Winston-Salem Chronicle*, April 5, 1990, http://newspapers.digitalnc.org/lccn/sn85042324/1990–04–05/ed-1/seq-1/#date1=04%2F05%2F1990&index=0&date2=04%2F05%2F1990&sequence=1&lccn=sn85042324&rows=20&words=&dateFilterType=range&page=1.

24 Phoebe Zerwick, "One Crime, Two Verdicts: The Death of Arthur Wilson," part 2 of two-part series, *Winston-Salem Journal*, June 13–14, 2004.

25 Rudy Anderson, "Hunt Looks at Future, Ponders Turbulent Past," *Winston-Salem Chronicle*, April 5, 1990, http://newspapers.digitalnc.org/lccn/sn85042324/1990–04–05/ed-1/seq-1/#date1=04%2F05%2F1990&index=0&date2=04%2F05%2F1990&sequence=1&lccn=sn85042324&rows=20&words=&dateFilterType=range&page=1.

Chapter 11

1 Phoebe Zerwick, "One Crime, Two Verdicts: The Death of Arthur Wilson," part 1 of two-part series, *Winston-Salem Journal*, June 13–14, 2004.

2 Seth Kotch and Robert P. Mosteller, *The Racial Justice Act and the Long Struggle with Race and the Death Penalty in North Carolina, North Carolina Law Review* 88, no. 6 (2010), http://scholarship.law.unc.edu/nclr/vol88/iss6/4.

3 Phoebe Zerwick, "Murder, Race, Justice: The State vs. Darryl Hunt," part 5 of eight-part series, *Winston-Salem Journal*, Nov. 16–23, 2003, http://www.journalnow.com/app/specialreports/hunt/about.html.

4 Richard McGough, interview with the author, Sept. 6, 2019.

5   James Ferguson, interview with the author, Sept. 27, 2019.

6   Philip N. Meyer, *Storytelling for Lawyers* (New York: Oxford University Press, 2014), Introduction.

7   "Transcripts," Darryl Hunt Collection, Wake Forest Law Library Special Collections and Archives, Wake Forest University School of Law, Winston-Salem, NC.

8   Transcripts, 193, Hunt Collection.

9   Transcripts, 195, Hunt Collection.

10 The summary and passages of James Ferguson's closing arguments are drawn from the trial transcript, 139–269, Hunt Collection.

11 Zerwick, "Murder, Race, Justice" (part 6).

12 Transcripts, 139–269, Hunt Collection.

13 "Darryl Hunt Journals," section titled "Darryl Hunt Prison Journal," Darryl Hunt Collection, Wake Forest Law Library Special Collections and Archives, Wake Forest University School of Law, Winston-Salem, NC.

14 The summary and passages from Dean Bowman's closing argument are drawn from the trial transcript, 269–360, Hunt Collection.

15 Transcripts, 354, Hunt Collection.

16 McGough, interview.

17 McGough, interview.

18 Hunt, Journals, section titled "Darryl Hunt Prison Journal."

19 Tracy L. Prosser, "Hunt Supporters Say He Never Stood a Chance," *Winston-Salem Chronicle*, Oct. 18, 1990, http://newspapers.digitalnc.org/lccn/sn85042324/1990–10–18/ed-1/seq-1/.

20 McGough, interview.

21 Hunt, Journals, section titled "May 4, 1989–1991."

Chapter 12

1   Richard McGough, memo to Mark Rabil, Ben Sendor, and Jim Ferguson, Oct. 31, 1994, Darryl Hunt Collection, Wake Forest Law Library Special Collections and Archives, Wake Forest University School of Law, Winston-Salem, NC.

2   Phoebe Zerwick, "Murder, Race, Justice: The State vs. Darryl Hunt," part 7 of eight-part series, *Winston-Salem Journal*, Nov. 16–23, 2003.

3   National Registry of Exonerations, A Project of the University of California Irvine, University of Michigan Law School, and Michigan State University College of Law, accessed Dec. 2020, http://www.law.umich.edu/special/exoneration/Pages/browse.aspx?View={b8342ae7–6520–4a32–8a06–4b32 6208baf8}&SortField=Exonerated&SortDir=Ascs.

4   McGough, memo to Rabil et al., Oct. 31, 1994, Hunt Archive.

5   "Darryl Hunt Journals," sections titled "Darryl Hunt Prison Journals, May 4, 1989–1991" and "Darryl Hunt Prison Journal, March 25, 1998–Sept. 4, 1998," Hunt Collection.

6   Hunt, Journals, section titled "Darryl Hunt Prison Journal, March 25, 1998–Sept. 4, 1998."

7   Hunt, Journals, section titled "Darryl Hunt Prison Journal, March 25, 1998–Sept. 4, 1998."

8   Gail Burnette, note to Adam Stein, Jan. 4, 1991, Box 2, File 7, Hunt Collection.

9   Darryl Hunt, "Reader Has Faith He Will Prove His Innocence," letter to the editor, *Winston-Salem Chronicle*, Jan. 3, 1991, https://newspapers.digitalnc.org/lccn/sn85042324/1991–01–03/ed-1/seq-4/.

10 Hunt, letter to the editor, Jan. 3, 1991.

11 Adam Stein, letter to Aaron Johnson, secretary, NC Department of Correction, Jan. 22, 1992, Hunt Collection.

12 J. C. Pinion, Superintendent IV, Piedmont Correctional Institution, letter to Adam Stein, Feb. 6, 1991, Hunt Collection.

13 NC Department of Public Safety, email to the author, July 10, 2017.

14 Hunt, Journals, section titled "Darryl Hunt Prison Journals, May 4, 1989–1991."

15 Ronald Cotton, interview with the author, Oct. 29, 2019.

16 Hunt, Journals, section titled "Darryl Hunt Prison Journal, 1991–1992."

17 Hunt, Journals, section titled "Darryl Hunt Prison Journal, 1991–1992."

18 Hunt, Journals, section titled "Darryl Hunt Prison Journal, 1991–1992."

19 Michelle Alexander, *The New Jim Crow: Mass Incarceration in the Age of Colorblindness* (New York: New Press, 2010).

20 "Caledonia Plantation," in *Plantations of North Carolina*, NCGENWEB Special Project, 2016, http://www.ncgenweb.us/ncstate/plantations/caledonia_halifax.htm.

21 Elijah Gaddis, "Caledonia," NCPedia, Aug. 27, 2012, https://www.ncpedia.org/caledonia.

22 Department of Correction, Overview, 1990, on loan to the author by the NC Department of Public Safety press office.

23 NC Department of Public Safety, "Caledonia Correctional Institute," last updated Oct. 1, 2020, https://www.ncdps.gov/adult-corrections/prisons/prison-facilities/caledonia-correctional-institution.

24 Ricky Duke, interview with the author, Nov. 7, 2019.

25 Duke, interview.

26 Ronald Cotton, interview with the author, Oct. 29, 2019.

27 Darryl Hunt, petition signed March 12, 1993, attached to a letter from Gail Burnette to Mark Rabil, March 16, 1993, Hunt Collection. Inmate death referred to in petition confirmed on NC Department of Public Safety website: https://webapps.doc.state.nc.us/opi/viewoffender.do?method=view&offenderID=0385762&searchLastName=squire&searchFirstName=glen&searchGender=M&searchDOBRange=0&activeFilter=4&listurl=pagelistoffendersearchresults&listpage=1.

28 Ayyub Rasheed, interview with the author, Oct. 31, 2019.

29 Hunt, Journals, section titled "Darryl Hunt Journals, May 4, 1989–1991."

30 NC Department of Public Safety, email to the author, July 10, 2017.

31 Darryl Hunt, letter to Mark Rabil, Dec. 3, 1992, Hunt Collection.

32 Mark Rabil, letter to Darryl Hunt, Dec. 8, 1992, Hunt Collection.

33 Tarrah Callahan, interview with the author, Sept. 9, 2019.

34 Ayyub Rasheed, interview with the author, Jan. 15, 2020.

35 Hunt, Journals, section titled "Darryl Hunt Journals, Sept. 22, 1992–Oct. 23, 1994."

36 Zerwick, "Murder, Race Justice" (part 7); and Mark Rabil, interviews with the author, 2016–2020.

37 Hunt, Journals, section titled "Darryl Hunt Prison Journals, Sept. 22, 1994–Oct. 23, 1994."

38 Mark Rabil, unpublished journal, shared with the author, Nov. 1994.

39 Zerwick, "Murder, Race, Justice" (part 1).

40 Rabil, journal.

41 Rabil, journal

42 Mark Rabil, interviews with the author, 2016–2020.

43 Morgan Melzer, ruling, Nov. 10, 1994, CRS 42263, "DNA Order," *Winston-Salem Journal* Special Report, http://www.journalnow.com/app/specialreports/hunt/documents.html.

44 Rabil, letter to Hunt, Nov. 10, 1994, Hunt Collection.

45 Phoebe Zerwick, "The Last Days of Darryl Hunt," Atavist, May 2017, available on WordPress, https://thelastdaysofdarrylhunt.wordpress.com/.

46 Hunt, letter to Rabil, Nov. 10, 1998, Hunt Collection.

Chapter 13

Much of this chapter relies on dozens of conversations—some formal interviews, others informal—which began in 2003 and continued through 2021.

1 *The Trials of Darryl Hunt*, documentary directed by Ricki Stern and Annie Sundberg (New York: Break Thru Films, 2006).

2   Phoebe Zerwick, "Murder, Race, Justice: The State vs. Darryl Hunt," part 7 of eight-part series, *Winston-Salem Journal*, Nov. 16–23, 2003.

3   Allen J. Beck and Darrell K. Gilliard, "Prisoners in 1994," *Bureau of Justice Statistics*, Aug. 17, 1995, NCJ 151654, https://www.bjs.gov/index .cfm?ty=pbdetail&iid=1280.

4   Patrick Langan et al., "Historical Statistics on Prisoners in State and Federal Prisons Yearend 1925–1986," *Bureau of Justice Statistics*, May 1988, https:// www.bjs.gov/content/pub/pdf/hspsfiy25–86.pdf.

5   Beck and Gilliard, "Prisoners in 1994."

6   Lauren-Brooke Eisen, "The 1994 Crime Bill and Beyond: How Federal Funding Shapes the Criminal Justice System," Brennan Center for Justice, Sept. 9, 2019, https://www.brennancenter.org/our-work/analysis-opinion/1994 -crime-bill-and-beyond-how-federal-funding-shapes-criminal-justice.

7   Elizabeth Hinton, "The War on Crime, LBJ and Ferguson: Time to Reassess the History," *Time*, March 20, 2015, https://time.com/3746059/ war-on-crime-history/.

8   Much of the author's thinking in this section is shaped by Marie Gottschalk, *Caught: The Prison State and the Lockdown of American Politics* (Princeton, NJ: Princeton University Press, 2016).

9   Frank Stasio, "Frank Stasio's Fondest Shows: 19 Years Wrongfully Imprisoned: Meet Darryl Hunt," *The State of Things*, WUNC Public Radio, Dec. 8, 2020, https://www.wunc.org/post/frank-stasios-fondest-shows-19-years -wrongfully-imprisoned-meet-darryl-hunt.

10   Darryl Hunt, letter to Mark Rabil, Jan. 15, 1995, Darryl Hunt Collection, Wake Forest Law Library Special Collections and Archives, Wake Forest University School of Law, Winston-Salem, NC.

11   Hunt, letter to Rabil, Jan. 15, 1995, Hunt Collection.

12   "Darryl Hunt Journals," section titled "Darryl Hunt Prison Journal 1995 . . .", Darryl Hunt Collection, Wake Forest Law Library Special Collections and Archives, Wake Forest University School of Law, Winston-Salem, NC.

13   Hunt, Journals, section titled "Darryl Hunt Prison Journal 1995 . . ."

14   Hunt, Journals, section titled "Darryl Hunt Prison Journal 1995 . . ."

15   Hunt, Journals, section titled "Darryl Hunt Prison Journal 1995 . . ."

16   Darryl Hunt, letter to Mark Rabil, Feb. 8, 1996, Hunt Collection.

17   Darryl Hunt, letter to Mark Rabil, March 19, 1997, Hunt Collection.

18   Hunt, Journals, section titled "Darryl Hunt Prison Journal 1995 . . ."

19   Hunt, Journals, section titled "Darryl Hunt Prison Journals, March 25, 1998– Sept. 4, 1998."

20   Hunt, Journals, section titled, "May 4, 1989–1991," Hunt Collection.

21   April Hunt, phone interview with the author, Dec. 10, 2019.

22 Hunt, Journals, section titled "Darryl Hunt Journals, March 10, 1998–March 30, 1998."

23 Justin Sowa, "Gods Behind Bars: Prison Gangs, Due Process, and the First Amendment," *Brooklyn Law Review* 78, no. 1 (2012), https://brooklynworks. brooklaw.edu/blr/vol78/iss1/10/.

24 J. E. Blalock, special assistant to the secretary of the NC Department of Correction, letter to Darryl Hunt, Aug. 20, 1998, Hunt Collection.

25 Hunt, Journals, section titled "Darryl Hunt Journals, March 10, 1998–March 30, 1998."

26 Hunt, Journals, section titled "Darryl Hunt Prison Journals, March 25, 1998– Sept. 4, 1998

27 Hunt, letter to April Johnson, June 4, 1998, in "Darryl Hunt Personal Papers," Hunt Collection.

28 NC Department of Public Safety, email to the author, July 6, 2017.

29 April Hunt, interviews with the author, Dec. 10 and 12, 2019.

30 Phoebe Zerwick, "The Last Days of Darryl Hunt," Atavist, May 2017, available on WordPress, https://thelastdaysofdarrylhunt.wordpress.com/.

31 Hunt, letter to Rabil, March 23, 2000, Box 3, File 8, Hunt Collection.

32 Bessel van der Kolk, *The Body Keeps the Score: Brain, Mind, and Body in the Healing of Trauma* (New York: Viking, 2014).

33 Supreme Court of the United States, "About the Court," accessed Dec. 2020, https://www.supremecourt.gov/about/faq_general.aspx.

34 April Hunt, interviews with the author, 2016–2020.

Chapter 14

1 Ted Richardson, photograph, in Phoebe Zerwick, "Murder, Race, Justice: The State vs. Darryl Hunt," part 2 of eight-part series, *Winston-Salem Journal*, Nov. 16–23, 2003.

2 Phoebe Zerwick, "Murder, Race, Justice: The State vs. Darryl Hunt" (part 1).

3 Les Gura, interview with the author, Aug. 7, 2020. (He remembers things slightly differently, that he came to me the next day.)

4 James McCool, Autopsy Report on Arthur Wilson, Sept. 17, 1983, NC Innocence Inquiry Brief, The State v. Williams, 61, https://innocencecommission-nc .gov/wp-content/uploads/state-v-merritt-williams-drayton/commission-brief .pdf.

5 Zerwick, "Murder, Race, Justice" (part 5).

6 Estella McFadden, interview with the author, 2003, date unknown.

7 Zerwick, notes to prepare for June 25, 2003, interview with Darryl Hunt, collection of the author.

8   Darryl Hunt, interview with the author, June 25, 2003, Phoebe Zerwick Collection, Wake Forest Law Library Special Collections and Archives, Wake Forest University School of Law, Winston-Salem, NC.
9   Zerwick, "Murder, Race, Justice" (part 1).
10   Zerwick, "Murder, Race, Justice" (part 7).
11   Hunt, interview, June 25, 2003.
12   Zerwick, June 25, 2003, interview notes.
13   Hunt, interview, June 25, 2003.
14   Zerwick, "Murder, Race, Justice" (part 1).
15   Mark Rabil, "My Three Decades with Darryl Hunt," *Albany Law Review* 75 (2012), http://www.albanylawreview.org/Articles/Vol75_3/75.3.0014%20 rabil.pdf.
16   Zerwick, "Murder, Race, Justice" (part 4).
17   Zerwick, "Murder, Race, Justice" (part 8).
18   Zerwick, "Murder, Race, Justice" (part 1).
19   Zerwick, "Murder, Race, Justice" (part 7).
20   Zerwick, "Murder, Race, Justice" (part 4).
21   Zerwick, "Murder, Race, Justice" (part 4).

Chapter 15

1   Andrew Cromer, email exchange with Mark Rabil, the NC Crime Lab, and others, Nov. 11, 2003, "Correspondence," Darryl Hunt Collection, Wake Forest Law Library Special Collections and Archives, Wake Forest University School of Law, Winston-Salem, NC.
2   Mike Rowe, Supplement Report, July 3, 2006, Winston-Salem Police Department, Appendix 10–2, Sykes Administrative Review Committee Report, City of Winston-Salem, 2007, https://www.cityofws.org/1957/ Sykes-Administrative-Review-Committee-Re.
3   Rowe, Supplement, Sykes Committee Report.
4   Rowe, Supplement, Sykes Committee Report.
5   Rowe, Supplement, Sykes Committee Report.
6   NC Department of Public Safety, Offender Public Information, "Willard E. Brown," accessed Dec. 2020, https://webapps.doc.state.nc.us/opi/viewof-fender.do?method=view&offenderID=0052172&searchLastName=brown& searchFirstName=willard&searchGender=M&searchRace=2&searchDOBR ange=0&listurl=pagelistoffendersearchresults&listpage=1.
7   Willard Brown, Statement, Sykes Committee Report.
8   April Hunt, interview with the author, Dec. 24, 2003.
9   Darryl Hunt, interview with the author, Dec. 20, 2003.

10 Patrick Wilson and Phoebe Zerwick, "Hunt Release Delayed," *Winston-Salem Journal*, Dec. 24, 2003, http://www.journalnow.com/app/specialreports/hunt/epilogue/20031224.html.

11 Motion and Order for Release from Custody, Dec. 24, 2003, reprinted in the *Winston-Salem Journal*, Dec. 25, 2003, http://www.journalnow.com/app/specialreports/hunt/documents/motiontorelease/motiontorelease.pdf.

12 Phoebe Zerwick, "He Is Free: Hunt Gives Thanks to His Supporters," *Winston-Salem Journal*, Dec. 25, 2003, http://www.journalnow.com/app/specialreports/hunt/epilogue/epilogueprint25a.html.

13 Zerwick, "He Is Free."

14 Phoebe Zerwick, Michael Hewlett, and Paul Garber, "I Always Had Faith," *Winston-Salem Journal*, Dec. 25, 2003, http://www.journalnow.com/app/specialreports/hunt/epilogue/20031225.html.

15 Andrew Cromer, motion to release, Dec. 24, 2003, http://extras.journalnow.com/hunt/documents/motiontorelease/motiontorelease.pdf.

16 Zerwick, notes from Dec. 24, 2003, collection of the author.

17 Michael Hewlett and Titan Barksdale, "Regaining Footing on Open Ground," *Winston-Salem Journal*, Dec. 31, 2003, http://journalnow.com/app/specialreports/hunt/epilogue/20031230.html.

18 *The Trials of Darryl Hunt*, documentary directed by Ricki Stern and Annie Sundberg (New York: Break Thru Films, 2006).

19 *The Trials of Darryl Hunt*, documentary.

Chapter 16

1 Chuck Byrom, interviews with the author, June 27, July 17, Sept. 26, and Oct. 10, 2019.

2 Byrom, interviews.

3 Sykes Administrative Review Committee Report, Appendix 13, City of Winston-Salem, 2007, https://www.cityofws.org/DocumentCenter/View/7241/Appendix-13-Arthur-Wilson-Trial-Doodles-and-Drawings-PDF.

4 Byrom, interviews.

5 Byrom, interviews.

6 Byrom, interviews.

7 Sykes Committee Report, Appendix 17, 300, https://www.cityofws.org/DocumentCenter/View/7235/Appendix-17-2005-to-2006-Committee-Investigators-Interviews-PDF.

8 Sykes Committee Report, interview with Kevey Coleman, Appendix 17, 304, Nov. 22, 2005, https://www.cityofws.org/DocumentCenter/View/7235/Appendix-17--2005-to-2006-Committee-Investigators-Interviews-PDF.

9   Byrom, interviews.

10 Sykes Committee Report, Appendix 7, https://www.cityofws.org/
    DocumentCenter/View/7251/Appendix-7--Linda-E-Case-File-PDF.

11 Sykes Committee, Appendix 9, https://www.cityofws.org/DocumentCenter/
    View/7246/Appendix-9-Kathleen-D-Case-File-PDF.

12 Byrom, interviews.

13 Byrom, interview with the author, Oct. 10, 2019.

14 Much of this section is based on Regina Lane and Linda F. Felker, *From
    Victim to Victory* (Winston-Salem, NC: Clear Light Books, 2012).

15 Regina Lane, interview with the author, Sept. 19, 2019.

16 Lane, interview.

17 Lane, interview.

18 W. C. Crump, police report dated May 28, 1985, Appendix 10–1, 54,
    Sykes Administrative Review Committee Report, https://www.cityofws
    .org/ DocumentCenter/View/7245/Appendix-10–1-Regina-K-Case
    -File-PDF.

19 Regina Lane, interview with the author, Sept. 12, 2019.

20 Phoebe Zerwick, "Judge Releases Interview with Brown from 1986," *Winston-
    Salem Journal,* Jan. 6, 2004.

21 Carter Crump, Supplement Report, Sept. 10, 1989, Appendix 10–2, 35,
    Sykes Administrative Review Committee Report, https://www.cityofws.org/
    DocumentCenter/View/7244/Appendix-10–2-Regina-K-Case-File-PDF.

22 Lane, interview, Sept. 12, 2019.

23 Lane and Felker, 59.

24 Lane and Felker, 133.

25 Lane and Felker, 134.

26 Lane and Felker, 134.

27 Byrom, interview with the author, Sept. 26, 2019.

28 Richard McGough, interview with the author, Sept. 6, 2019.

29 Innocence Project, "Compensating the Wrongly Convicted," accessed Dec.
    2020, https://innocenceproject.org/compensating-wrongly-convicted/.

30 Mark Rabil, letter to Ron Seeber, City Attorney, Jan. 26, 2007, Darryl Hunt
    Collection, Wake Forest Law Library Special Collections and Archives,
    Wake Forest University School of Law, Winston-Salem, NC.

31 Bert Gutierrez and Dan Galindo, "Council Agrees to Pay Hunt $1.65 mil-
    lion," *Winston-Salem Journal,* Feb. 20, 2007, https://www.journalnow.com/
    news/local/council-agrees-to-pay-1-65-million-to-hunt/article_9976ec6a
    -24c0-11e4-9768-001a4bcf6878.html.

32 Mark Rabil, interviews with the author, 2016–2020.

33 Rabil, letter to Seeber.

Chapter 17

1 *The Trials of Darryl Hunt*, documentary directed by Ricki Stern and Annie Sundberg (New York: Break Thru Films, 2006).

2 John Hinton, "Darryl Hunt Project Scaling Back Operations," *Winston-Salem Journal*, Dec. 23, 2011, https://www.journalnow.com/news/local/darryl-hunt-project-scaling-back-operations/article_54444bba-1349–55b1–8122-d16e55cd01be.html.

3 Dale McCants, interview with the author, Oct. 24, 2019.

4 Jo Anne North Goetz, *Long Time Coming*, as told to Leigh Summerville McMillan (Bloomington, IN: AuthorHouse, 2007), 121.

5 Les Gura, "Darryl Hunt Reflects on His Life Since He Was Released from Prison," *Winston-Salem Journal*, Dec. 21, 2008, https://journalnow.com/news/local/darryl-hunt-reflects-on-his-life-since-he-was-released-from-prison/article_56821241-a716–508f-8f27-b451c3b7769d.html.

6 Darryl Hunt, "Darryl Hunt Journals," n.d., section titled "Darryl Hunt Prison Journals," Darryl Hunt Collection, Wake Forest Law Library Special Collections and Archives, Wake Forest University School of Law, Winston-Salem, NC.

7 Blair Ames, "NIJ Funded Research Examines What Works for Successful Reentry," *NIJ Journal* 281 (Nov. 2019), https://nij.ojp.gov/topics/articles/nij-funded-research-examines-what-works-successfu-reentry.

8 Ames, "NIJ."

9 Ames, "NIJ."

10 NC Department of Public Safety, "Reentry Programs and Services," accessed April 2021, https://www.ncdps.gov/adult-corrections and https://www.ncdps.gov/our-organization/adult-correction/reentry-programs-and-services.

11 The Sentencing Project, "Criminal Justice Facts," https://www.sentencingproject.org/criminal-justice-facts/, retrieved April, 2021.

12 US Department of Justice, Office of Justice Programs, Press Release, Sept. 29, 2020, "Justice Department Awards More than $92 Million to Support Offenders Returning to Communities," https://www.justice.gov/opa/pr/department-justice-awards-more-92-million-support-offenders-returning-communities.

13 US Department of Justice, FY 2020 Budget Request, https://www.justice.gov/jmd/page/file/1142306/download#:~:text=The%20DOJ%20FY%202020%20Budget,technology%2Fother%20(2.9%25).

14 Peter Wagner and Bernadette Rabuy, "Following the Money of Mass Incarceration," Prison Policy Initiative, Jan. 25, 2017, accessed April 2021, https://www.prisonpolicy.org/reports/money.html.

15 Marie Gottschalk, *Caught: The Prison State and the Lockdown of American Politics* (Princeton, NJ: Princeton University Press, 2015), 241.

16   Reuben J. Miller, "How Thousands of American Laws Keep People 'Impris-
      oned' Long After They're Released," *Politico*, Dec. 30, 2020, https://www
      .politico.com/news/magazine/2020/12/30/post-prison-laws-reentry-451445
      and Collateral Consequences of Conviction Project, American Bar Asso-
      ciation, accessed December 2020, https://www.americanbar.org/groups/
      criminal_justice/niccc/.

17   Beth Avery and Han Lu, "Ban the Box: US Cities, Counties, and States
      Adopt Fair Hiring Policies," National Employment Law Project, Sept. 30,
      2020, https://www.nelp.org/publication/ban-the-box-fair-chance-hiring
      -state-and-local-guide/.

18   The Sentencing Project, "Felony Disenfranchisement Laws in The United
      States," April 28, 2014, https://www.sentencingproject.org/publications/
      felony-disenfranchisement-laws-in-the-united-states/.

19   "Darryl Hunt Project for Freedom and Justice, Inc. Business Plan," March
      2005, Darryl Hunt Collection, Wake Forest Law Library Special Collections
      and Archives, Wake Forest University School of Law, Winston-Salem, NC.

20   Gura, "Darryl Hunt Reflects."

21   Ricki Stern, interview with the author, Feb. 28, 2020.

22   Hinton, "Darryl Hunt Project Scaling Back."

23   McCants, interview.

24   David Harold, interview with the author, Sept. 26, 2019.

25   Gura, "Darryl Hunt Reflects."

26   Gura, "Darryl Hunt Reflects."

27   Angela Hattery and Earl Smith, *Prisoner Reentry and Social Capital: The Long
      Road to Reintegration* (Plymouth, UK: Lexington Books, 2010), 145.

28   David Moore, interview with the author, Oct. 2, 2019.

29   NC Department of Public Safety, Offender Public Information, "David
      M. Moore," accessed Dec. 2020, https://webapps.doc.state.nc.us/opi/
      viewoffender.do?method=view&offenderID=0755712&searchLastName=
      moore&searchFirstName=david&searchMiddleName=m&searchDOB=
      08/04/1960&searchDOBRange=0&listurl=pagelistoffendersearchresults
      &listpage=1.

30   Moore, interview.

31   Moore, interview.

32   McCants, interview.

33   Tarrah Callahan, interview with the author, Sept. 9, 2019.

34   Callahan, interview.

35   Callahan, interview.

36   Mark Rabil, interviews with author, 2016–2020.

37 Mark Rabil, interview with the author, Aug. 5, 2019; Hannah McMahan King, interview with the author, Sept. 23, 2019; and email from Stephen Boyd, Sept. 7, 2019.

38 Hunt, Journals.

39 Hunt, Journals.

40 Darryl Hunt, email to Tanya Wiley, Dec. 21, 2011, shared with the author by Mark Rabil.

41 April Hunt, interview with the author, June 23, 2020.

42 Rabil, interviews.

43 Carter Center, "Former US President Jimmy Carter Calls for Clemency for Troy Davis," Sept. 18, 2008, https://www.cartercenter.org/news/pr/clemency_troy_davis.html; and Innocence Project, "Remembering Troy Davis," Sept. 24, 2012, https://innocenceproject.org/remembering-troy-davis/.

44 Callahan, interview.

45 Ed Pilkington, "Troy Davis Executed after Supreme Court Refuses Last-Minute Reprieve," *Guardian*, Sept. 21, 2011, https://www.theguardian.com/world/2011/sep/22/troy-davis-execution-goes-ahead; and Kim Severson, "Davis Is Executed in Georgia," *New York Times*, Sept. 21, 2011, https://www.nytimes.com/2011/09/22/us/final -pleas-and-vigils-in-troy-davis -execution.html.

46 Callahan, interview.

47 Campbell Robertson, "Bias Law Used to Move a Man Off Death Row," *New York Times*, April 20, 2012, https://www.nytimes.com/2012/04/21/us/north-carolina-law-used-to-set-aside-a-death-sentence.html; Anne Blythe, "NC Justices Hear Arguments in Racial Justice Act Cases," *Charlotte Observer*, April 14, 2014, https://www.charlotteobserver.com/news/local/article9112868.html; Paul Woolverton, "NC Supreme Court to Hear Racial Justice Act Death Row Cases," *Fayetteville Observer*, March 2, 2018, https://www.fayobserver.com/news/20180302/nc-supreme-court-to-hear-racial-justice-act-death-row-cases; and Ken Rose, attorney with the NC Center for Death Penalty Litigation, email exchange with the author, July 31, 2020.

48 Callahan, interview.

Chapter 18

1 NC Department of Public Safety, Offender Public Information, "Ayyub Rasheed," accessed Dec. 2020, https://webapps.doc.state.nc.us/opi/viewoffender.do?method=view&offenderID=0142419&searchLastName=Rasheed&searchFirstName=Ayyub&searchDOBRange=0&listurl=pagelistoffendersearchresults&listpage=1.

2   The sections dealing with Ayyub Rasheed rely on a series of interviews with the author that began July 13, 2016, and picked up Oct. 31, 2019, through Jan. 6, 2021 (Dec. 7, 2019, Dec. 17, 2019, Jan. 15, 2020, Feb. 21, 2020, March 22, 2020, July 13, 2020, July 28, 2020, Sept. 22, 2020).

3   Ayyub Rasheed, letter to Darryl Hunt, Jan. 1, 2004, Darryl Hunt Collection, Wake Forest Law Library Special Collections and Archives, Wake Forest University School of Law, Winston-Salem, NC.

4   Phoebe Zerwick, "The Last Days of Darryl Hunt," Atavist, May 2017, available on WordPress, https://thelastdaysofdarrylhunt.wordpress.com/.

5   Rasheed introduced the author to Anthony Wright on Jan. 15, 2020, leading to follow-up interviews that lasted through Jan. 6, 2021 (Jan. 21, 2020, Feb. 15, 2020, March 22, 2020, July 28, 2020, Sept. 22, 2020).

6   Wright, interviews.

7   Wright, interview, March 22, 2020.

8   Rasheed, interviews.

9   Les Gura, "Darryl Hunt Reflects on His Life Since He Was Released from Prison," *Winston-Salem Journal,* Dec. 21, 2008, https://journalnow.com/news/local/darryl-hunt-reflects-on-his-life-since-he-was-released-from-prison/article_56821241-a716-508f-8f27-b451c3b7769d.html.

10 April Hunt, interview with the author, Dec. 12, 2019.

11 Rasheed, interviews.

12 Mark Rabil, interview with the author, Aug. 12, 2020.

13 Mark Rabil, "My Three Decades with Darryl Hunt," *Albany Law Review* 75 (2012), http://www.albanylawreview.org/Articles/Vol75_3/75.3.0014%20rabil.pdf.

14 John Healy, "Man Already in Jail Is Charged with Sykes Murder," *Winston-Salem Journal,* Sept. 15, 1984.

15 Virginia Lefever, interview with the author, June 16, 2020; and Lefever, "Effects of Wrongful Conviction on the Health of Exonerees," Health Promotion Project: Nursing 6999, South University (unpublished project shared with the author, n.d.).

16 Saundra Westervelt and Kimberly Cook, "Continuing Trauma and Aftermath for Exonerated Death Row Survivors," in *Living on Death Row: The Psychology of Waiting to Die,* ed. H. Toch, J. R. Acker, and V. M. Bonventre (Washington, DC: American Psychological Association, 2018), 301–329, https://psycnet.apa.org/doiLanding?doi=10.1037%2F0000084-013.

17 Kimberly Cook and Saundra Westervelt, "Power and Accountability: Life after Death Row in the United States," in *The Routledge Handbook of Critical Criminology,* ed. Walter Dekeseredy and Molly Dragiewicz (London: Routledge, 2018), https://doi.org/10.4324/9781315622040.

18 Westervelt and Cook, "Continuing Trauma and Aftermath."
19 Saundra Westervelt, interview with the author, Feb. 21, 2020.
20 April Hunt, interviews.
21 Rasheed, interview with the author, July 13, 2016.
22 Gura, "Darryl Hunt Reflects."
23 Zerwick, "The Last Days of Darryl Hunt."
24 Zerwick, "The Last Days of Darryl Hunt."
25 Rasheed, interview, Dec. 17, 2019.
26 Khalid Griggs, interview with the author Feb. 25, 2020; and Zerwick, "The Last Days of Darryl Hunt."
27 Mark Rabil, interview with the author, Aug. 12, 2020.

Chapter 19

1 Phoebe Zerwick, "Attack at the Silk Plant Forest," *Winston-Salem Journal*, Nov. 21–25, 2004.
2 Zerwick, "Attack."
3 Silk Plant Forest Report Documents, "Findings and Recommendations of the Silk Plant Forest Citizen's Review Committee," City of Winston-Salem, July 24, 2009, https://www.cityofws.org/DocumentCenter/View/7649/Final-Report-of-the-Silk-Plant-Forest-Citizens-Review-Committee-redacted-including-Attachments-One-and-Two-PDF.
4 Mark Rabil, "Proposal to Formalize Relationship between Wake Forest University and Darryl Hunt," Aug. 2014, provided by Mark Rabil to the author, in the author's collection.
5 Phoebe Zerwick, "The Last Days of Darryl Hunt," Atavist, May 2017, available on WordPress, https://thelastdaysofdarrylhunt.wordpress.com/.
6 Michael Hewlett, "Darryl Hunt's Wife Files for Domestic Violence Restraining Order," *Winston-Salem Journal*, Sept. 15, 2014, https://journalnow.com/news/local/darryl-hunt-s-wife-files-for-domestic-violence-restraining-order/article_07343a9a-3cfa-11e4-8d43-0017a43b2370.html.
7 Zerwick, "The Last Days of Darryl Hunt."
8 April Hunt, interview with the author, Dec. 12, 2019.
9 Zerwick, "The Last Days of Darryl Hunt."
10 Zerwick, "The Last Days of Darryl Hunt."
11 Zerwick, "The Last Days of Darryl Hunt."
12 Jamika Burnette, interview with the author, Oct. 15, 2019.
13 Gail Burnette, letter to Charles Stevens, Oct. 10, 1988, Darryl Hunt Collection, Wake Forest Law Library Special Collections and Archives, Wake Forest University School of Law, Winston-Salem, NC.
14 Ayyub Rasheed, interview with the author, Oct. 17, 2019.

15 National Institute of Justice, "Exonerees and Original Victims of Wrongful Conviction: Listening Sessions to Inform Programs and Research," Office of Justice Programs, Washington, DC, Feb. 22–24, 2016, p. 18.

16 "Free Kalvin Michael Smith Rally - Winston-Salem, NC," YouTube video, Feb. 21, 2016, https://www.youtube.com/watch?v=vVrGcFOgv_c&t=3294s; and Darryl Hunt, "Darryl Hunt (1965–2016) Last Public Speech at Kalvin Michael Smith Rally," March 14, 2016, YouTube video, https://www.youtube.com/watch?v=mmb5yBNegTw.

Chapter 20

Portions of this chapter were printed earlier in Phoebe Zerwick, "The Last Days of Darryl Hunt," Atavist, May 2017, available on WordPress, https://thelastdaysofdarrylhunt.wordpress.com/.

1 Phoebe Zerwick, "The Last Days of Darryl Hunt," Atavist, May 2017, available on WordPress, https://thelastdaysofdarrylhunt.wordpress.com/.

2 Zerwick, "The Last Days of Darryl Hunt."

3 Zerwick, "The Last Days of Darryl Hunt."

4 Ayyub Rasheed, interview with the author, April 5, 2021.

5 Zerwick, "The Last Days of Darryl Hunt."

6 Zerwick, "The Last Days of Darryl Hunt."

7 Zerwick, "The Last Days of Darryl Hunt."

8 Zerwick, "The Last Days of Darryl Hunt."

9 Jennifer Cotton, interview with the author, Aug. 18, 2019, Chapel Hill, NC.

10 National Registry of Exonerations, A Project of the University of California Irvine, the University of Michigan Law School, and Michigan State University College of Law, accessed Dec. 2020, https://www.law.umich.edu/special/exoneration/Pages/about.aspx.

11 Lara Bazelon, *Rectify: The Power of Restorative Justice after Wrongful Conviction* (Boston: Beacon Press, 2018), 95–97 and 156–165.

12 Mike Rose, interview with the author, June 29, 2020.

13 Joseph Neff, "They Did 30 Years for Someone Else's Crime. Then Paid for It," *New York Times*, April 7, 2018, https://www.nytimes.com/2018/04/07/us/mccollum-brown-exoneration.html.

14 Ronald Cotton, interview with the author, Oct. 29, 2019.

Epilogue

1 Frank Stasio, "Frank Stasio's Fondest Shows: 19 Years Wrongfully Imprisoned: Meet Darryl Hunt," *The State of Things*, WUNC Public Radio, Dec. 8, 2020, https://www.wunc.org/post/frank-stasios-fondest-shows-19-years-wrongfully-imprisoned-meet-darryl-hunt.

2   WFMY News 2, "Silk Plant Forest Case: Kalvin Smith Released From Prison," Nov. 10, 2016, https://www.wfmynews2.com/article/news/local/silk-plant-forest-case-kalvin-smith-released-from-prison/83–350479327.

3   Augustus Dark, interview with the author, Nov. 22, 2020.

4   Dark, interview with the author, Dec. 21, 2020.

5   Michael Hewlett, "Kalvin Michael Smith Is Out of Prison But He's Still Not Free," *Greensboro News & Record*, June 4, 2017, https://greensboro.com/news/local_news/kalvin-michael-smith-is-out-of-prison-but-hes-still-not-free/article_97968afe-9c3f-5d75-b06b-fb4fea328958.html.

6   Phoebe Zerwick, "Attack at the Silk Plant Forest," *Winston-Salem Journal*, Nov. 21–25, 2004.

7   Michael Hewlett and Bertrand M. Gutierrez, "Judge Asked to Review Ex-FBI Agent's Report in Kalvin Michael Smith Case," *Winston-Salem Journal*, July 19, 2012, updated April 8, 2019, https://journalnow.com/article_e72a6a9c-833e-5c40-95bb-ad92043fb102.html.

8   Hewlett and Gutierrez, "Judge Asked."

9   Dark, interviews.

10 Dark, interviews.

11 Dark, interview, Dec. 21, 2020.

12 Dark, interview, Dec. 21, 2020.

13 Dark, interview, Nov. 22, 2020.

14 Mark Rabil, multiple conversations with the author.

15 Carlton Eversley, interview with the author, April 18, 2016.

16 Michael Hewlett, "Death Row Inmate Convicted of Killing a Winston-Salem Police Officer Claims Racial Discrimination in Case," *Winston-Salem Journal*, Aug. 24, 2019, https://journalnow.com/news/crime/death-row-inmate-convicted-of-killing-a-winston-salem-police-officer-claims-racial-discrimination-in/article_f92b95bc-f0a6-530d-a686-46d0dcdcbdf7.html.

17 National Registry of Exonerations, A Project of the University of California Irvine, the University of Michigan Law School, and Michigan State University College of Law, accessed Dec. 2020, https://www.law.umich.edu/special/exoneration/Pages/about.aspx.

18 NC Department of Public Safety, "Adult Corrections," accessed Dec. 2020, https://www.ncdps.gov/Adult-Corrections.

19 Matt Clarke, "Long Term Recidivism Studies Show High Arrest Rates," *Prison Legal News*, May 3, 2019, https://www.prisonlegalnews.org/news/2019/may/3/long-term-recidivism-studies-show-high-arrest-rates/.

20 *Politico Magazine*, "5 New Policy Ideas for Fixing Life After Prison," Dec. 30, 2020, https://www.politico.com/news/magazine/2020/12/30/reentry-after-prison-solutions-450299.

21 Stasio, "Meet Darryl Hunt."

Acknowledgments

I write this book with deep gratitude to Darryl Hunt, for the life you led, the little bit of time we spent together, and the journals, letters, interviews, and talks you left behind. I hope I have done justice to your story.

This book would not have been possible without the generosity of Hunt's friends and others close to him who trusted me to treat their words with the care they deserved. I am grateful to everyone who fought for Hunt's freedom and who helped me understand his life.

To Mark Rabil for spending countless hours with me and for making your papers available through the Darryl Hunt Collection at the Wake Forest Law Library at the Wake Forest University School of Law. These papers provide an intimate portrait of your friendship with a man you represented for more than nineteen years.

To April Hunt for sharing your love story with me.

To Ayyub Rasheed for your trust and guidance. To Anthony Wright for showing me the spirit of your friendship with Hunt through your laughter. To the late Gail Burnette for sharing as much as you felt you could.

To Khalid Griggs, John Mendez, Richard McGough, and the late Carlton Eversley, who fought so hard for Hunt's release. And to

Larry Little for your dedication to Hunt and the many interviews you have granted over the years to me and to others.

To Regina Lane for your dignity and your book *From Victim to Victory.* To Chuck Byrom for your courage to disclose what your former colleagues in the police department had done. To Augustus Dark for your honest discussion of your family's struggle. And to Tarrah Callahan for your memory of detail and your marvelous stories.

I am ever grateful to the authors and filmmakers whose work has influenced me. To Ricki Stern and Annie Sundberg for your documentary *The Trials of Darryl Hunt.* To Allen Johnson for your reporting on Hunt's trials in the *Winston-Salem Chronicle.* To Jo Anne North Goetz and Leigh Somerville for your *Long Time Coming* and to Stephen Boyd for your *Making Justice Our Business.* To Robert Korstad for your research into the case of Clyde Brown. To Albert Woodfox for your book *Solitary.* To the many contributors to *The Marshall Project*'s "Life Inside," whose words remind us of the range of human experience found in prison. To Lara Bazelon for introducing me to the notion of restorative justice with your book *Rectify.* To Jennifer Thompson and Ronald Cotton for your book *Picking Cotton.* And to Ta-Nehisi Coates for helping me better understand the full impact of the carceral state with your work for the *Atlantic.*

This work would not have been possible without the guidance of editors who have shaped me over many years in journalism. To Carl Crothers for seeing in 2003 that Hunt's story deserved to be reexamined by the *Winston-Salem Journal.* To Les Gura for teaching me how to tell a long-form narrative and for reading an early manuscript of this book, and to Ken Otterbourg for believing I was up to the task. To Andrew Park for finding support at Duke University School of Law for "The Last Days of Darryl Hunt" and for your brilliant editing.

I could not have done the research alone. To Leslie Wakeford for curating the Darryl Hunt Collection at the Wake Forest University School of Law. To Alice Brooke Wilson for your help with the endnotes. To journalists Jonathan Michels and Jordan Green for steering me to your work related to the local Black Panther Party and the Clyde Brown case. To Hilorie Baer and Cristin Whiting, wise therapists and teachers, for sharing your knowledge of trauma and addiction. To my former writing and journalism students Lillian Johnson, Ren Schmit, and Mia Pearsall, who assisted with research and fact-checking. And to all my writing and journalism students at Wake Forest University, I have learned much about writing by teaching you.

None of this would be possible without Stephanie Steiker, my agent at Regal Hoffman & Associates, for initiating this project and believing in me. To George Gibson, my editor at Grove Atlantic, for your kindness, keen eye, and steady support. And to those at Grove who transformed a manuscript into a book, especially to managing editor Julia Berner-Tobin for your attention to detail, to Emily Burns, assistant editor, for your sound judgment, to Becca Fox, designer, for your elegant taste, to Jill Twist, for your careful copyediting, and to Kaitlin Astrella, for finding a wide audience for Hunt's story.

To my mother, Chloe Zerwick, who in the year before your death encouraged me to press forward with this project. To my children, Corinne and Henry White and Jackson LaBrecque, for giving me space and time when I needed it. And most of all, to my husband, Mark LaBrecque, you supported me and believed in me when I wavered. Thank you.

Index

322   Index